THE ART OF INTIMACY

The Art of INTIMACY

Thomas Patrick Malone, M.D.
Patrick Thomas Malone, M.D.

A FIRESIDE BOOK
Published by Simon & Schuster
New York London Toronto Sydney Tokyo Singapore

The following publishers have generously granted permission to use quotations from copyrighted works. From "i shall imagine life," by e. e. cummings. Copyright 1958 by e. e. cummings. Reprinted from "i shall imagine life" in his volume *Complete Poems 1913–1962* by permission of Harcourt Brace Jovanovich, Inc., and Grafton Books. Excerpt from page 221 of *Seven Arrows* by Hyemeyohsts Storm. Copyright 1972 by Hyemeyohsts Storm. Reprinted by permission of Harper & Row, Publishers, Inc. From *The Way of Chuang Tzu,* by Thomas Merton. Copyright 1965 by The Abbey of Gethsemani. Reprinted by permission of New Directions Publishing Corporation. From "a total stranger one black day," by e. e. cummings. Copyright 1957 by e. e. cummings. Reprinted from his volume *Complete Poems 1913–1962* by permission of Harcourt Brace Jovanovich, Inc., and Grafton Books. From *Sunflower Splendor,* by Wu-Chi Liu and Irving Yuchung Lo. Published in 1975 by Doubleday & Company. Reprinted by permission of Doubleday & Company, Inc. From "maggie and milly and molly and may," by e. e. cummings. Copyright 1956 by e. e. cummings. Reprinted from "maggie and milly and molly and may" in his volume *Complete Poems 1913–1962* by permission of Harcourt Brace Jovanovich, Inc., and Grafton Books. From *Illusions* by Richard Bach. Copyright 1977 by Richard Bach. Reprinted by permission of Delacorte Press.

FIRESIDE

Rockefeller Center
1230 Avenue of the Americas
New York, New York 10020

Manufactured in the United States of America

10 9

First Fireside Edition 1992

Library of Congress Cataloging-in-Publication Data
Malone, Thomas Patrick, 1919–
The art of intimacy/Thomas Patrick Malone, Patrick Thomas Malone.—1st pbk ed.
p. cm.
1. Interpersonal relations. 2. Intimacy (Psychology) I. Malone, Patrick Thomas, 1944– . II. Title.
[HM132.M325 1988]
158'.2—dc19 88-4821
CIP
ISBN: 0-671-76152-8

Dedicated

to

Generations

Acknowledgments

We begin by thanking our immediate colleagues at the Atlanta Psychiatric Clinic for their patient acceptance of our unbridled enthusiasm with our ideas. They never dampened us but spoke out clearly in both agreement and disagreement. We also thank our clients; our ideas were shaped by our experience with them.

We gratefully acknowledge the help of a son and brother, himself a writer, Michael Malone, who did the final editing of the book. The book would not have been what it is without his talent and love. He also shepherded us through the trials and perils of publication.

We would also like to thank our editor, Phil Pochoda, for his enlightened enthusiasm, and for presenting us with so few trials.

We are grateful for the help from our families. Their patience while we wrote late at night and on weekends was appreciated. We are particularly grateful to Elaine Malone and Tom Malone II, for their loving efforts to bring this manuscript to a reality.

We also want to thank Joan Hussey for her help. She took on the original task of preparing the manuscript for publication. Because of her knowledge and love of the English language, she enabled two writers, who never disagreed with each other, to merge two very different styles into some semblance of coherent prose.

Contents

THE ART OF INTIMACY

Prologue

I know well what I am fleeing from
but not what I am in search of.

—MICHEL DE MONTAIGNE

Why do you think Archimedes jumped out of the bath and yelled "Eureka!"? Why was Galileo so profoundly changed when he saw the four major moons of Jupiter and the craters of our moon? How did Shakespeare feel when he "found" Falstaff, or Madame Curie when she discovered radium, or Michelangelo when he brought David from the stone? Surely they derived satisfaction from their skill and talent, but also they must have experienced the energizing, enhancing sense of seeing and feeling a real connection, of being in touch with some aspect of the integral truth that is the universe.

We can say that these were special people who had special experiences. But if we do, we make the mistake of "civilized man": the mistake of believing that being connected to the universe and to the universality of truth is "special"; that only the few who are talented or powerful, beautiful or rich, socially titled or spiritually saved—or whatever the hierarchies of the times valued most—only those few can feel themselves at the center.

Similarly, we make the mistake of thinking that this special experience can happen to us only by mediation through another: a priest, minister, shaman, guru, or psychotherapist; or only by mediation through drugs or sex. But the truth is that we *are,* all of us, a connected part of the whole, even though not knowing it. As *selves* we participate in nature; this participation is beyond our control. That we do try to control it is why we often do it so poorly.

Why our lasting fascination with the "great lovers," with Samson and Delilah, Antony and Cleopatra, Tristan and Isolde, Lancelot and

Guinevere, with Henry VIII and Anne Boleyn, or more recently with Richard Burton and Elizabeth Taylor? The high drama and titillation of passion are no doubt entertaining. But, more profoundly, these famous relationships represent windows into that same kind of connection that we sense in nature. Lovers are, on a human level, a picture of a truth of nature.

If you walk on the beach, especially in a protected area, like Acadia, Point Reyes, or the Outer Banks of North Carolina, you experience a different ecosystem—the unspoiled face of nature. That what you see is different, new, and strange to you heightens your seeing, and you feel an increased sense of connection to your surroundings. If you are out at night on that beach, you may look up and see a broad band of light sweeping across the sky—the Milky Way. You can actually see satellites go by overhead. You can actually see nebulas and other galaxies. In short, you *see* the night sky, in a way that most likely you no longer can where you live. Seeing it this way, you suddenly realize why earlier people cared so deeply about the heavens, why they named the constellations, why they charted the planets, why they *looked* at the sky. You feel how they could be connected, and sense how powerful an experience that connection is. In doing so, you connect yourself, in space to your stars and sky, and in time to your ancestors and descendants.

The Art of Intimacy is about experiencing such connection, such energy, such seeing. Connection is the most direct form of relatedness, of relationship. Whether we talk of nations and war, marriage and divorce, families and delinquency, health and pollution, or earth and the rest of the universe, we are talking about relationships. Relationship is universal at and between all levels of existence: one cannot "not relate." Connection is simply our personal participation in truth. We are going to call this experience of connectivity *intimacy*.

It is our basic conviction that the keystone of all relationships knowable to humans, the prototype out of which all our other relational models, whether familial, social, or cultural, are derived, is the human-to-human relationship. Does this mean that our prototype is special or unique? No, only that it is most fundamentally knowable to us. Stars would have to understand the relationship between two humans in terms of their relationship to other stars. Each of us can know only what we are, with whom we are; perhaps we should say each of us can know only *through* what we are. Leonardo da Vinci summarized this fundamental truth by saying, "All our knowledge has its origins in our perceptions." We project our inner experience out. For us as perceivers, living in our middle-order reality (we are neither stars nor atoms), the connection between humans is the prototype for all relationships.

We must learn to understand the nature of intimacy and the intimate self, because in that connectivity we are looking at the central energizer of life, not just an aspect of humanness. What we are calling *intimacy* has been called many other names through history: "the way," "the creator," "the source," "nirvana," "soul principle," even "the force." Most often, it is defined as transcendental and inexpressible. We, however, feel that it is both experiential and describable.

Systemic Connections and Dyadic Connections

We humans have become lost in our preoccupation with systems, the hierarchical, fixed organization of relationships, from the large systems of government, economy, society, religion, or work to the smaller systems of family, marriage, or simply you and me. In themselves, systems are neither always bad nor never necessary; they are very useful; society could not function without them. The problem is that, having gotten too caught up in our systems, we have progressively lost awareness of our experience of connection, can no longer *see* the basic connecting interactions that are the building blocks of systems: of pairings, marriages, families, nations, or ecology itself. This ignored, and basic, dyadic connection we call the *I-other,* whether it is flower-soil, water-fish, lover-lover, sun-earth, husband-wife, or you-me. It is *intimacy. Dyadic* simply means "of two parts," two parts interacting in balance.

When we become captured by our systems, we lose connection as *I-other* and embroil ourselves in closeness: in fixed systems. In this closeness, we are no longer *I-other* but instead are a "part of" something—a marriage, an office, a company, a country. Our desire for systems reflects our concern with maintenance and familiarity, and our neglect of creativity and energizing connections. Closeness is certainly important and necessary, but it has become a neurotic, obsessive preoccupation, and a destructive overconcern in current human societies. The pendulum that with the start of agriculture and urbanization began to swing away from the natural balance in life has swung too far in the direction of conserving those familiar systems. Cyclic, as is the case in all of nature, the pendulum needs now to swing back the other way. The ways in which we are being captured by our systems reveal our lack of understanding of them, our current inability to move freely from one position to another, and our diminished capacity freely to choose where and when we want to move, who and how we want to be.

Systems and dyadic relationships are not mutually exclusive, nor are they antithetical. They are mutually explanatory. The emphasis in *The Art of Intimacy* is on the dyadic connection, in order to address the need to reestablish some balance, to help the pendulum reverse direction. But intimacy is not the more fundamental unit; system and intimacy are a pair. We do, however, believe that the emphasis on system has diminished our interest in the intimate, energizing dyadic connection and thus jeopardized our ability to understand either the system or the self.

As psychiatrists, we see this imbalance every day in our work with clients. In dealing with the different experiences of family therapy, couple therapy, and individual therapy, we deal with both systems and dyads. We have dealt with, and will be discussing in these chapters, both the power and pain of closeness (systems) and the creativity and risks of intimacy (the *I-other* dyad). We believe that the *human* position as the prototype for relatedness can be a key to new understandings only if we stay in touch with this complementary existence of closeness and intimacy.

There are many words used to attempt to describe the functional (useful) human relationship, the healthy, growthful, prototypical dyad. The most common are *love, openness, commitment, genuine closeness, supportiveness, affirming awareness, mature relationship.* We speak of being yourself with others, of honestly relating. All of these terms have specific significance and are subtly different from one another. They each describe some particular aspect of relationship. Normally, however, we use them not specifically but interchangeably: to be open is to be aware; to be aware is to be mature, honest, and committed in relationship; to be all of these is to be genuinely close. This is not true. These different aspects of relationship are each important in their own way, but many of them are not at all what we mean by the term *intimate.*

Sarah is twenty-nine years old, married for nine years, the mother of two children, and chronically depressed. She comes into therapy by herself, because she does not think her husband would agree to come with her; in fact, she had not even told him that she is coming in. She is afraid that he would not understand, would be angry, or would think that she is betraying their relationship. She talks about herself: her history, her problems, the children—everything but her marriage. Why is she really here? She probably does not know. After a gentle inquiry about the marriage, we see a change in her posture, voice tone, and personal presence. Are she and her husband close? Honest? Mature? Genuine? Committed? Open? She is not sure. She is not sure what they are or are not. She just knows that something is missing, something very important.

Love, Closeness, and Intimacy

Of all these significant, encompassing words and phrases for describing the "good, healthy," satisfying growing relationship, the most common and important are *love, closeness,* and *intimacy.* We are convinced from our clinical experience that these three concepts describe the most fundamental dimensions of human relatedness, and therefore relatedness in all its forms. They each represent a separate experience of reality. Each is valid, each different, each important, and each has its own contribution to relationship.

Sarah is sure that her husband "loves" her and that she "loves" him. Like most of us, she is not exactly sure what she means by this. Love is hardly definable, and when specifically described is often confusing. Other people will argue with almost any definition you may offer. Nevertheless, it is "love" that not only operatively makes relationships work, but also makes them growthful systems. When *I-other* relationships work as love (the most basic example is a primary pairing, traditionally called *marriage*), then families work. When families work, societies work; when societies work, nations work; when nations work, worlds work; when worlds work, nature works; and when nature works, the universe works. That is how humans as the perceivers of these realities live in the world. But, in truth, this list can as easily be presented backward. Nations could work, helping societies to work, helping families to work, if we were capable of living in the world as intimate selves. This assumption is not teleological; we simply mean that as dyadic connections these pairings are all equivalent. Love is both immanent and transcendental. It is the force that forms the canvas on which we humans paint. Along with the concepts *truth* and *beauty*, it is our way of naming this canvas, the ground substance of existence. It is a level above those things that make it up—closeness and intimacy. Love cannot be understood if we do not understand its twofold makeup, and if we do not understand the difference between intimacy and closeness. Nor can it be understood if we do not comprehend that the power of love depends precisely on the *balanced* interaction between being close and being intimate in our relationships.

This love is what Sarah finds missing in her life. She needs to begin to understand the difference between being close and being intimate. She is *close* enough to her husband to "know" that he would not come in with her for therapy, to know not to tell him what he does not want to hear (that she is distressed and sought help), to know that he loves her. She is seldom *intimate* enough to be herself with him.

Learning more about closeness (the "being part of") is easy. Just study systems: large, small, independent, dependent, functional, nonfunctional, real, imagined. There are a myriad of well-structured, detailed systems. The how-to literature on counseling, management, religion, friendship, warfare, supervising, on adjusting, coping, fixing, maintaining, on psychological stratagems, and so on ad infinitum, are all discourses about closeness. Most of the many concepts of relationship that we mentioned earlier (supportiveness, commitment, etc.) are also aspects of closeness. We are as imbalanced in our literature as we are in our living. Read the scholarly treatises in psychiatry and psychology, and in the vast majority you will see a preoccupation with the ego (the engineer of closeness) and an ignoring of the unconscious (the source of intimacy). Go to the popular-psychology section at a bookstore. You will be overwhelmed by the number of books on how to be close.

This cultural imbalance is part of Sarah's confusion. She has read many of these books but has not found what is missing. Instead, she finds how to be a better wife, woman, mother, communicator, or whatever, but not how to be joyfully Sarah herself, with her husband. It is not that all of these books, or television shows, or discussions with friends about how to be "better," are not good and worthwhile and important. It is simply that they only reinforce the side of relationship that is already overly present.

To learn more of *intimacy* is much more difficult. Culturally, we have little insight into or even literature about intimacy. You can read existentialists like William James, Husserl, Dilthey, Maritain, Camus, Sartre, and de Beauvoir. There are theologians like Saint Augustine, Kierkegaard, Tillich, and Gabriel Marcel. Only a few writers on psychology deal with intimacy. Among them are Carl Jung, Rollo May, R. D. Laing, Harry Stack Sullivan, Erich Fromm, Medard Boss, Ludwig Binswanger, and a few less-well-known writers such as Georg Groddeck (*The Book of the It*). Most others concern themselves only with closeness when they deal with relationship; the pendulum has swept most before it. Insight into intimacy is, perhaps not surprisingly, more evident in the immediacy of lyric poets like John Keats or e. e. cummings, or short-story writers like Stephen Crane or William Trevor, than in abstract discourse, or even in longer literary genres, like the novel, in which systems of closeness are developed and explored. Readers have also turned to folk literature and to the stories and writings of such cultures as the American Indian, whose approach (as in the works of Hyemeyohsts Storm) is grounded in the particularity of connectivity. As the contemporary Czechoslovakian writer Milan Kundera has said, "Truth lies in detail." The detail of a moment can be intimate; hundreds of pages of verbalization can bury you in the closeness of "being part of."

Once we are clear that being close and being intimate are different experiences that naturally are in balance, the pressing issue then becomes to clarify and describe the specific qualities and dynamics of the intimate experience, the forgotten and neglected component in relationship.

Intimacy

Most writers have described intimacy in terms of sentimentality or romanticism. To do so is to falsify it. Our capacity for, our experience of, intimacy is part of nature. One of the beauties of what little written literature there is by Native Americans is their clarity on this point. For example, the Hopi word *koyaanisqatsi,* "life out of balance," summarizes succinctly and directly the consequences of our experiential loss. This word, meaning crazy life, life in turmoil, life disintegrating, or, perhaps most significant, a state of life that calls for another way of living, poignantly expresses our current imbalance. What we need is a life *in* balance. *Truth, beauty,* and *love* are our culture's names for this "life in balance," a balance between intimacy and closeness. We hear this from the ancients as well as the writers of the present. Zeno said, "The goal of life is living in agreement with nature." Thousands of years later, Buckminster Fuller spoke to the same issue: "When I am working on a problem, I never think about beauty. I think only how to solve the problem. But when I have finished, if the solution is not beautiful, I know it is wrong." "Life in balance" is experienceable.

To begin with, being intimate is natural. Nonhuman relationships are organically intimate. Students of astronomy, botany, zoology, physics, chemistry, geology, or any of the other disciplines not directly studying humans, can feel the "connections" and describe them to you. Ask the astronomer about comets and you will hear of the interrelationships of gravity, ellipses, mass, ice, tails, of the sun and its solar winds. If they enjoy their work, it is exactly this connectivity that attracted them to their field. In their areas of study, they can feel the intimacy, because intimacy is a basic quality of nature—a quality or dimension, not an intellectual or social construct. This distinction is critical. Intimacy represents a dimension of reality, not a social position.

We see the naturalness of intimacy on the nonhuman level all the time. Creatures, objects, remain *how* and *what* they are in the presence of apparent dissonance among their relationships. Among animals in the wild, the death of one may cause sadness (as humans define sadness) in another, but it does not cause depression. You will see depression only in domesticated animals, those who have learned to be too involved in closeness. You can remain yourself and still be sad; you can retain your *nature.* You cannot do this when you are depressed. Sadness is a natural feeling; depression is turning against your *self.* In nature, nonhumans persist on being who or what they are in relationship, be they stars, wolves, trees, or mountains.

To say so is not to impose some philosophical schema on nature. Nature is not philosophical. It is pragmatic. Nonhuman species retain their natures because it is to their evolutionary advantage to do so. They stay healthier, stronger, more energized, more connected to their environment, and therefore safer in it. They grow and change from natural experiences such as sadness instead of stagnating from the unnatural tribulations of depression. The unique, central importance of the intimate dyad is that it is the operative place, and dimension, in which growth, change, evolution, and the transfer of energy occur. The intimate dyad is the radical experience; not radical in the political sense so much as in the chemical one. In chemistry, radicals are the "relationally" active components. The intimate dyad is the interactive position. It is no less (or more) important than the conservative experience of closeness. Conservation instead of interaction, security instead of change (taking risks), are "sides" of the same sphere. But as security has become an obsessive concern of humans in an increasingly stressful and uncertain world, more and more attention is paid to closeness; more and more is written about it. Less and less attention is paid to intimacy—although it is intimacy that energizes and promotes change, offers the prospect of accelerating and driving our evolution, both personally and biologically, and therefore contains our hope for the future.

Seen this way, understanding intimacy is crucial to our understanding relationship, marriage, family, and parenting. But it is just as important in our preparation for, our capacity for, societal intimacy and closeness, national intimacy and closeness, international intimacy and closeness, human and nonhuman intimacy and closeness. It is vital to our understanding of biology, botany, ecology, and even our relationship to infinite space, including whatever others there may be out there, be they "people" or stars.

For Sarah to be joyfully Sarah, she will have to be able to make connection not just to her husband but to her children, her friends, her community, her trees, her stars, and her universe. In short, she must *experience* the dimension of her own universality.

The Art of Intimacy speaks not only to a somewhat radical departure from the traditional developmental-causality paradigm of human psychology—in which childhood causes of adult problems are diligently traced in a cause-and-effect manner—but to the whole issue of how any of "us"—persons, stars, wolves, trees, or mountains—can continue to be and grow in this world, to be "in this world in good faith." If the question is not as interesting to the ecologist as it is to the psychologist, then we have failed.

1

Personal Spaces . . . Love, Intimacy, and Closeness

You are free and that is why you are lost.

—FRANZ KAFKA

When we spoke of Sarah's not knowing for sure what love was, and of how most of us share in this confusion, we cautioned against trying to define love with words. But since we have to have some descriptive parameters as we look at the union of intimacy and closeness that together form love, we will have to ignore our own caution. Having some *agreed* ground regarding what love is may be more important than thinking that we are actually defining it. In 1970 I *(Tom)* published the following short essay. The response was enlightening to me: on the one hand, I received a great deal of support and many requests for reprints. On the other hand, I received a great many complaints that it was not possible for humans to achieve this level of love. I took the divided response to indicate that I had sounded a meaningful note. If everyone agrees with what you say, most likely what you have said has compromised any real substance.

Love

The experience of loving is unilateral. It asks no response, nor does it demand the other to be deserving. Any and every human being deserves love. It is not earned; one deserves it. So every human being offers us the opportunity of loving them. The loving rewards, not the being loved. Being made in the image of God, each of us deserves love. Our loving is our striving toward godliness. It is our privilege, not our duty. Love has no rewards beyond the experience of it, nor does it require any.

"I love you" is most deeply a feeling, then an activity, and least of all, words. As words, it is often used to stop loving, or reassure, or push away. When the feeling forms the words, the words are not merely heard, but are seen and touched. As a feeling, it brings the loved into being and the lover to the experience of another being. Alone, each is beautiful; experienced together, they create.

The feeling of love arises out of your person, unreasonably and wonderfully thrusting itself on, and contagiously evoking response in the other. When felt unreservedly without hesitance, shame, or fear, the loved has no choice but to love. The slightest hesitance or most meager reservation in loving can undo. If the love feeling in you does not wake a love response, do not chastise the other, but look into your own heart to find wherein your loving lacks fullness or is crippled by your hesitance.

Many good and bad feelings are mistaken for love. Caring for, forgiveness of, tolerance of, infatuation with, dependence on, feeling close to, being friendly with, going to, accepting from, sacrificing to, being excited by, understanding of, and countless others. These feelings are not only *not* love, they are seldom part of loving. They are part of living with, but not loving of.

"I love you" means something very special and very concrete. It means that I surround you with the feeling that allows you—perhaps even requires you—to be everything you really are as a human being at that moment. When my love is fullest, you are most fully you. You may be good, or bad, or both; tender, or angry, or both; but you are you, which is the very most I could ever ask or expect. And so I experience you in all your beauty and all your ugliness. But *you,* not what I expect, or want, or what you feel you should be, or were fashioned to be, but really *you.* I do not love you for what you are. My love of you enables you to be what you are. Love shatters roles and illuminates persons. The acquired masks are discarded, and we face each other as we are—really and usually wonderfully. Because being loved allows the other to be what he or she really is, it is much easier to know when you are loved than it is to know when you are loving. The affirmation of your love is in the other person's being; the confirmation of being loved lies in your experience of being yourself. This you can most readily and reliably know. Since it is easier to know when you are loved than when you are loving, the most serious personal distortions of human experience lie in the loving, not the loved experience. Most psychiatric problems arise out of confusion of loving; mistakes about being loved are rare, if they occur at all.

What are the prerequisites to our loving? I am convinced that if one is really one's self, one is loving, if for no other reason than that loving is so natural, so practical, and so rewarding. The reasons for nonloving must of necessity be unnatural, formidable, and powerful. I suspect these outrageous reasons stem from a fear of being alone or separated, since the need to belong is the second most powerful feeling I know of—second only to love. But to love is to be alone, at least initially and momentarily, since it is unilateral and not dependent on response from the loved one. And since the fear of being separated makes us concerned with the response of the other, and so keeps us from loving, the very fear of aloneness and separation oddly enough results in our awful aloneness and deadly separation.

Can one set out to love? Love by nature is involuntary if it is meaningful. So do I have to sit around and wait for it? Hardly, though most of us do. I can bring it about, but not by trying to love. One of the oddest and most frustrating experiences I have had is the experience of loving my wife when I am not with her. We encounter each other and something goes wrong; I am hurt and confused. I go to my work and, in my inner experience, feel my love and am determined to let her know of this when I see her next. I see her and find the same awful troubles, now more convinced than ever that she does not appreciate the wonderful loving person I am. I have no humility, and so I do not really love. I am alone and so I reflect. I reflect on myself. This reflection is a feeling, not thought. The self-reflection arising out of aloneness quiets and stills. Gradually, it illuminates my surroundings. I sit in the autumn sun and feel quiet, and know surely that there is a larger, and incomprehensibly beautiful universe of which I am only a part, but a moving part. Ultimately this feeling will include my wife. I go to her and see her and me as something more wonderful and larger than the alone of me. My self reflection illuminates her for me. Then I participate in us, and really know her deservingness, and I love without requiring response. We know each other. My humility in the experience of our relationship has suddenly made it possible for me to love and be loved. My humility is not my experience of my insignificance, but my experience of my being part of—belonging—and being extended the privilege of loving what I am so meaningfully a part of. So humility breeds love. Perhaps equally important, such a humility enables me to experience the identity I have with her. We are felt as two alikes, and love of her becomes love of me.

However complicated this seems to you, I tell you it is simple. Without it I am empty, and within it I am. Without it I know you feel empty, and within it I know I could love you. And so the importance of *I Love You* is its importance to me.

Let us take this description as an operative definition, one we can start with. The concept of love is powerful when it is used congruently, but it is much misused casually. Real love moves relationships to greater real experience. Unreal love, which can vary from constructive to destructive, can create plastic relationships, can be used to manipulate others, can have damaging effects on the other's person. For *love* can mean sundry, ambiguous, and sometimes even evil things. Intimacy is a dimension of real love, not of the multitude of other things that get so labeled. Recall that Sarah was very clear about the mutual love between her and her husband; it was their lack of intimacy that was making that love painful.

What Love Is Not

Love is often the mislabel used to describe good and worthwhile feelings, feelings that may even increase closeness in relationships. Respect, enthusiasm, admiration, and camaraderie are all positive but are not love. They may be very important to closeness, and therefore form part of the matrix of love, but they are not love in themselves. We confuse relationships by saying "I love you" when we mean "I am concerned about you" or "I am feeling sorry for you." We care *for* people in many ways and care *about* people in yet other ways. These feelings are useful, spiritually valuable, and important to relationship; but they are not love.

We can even be "in love" without truly loving the other. This particular experience probably causes more relational misery and confusion than any other emotion mistaken for love. Sometimes being "in love" is a precursor to a real love in which we may then grow and learn. Too often, however, it makes loving more difficult. We do not want to give up our fantasy and grow into the reality of actually loving the other as he or she is, rather than how we wish they were. The stepparent who so fantasizes a "perfect" relationship to the stepchild that he or she cannot experience the reality of the child is thereby effectively blocked from loving that child.

The most common example of this fantasy love is infatuation or "puppy love," that first "love" by which we are struck in adolescence. Unfortunately, the experience is not confined to teenagers. When we are infatuated, we do not see the loved other as a real person at all; we are in love with our own idealization. The expressions we use about being "in love" point out this unreality: we are "head over heels," "blind," "in a daze," or so "crazy" about someone we "cannot sleep." What are these but dreams? Perhaps we need to have this wonderful human dream experience of being in love with love first. Children, after all, grow into reality through their freedom to have their fantasies. So being "in love" may prepare us for loving, but it is not love. Giving up the dream saddens us, but allows us to go on.

Evan is so "in love" that he does not see his lover's manipulativeness. His friends do; they see him being used and cannot understand why he does not feel it also. We can talk to Evan about this, but for now he has his own way of seeing "reality." He sees what he is looking for inside himself, not what is actually there in the other. If his lover leaves him, Evan will, as most of us would, feel rejected. He will feel he has "lost a part of himself." This is, in a way, true; his "reality" has been changed. Without intimacy, "reality" is individualistic, because there is no *real* connection. Being "in love" is not an intimate experience.

Usually, being "in love" wears out. It is then that love becomes a possibility. Surviving the disenchantment and the depressions we all felt as adolescents, we move on to really loving each other. Like the players in a play, we move from loving the characters to actually loving our fellow actors.

Love is also confused with tolerance. Tolerance nurtures communal life and is valuable to society, but it is not love; it lacks love's power of acceptance. Tolerance is social graciousness, while acceptance, as we will discuss later, is an integral part of love. Tolerance sometimes helps us move to acceptance and love, but sadly is more often experienced as a self-righteous rationalization for never accepting in love what we tolerate. We tolerate those with whom we feel no connection; indeed, to whom we usually feel superior. The "religious" person who tolerates another's spirituality must seriously question his or her own spirit. The "religious" person who does not even tolerate another's spirituality is neither tolerant nor loving—but righteous.

Forgiveness is sometimes felt as love, but it is not. You may ask, "But isn't forgiveness an integral part of love?" We are saying no. When I feel forgiven, I feel once again a part of my community—a wonderful feeling, but different from being loved. Not better, not worse, just different. Forgiveness may pave the way to my being loved, but, however nurturing, it is not love. "He that cannot forgive others," the English clergyman and author Thomas Fuller said, "breaks the bridge over which he must pass himself; for every man has need to be forgiven." But every man also has the need to be loved.

The feeling most frequently confused with love is "taking care of" someone who is dependent on you. A new couple come in together for their first therapeutic visit. They are fairly quiet and very protective of each other's feelings. As the story of their relationship slowly unfolds, it becomes clear that they have been "taking care of" each other this way since their relationship began. They have two children and are very involved in "taking care of" them as well. It is difficult to bring out why, but they both feel dissatisfied in some vague way. They will not and cannot "hurt" each other, even when that is what needs to be done. They cannot say "I wish you would grow up" or "I was hurt by your behavior the other night" or "I think you need to work on how you make love." They are already starting to have the same difficulty with their children. They take care *of* them in the misbelief that this is caring *for* them.

Suggesting that care-ful parenting is not love is begging for trouble, but we are convinced that it is not. It is parenting, and despite its tremendous genuine importance and crucial place in human relating, it should not be mistaken for love. This is not to say that love is not a part of parenting, but it is a very special and particular part. You must love your children as well as parent them; simply parenting them is not enough. Parenting them prepares them to live in the world; loving them enables them to prosper emotionally in relationship and to find a quiet and beautiful delight in simply being, even when they are alone. We parent when we teach; we love when the sight of our children makes our hearts glad simply because they exist.

Phyllis is thirty-three and has two children, nine and five years of age. She works as a programmer during the day and as a parent at night. After the divorce, the children's father moved to the West Coast, and he has not seen them for three years. Phyllis talks about the difficult job of trying to be both parents, the tiredness she feels, the energy she lacks. She struggles with the guilt she experiences when she resents her children and knows at those times that something is not as she wants it to be. When she can feel the joy of her love with them, she more directly becomes aware of its too-frequent absence, and the anger and hurt she feels because of this.

Brian has a very different life experience. Since his divorce, he sees his three children every other weekend. These times are mostly filled with "doing" activities—movies or skating, visiting friends, eating out. He feels little connection to his children or their real lives, other than the pain he experiences from his deep love for them. He does not know how to change this. Just as he could not find what he sought with their mother, he cannot find it with them. He is not even sure where to look.

More children today suffer from a deficit of this love than did in the past of large extended families. We have too few extended families, too many one-parent families. These parents may be caring and responsible, but they are often so concerned with being "good" parents, so worn out from carrying the whole burden alone, that they lose the capacity to be joyful parents. Children in such families may get extra parenting but inadequate love, in that "eyes lighting up" sense. Of course, this deficiency also happens in families where both parents are present, but either have too much zeal about preparing their children to "be successful in the world," and not enough playful intimacy with them, or are so stressed by their struggle with life that they have nothing left to give their children. Such parents have not learned how to be themselves, and so cannot share those selves with their children.

Frances and Tim have been in therapy for about a year. They have a five-year-old child. They told us a story that illustrates the difference between loving and parenting. While traveling as a family, they stopped to eat. The waitress took the parents' order, then asked the child what he wanted. He said he wanted a hot dog with everything on it and a large Coke. Frances humorously and politely said, "Bring him some chicken, mashed potatoes, and peas." When the waitress returned, she placed the parents' food in front of them, and then set a hot dog with everything on it and a Coke in front of the child. She left, and there was a deep silence. Then the five-year-old said, "She must think I'm a real person." At that moment the child felt loved, not because he had gotten his way but because he was accepted for himself. Frances and Tim expressed their love in their silence. They had learned something: Parenting and loving are not the same thing.

We love specifically when we not only allow, but enable, enhance, and enjoy the "otherness" of our child, spouse, or lover. This is a special experience, for so much of the time we are instead caring for or caring about others by tolerating, taking care of, forgiving, or any of many other responses that are not love but aspects of closeness, a part of the matrix of love. They are essential parts of closeness and certainly not unloving, but closeness alone is not love. Liking is not love, understanding is not love, friendship is not love. They are profoundly important human relational experiences, but they are not love. We may indeed love a friend, but the experience of love is not the same as the experience of friendship. What we mean by love is the fully felt connection John Donne described in "A Lecture Upon the Shadow":

> Love is a growing, or full constant light,
> And his first minute after noon, is night.

Many relationships are tormented by confusion about loving and liking. But, where definitions of love are elusive, what we mean by *like* is fairly clear. We like people when we enjoy the way they love us. The difference has a startling implication: It suggests that others can love us in ways that we do not enjoy. We believe this to be absolutely true. Being loved, being moved by another's acceptance into knowing ourselves as we really are, is sometimes quite unenjoyable. The knowledge may bring us to an awareness of ourselves that confronts and troubles our preestablished mythology. The result can be painful. Since the new awareness comes about through love, and feels authentic—not a judgment or accusation, but a sharing by the other that cannot be rationalized away—we can grow with it. But we are not always overjoyed with those who bring us to such honesty. We can even dis*like* them. When others, by loving, make us be who we are in some way we *enjoy*, that is when we "like" them.

Being around Henry and Gail is not easy at best, and when they really get going they can drive their closest friends away. In the therapist's office they get downright mean with each other. Their usual mode is a perpetual round of nitpicking, bickering, and complaining that makes it difficult for others to be comfortable around them: "You never do anything right." "You're a rotten lover." "You get lost every time we go on a trip." "Why can't you get a decent job?" "Why do you let that person walk all over you?" "You're a wimp." "Why can't you ever tell the truth?" These are their terms of endearment. It seems clear to most who know them that they do not like each other. That they stay together anyway would seem to mean that they must love each other. There is *some* connection between them. Some couples stay together who neither like nor love each other. In them, there is no connection; there is simply the commitment to slowly die with each other.

It happens frequently in relationships and marriages that liking and loving are not experienced together. It seems to be easier to "like" a mistress or casual lover whose ways of loving suit our personal mythology; that, after all, is why we picked them. But the struggle of the primary relationship *does* have real importance. All of us need to learn to be loved in ways we have never been willing or able to be loved before. This need is where the critical importance of intimacy becomes clear. Love forces us to grow, and humans grow with extreme reluctance. We often resent those whose love forces our growth. The intimate experience is the only opportunity we have to resolve this dilemma. The intimate experience is available in all of our dyadic relationships. We *can* grow from intimacy with the flower, the mountain, or the painting, but the human-to-human relationship is where we learn, mislearn, and relearn most directly. The primary relationship is where we can relearn most profoundly.

How puzzling that so often we do not choose someone we like, with whom it would be easy and comfortable to live. And yet, we do not. Two friends seldom pair. "Incompatible" people often do. We are not talking here about partners who abuse each other, or even about those who childishly fight constantly. We are talking about our predilection to pair with someone with whom we then come to struggle, of choosing those whose ways of loving us we dislike. We choose for traits or reasons that quickly become our yokes. The yoke of any primary relationship is its truth. The relationship, if real, forces us to this struggle. There is an emergent sweet pain to any real relationship. Disliking someone can be the beginning of love, as even the movies know (as portrayed, for example, by Bogart and Hepburn in *The African Queen*). A primary life pairing formed of such a relationship is often called a marriage, but is, in reality, a living position, not a legal construct. It is a spiritual concept, not a religious one.

Not all feelings that in relationships masquerade as love are good in themselves: righteousness, control, or planned and relentless dependency on another are certainly not love. Gratitude, loyalty, deference, or placation may be useful and positive at times but are not love; psychopathy, depressive passivity, subtle rape, and manipulation are some more of the thousand distortions that are called love. Some of these qualities are evil in themselves, others only if they masquerade as love.

The Intima

Often our difficulty with knowing what love is and is not is really a matter of our failure to see the differences between intimacy and closeness, or to see the imbalance between the two. What is intimacy on the personal level? How can we understand Sarah's depression, her hurt with her marriage, her search for the person, Sarah? Inside each of us lies our *intima,* the deepest core of our person. It is the innermost part of ourselves, our most profound feelings, our enduring motivations, our sense of right and wrong, and our most embedded convictions about truth and beauty. Our *intima* also includes that behavior which congruently expresses these innermost aspects of our person.

We can survive our disapproval of, dislike for, or disrespect for others. The feeling can isolate us painfully, but it is nothing compared to the devastation we feel when we disapprove, dislike, or disrespect ourselves. Alienation from our *intima* can incapacitate us. To live in the world in good faith, I must care for, like, and respect myself. If I disdain others, I may be tormented; if I disdain myself, I am unlikely to survive. Likewise, I can survive others' dislike of me, but my personal well-being cannot withstand my dislike of myself.

What is this *intima* I must know, love, and respect in myself? What is it with which I need to be congruent in order to live in this world joyfully? *Intima* is not the same as soul. *Intima* is *our participation* in the soul experience. Soul is when there is no need at all for closeness, system, or accommodation, because all is connected. Soul is totally unconscious. Our *intima* is a bridge to soul, but is not in itself soul.

Kaye comes in to the therapist's office every week. She is painfully obsessed with the safety of her three children. She insists that they call her every hour or so when they do anything away from home. If they take a trip, they have to call her regularly to reassure her. She knows how destructive this obsession is to her, to her angry and silently disapproving husband, and to her patient but resentful children, who are outwardly good-natured most of the time, but underneath feel their self-confidence being undermined. (They also feel very embarrassed in front of their friends.)

Kaye comes in one day saying offhandedly that she thought about not coming because she has a cold and does not want to give it to the therapist. The therapist says, "I don't believe in the germ theory." This makes Kaye angry, and she says, "Damn you, what if I'm walking down the street and some careless maid knocks a flowerpot off the windowsill of the twelfth floor of an apartment building and it hits me on the head—would you ask me why I was out on the street?" The therapist replies, "Of course I would. Do you want to spend all of your life worried about careless maids, or every virus, or that at any moment, when one of your children is out of your sight, something dire is going to happen? You can only do something about you."

Like Kaye, we each have enough germs in our noses and throats to infect half the city. And, like her, we each have to rely on ourselves, our health, our spirit, our immune system—our will to live, our *intima.* We cannot live our lives in response to the muggers, or to the angry lover, the paranoid neighbor, the misunderstanding colleagues. They are out there; we have to deal with them and be aware of them. But we can *do* something only about ourselves.

We are each in charge of our own lives. What happens to us may be only 0.1 percent our own part and doing. It may be 90 percent. It makes no difference; it is the only part we can do anything about. Sartre wrote (in *Situations*), "We do not do what we want and yet we are responsible for what we are—that is the fact." And that is our responsibility to our *intima.*

The *intima* is the way in which we value and esteem ourselves. It contains our ongoing sense of who we are, how we are, and how significant we are in our being with others. It has little to do with how others think or feel about us. We know some of the ways these self-valuing qualities are established in childhood and adolescence; they include touching, unconditional positive regard, and the freedom to experience self-responsibility. What therapists do not know how to do well is amend the deficiency in self-esteem that we see in adults. Why do people persist in self-depreciation when they have repeated experiences of being valued and loved by others, be they friends, lovers, spouses, or therapists? Why are they so resistant to the love and respect of others who are significant to them? Often, we therapists have more respect and admiration for the people we see than they have for themselves. Why does it change nothing in them?

It changes nothing because there is an absence of intimacy. This intimacy is the dimension necessary to actualize self-love and self-esteem. Our clients are often more concerned with, and aware of, our feelings than with their own; not in the sense of refraining from hurting our feelings, though that is often present, but in the sense that they are more concerned with what *we* think or feel than what *they* think or feel. We are convinced that only if they experience such close feelings toward us, while they are also fully aware of themselves, can they change. Change happens so seldomly with spouses, lovers, friends, or therapists, because the experience has to be one of intimacy, not just supportive closeness. Our inability to choose freely to be our intimate selves is why we must try to understand intimacy's anatomy. We must regain our balance.

Defining Intimacy

Intimacy is derived from the Latin *intima,* meaning "inner" or "innermost." Your inside being is the real you, the you that only you can know. The problem is that you can know it only when you are being intimate with something or someone outside yourself. *Intimate* itself is revealing as a word. As an adjective it means "personal," "private," "detailed," "deep," "innermost." As a noun it describes a close friend or associate. As a verb it means "to make known indirectly" or "to hint at." This sense of touching our innermost core is the essence of intimacy: It contains all the qualities implied in its various definitions.

Melinda comes to therapy because in the last several years she has been in two relationships that ended painfully. Each time, she began by thinking that this one would make her happy, this one was an answer to her loneliness. After the first, she blamed her lover; after the second, she is questioning herself. Does she so misjudge the other, or is it her own inability to be joyful? She is not at peace. "I guess I want to know what happened. I thought I knew who I was, what I wanted. Now I'm not so sure."

William has been seeing a therapist for the past year. He is more comfortable and coping better with graduate school, but he is not really different. He still hurts in his innermost self; he is hurt by his dissonance with his *intima.* In William we see this dissonance in his inability to be spontaneous, playful, and relaxed, but he experiences it as a lack of joy with life. William cannot really understand when the therapist suggests that he "go out and play" or "go run around your house backward." He graciously takes these suggestions as intended to be helpful, even smiles a bit to signify that he knows they are meant playfully, but he cannot make the connection between them and his dissonance. He wants some "work" to do to get better. He cannot "see" how to do this work. Actually, William needs experiences that would allow him to be in touch with his insides, so he could "see," while in a place in which he could use the experience to change him. The only such place or experience we know of is intimacy.

The outstanding quality of the intimate experience is the sense of *being in touch* with our real selves. It allows us a fresh awareness of who, what, and how we are. It differs from introspection or meditation, which are ways of *looking* at ourselves. They are between us and ourselves, "alone" experiences, and, while valuable, do not energize, enhance, or create growth as intimacy does. In the intimate experience, our "seeing" happens in the presence of the other. It requires no looking or thinking but occurs directly; it is experiential. In this sense, we can be intimate with flowers, animals, trees, and stars, and be nourished by the experience. But the most powerful and profound awareness of ourselves occurs with our simultaneous opening up with another human. This is the most deeply and directly we humans are capable of experiencing our real selves in the world. It is the most meaningful and courageous of human experiences.

Sarah, Kaye, Melinda, and William all feel the absence of this experience in their lives. The lack is not something their spouses, lovers, children, or therapists are not doing; rather, they are estranged from a way of being in the world in good faith. Interestingly, most of us do not sense intimacy as courageous or meaningful at the time we are experiencing it. We perceive it simply as feeling good, being real. We long for it, search for it, wish for it, but still we seldom experience it, because we are so consumed by our closeness, our established systems of interaction. Consequently, both meaningfulness and courage are malnourished in our lives. This malnourishment is what Sarah, Kaye, Melinda, William, and so many others *are* in touch with: "I am not joyfully me, and I do not know why. Why is this, and how might I change it?"

Who knows you? Does your lover, spouse, parent, sibling, child, boss, or friend know you? Think of all the times you have actively thought about and struggled with the fact that they do not. They know parts of you, know you in certain ways, but they do not *know* you. But you yourself, do you *know* you? Unfortunately, for most of us the answer again is no. Here is where the deficit of the intimate experience is most apparent; for it is the only way in which we can both know and nurture ourselves. How can we define this experience in a way that helps us? How can Sarah, Kaye, Melinda, William, you, or I become rebalanced?

The Personal Space

Dick has had his Saturday planned for most of the week. He wants to work on his ship models and check through his supplies and equipment. He has even found a reasonably pleasant way to think about cleaning out the storage room, which he knows needs doing: He will use the time to think about building a small workshop there. But on Friday evening, Toni asks him to go to a movie with her on Saturday. He does not want to go but feels guilty about it. After some stilted conversation, they leave it that she will go to the movie and he will follow his own plans. Yet when Saturday arrives, Dick does not enjoy his models, he does not pleasantly daydream about workshops while cleaning the storage room; in truth, he does not enjoy his day much at all. What happened? Did Toni do something to him? By analyzing this situation, we can start to define the intimate experience.

All humans have spaces. We exist in several different ways with ourselves, and we can think of each of these ways as a "space." When you walk alone, musing to yourself, you are in your own personal space. That experience was Dick's plan for Saturday. Being able to have that space and go there is most important to our staying healthy and sane. We all know this intuitively—know when we need to get away, take a break, or retreat. When we are wise, we heed these feelings. When we deprive ourselves, we often end up physically, emotionally, spiritually, or relationally "sick."

On the other hand, surely you have had the experience of being alone but not freely and pleasantly having that space to yourself. Instead, your head is filled with others who are not there physically but nonetheless very much present. This is not the warm, pleasant feeling of remembering or sense of belonging that we will discuss later, but the intrusion of some other into your personal space. And this is how Dick did spend his Saturday. The invasion of our personal space by others is the essence of neurosis; that is, we do it to ourselves. When we are obsessed, compelled, anxious, depressed, or any of the many other ways we have devised to lessen our humanness, we are not alone in our personal space but unhappily sharing it with the other. Toni did not ruin Dick's day. Dick's guilt and then resentment and then anger about Toni and her desires spent the day with him Saturday, and ruined it for him. He did not enjoy being Dick that way. Most of us do not enjoy ourselves when we are struggling with ghosts in our own space.

This personal space is a unique and valuable part of us. When we are in it healthily, we are alone in a way that refreshes and enlivens us. We feel good about ourselves, without excuses or apologies; there is no one else there to listen to, report to, or alter ourselves for. What others think of us is not relevant or important. Here in our space we simply are who we are, without self-consciousness or apology. Most of us spend too little time in this space, both because of the real stresses of our external lives (all that closeness again) and because we collect others and let them move in as ghosts (another form of closeness).

Some mornings you wake up, sit on the side of the bed, and begin thinking about that interview with your boss today, or a difficult assignment, or conflict with a co-worker. You are not alone, quiet, or at peace with yourself. If you could find some way of thinking of these things without altering or changing yourself or your personal space, you could preserve your peace and calm. Learning how to do this is the real issue in healthy relationships.

Human beings are complicated creatures. There is a tendency to create more and more complicated theories to explain behavior and emotions. Behavior theory gives rise to learning theory. Simple psychology gives way to analytic theory or ego psychology theory. These theories then become less and less directly connected to the living process itself. Underlying all the theorizing remains a very basic problem: *How can we be ourselves while we are in relationship to another person?* It seems a simple question, but, as with Dick and Toni, in actual living it proves very complicated. Understanding what makes up the healthy, creative, relating human being must lie at the core of any theory attempting to explain behavior. The answer may simply be that the healthy person, the mature person, is the one who can do just this: remain himself or herself while in relationship to another. If, as some anthropologists and ethnologists have proposed, relationship is one of the driving forces in human evolution, then this concept is not just a psychological construct; it is a core biological issue for us as persons. In *Encounter with Anthropology,* Robin Fox writes:

> . . . the actual picture of the evolution of the brain is much more complex. But in essential outline it is true and, for immediate purposes, enough to make the point that man's uniqueness is a biological uniqueness and that culture does not in some mysterious sense represent a break with biology. The present human biological make-up is a consequence, among other things, of cultural selection pressures. Man is, therefore, biologically constituted to produce culture, not simply because by some accident he got a brain that could do cultural things, but because the cultural things themselves propelled him into getting a larger brain.

This conscious brain allows more effective relationship, but makes us vulnerable to capture by the very systems that helped drive its evolution.

If our premise—that psychic health is the ability to maintain the self in relationships—has some truth, then the neurotic person is one who has to accommodate, compromise, or alter who he or she is in order to stay, even uncomfortably, in relationship to another person. More radically, the psychotic is someone who can find no way to be who he or she is in relationship to another. This simplified concept demonstrates the operative reality of the theory of personal space.

When some other intrudes into our personal space, we are instantly aware of it. If the intrusion is loving, we feel loved, enjoyed, enlivened, and expanded. However, if it is unwanted and uninvited, we feel lessened, troubled, unloved, and assaulted. Our personal space is exquisitely sensitive to the motivations of the other. This is true whether the other is there physically or only "in our heads." We are *responsive* to these intrusions. We have an immediate feeling response; we do not have to think about it. We feel affirmed or disquieted, and in either feeling, we define that other.

Shared Space

Wilbur and Christie have been together for six years. They have built a support group of friends who get together on weekends to go skiing, play tennis, hike in the mountains, or just sit around and talk. The group can now move comfortably around one another emotionally and feel natural in doing so. Today, some of them are on an outing to the lake. They are sitting around relaxing when another member of the group arrives. There is no shifting or rearranging emotionally; this accepted other is immediately given space. Shortly after, however, Jim and Louis walk up. They are acquaintances, not close friends, and we now see a shifting as some new space has to be created. This is a real feeling, a tangible change. It may be an actual physical moving to create a "comfortable" distance, or just the psychological equivalent inside each person. If the group cannot find some way to make Jim and Louis part of itself, then this uneasy and disjointed feeling will remain.

We have another space as humans, a space we share with some few others with whom we are close. This is frequently just one person at a time, but may be a group (especially a family group) if we are close to all of the group's members. In our feelings, we know this space just as clearly and as well as we know our personal space. Wilbur or Christie or anyone else in that group can feel the difference immediately when Jim and Louis arrive. This new space, too, is immediately sensed and known. We know clearly when we are in one or the other, either the personal space or the shared space. The two form the basic experiential foundation of our lives. To whatever extent we are able fully to be ourselves in these two spaces, we are able fully to be in this world.

When we discussed Dick's unhappy Saturday we said that understanding these spaces would help us begin to understand intimacy. How? Dick was unable to be himself on Saturday: He moved from an unhealthy shared space to an unhealthy personal space. How capable each of us is of *combining these two spaces healthily* determines how capable each of us is of being intimate. Simply put, when you can be in your own personal space while you are also in the space you share with another, you are being intimate.

All of us experience our personal space most often when we are alone. We may be sitting on the porch musing, or playing golf, working in the garden, sleeping and dreaming, or even drifting away while at work. What we are doing is not important so long as relationship to another is not the issue at hand. Our awareness is not focused on the other. We *can* be in our personal space while around others, but it is difficult, and our behavior is often misinterpreted as uncaring or hostile. Conversely, we most often experience our shared space when we are with someone we deeply care about. We may be talking, eating, working in the garden together, or merely sitting quietly with each other. Again, the activity is not important; it is the fact that relationship to another is filling our consciousness and that we are as aware of the other as we are of ourselves. Moreover, it is possible to be in this shared space when alone. The other then is there in your thoughts and feelings. The point again is that you are as aware of them as of yourself.

If we go back and look at Sarah, the first person we discussed, we see that she certainly experienced the shared space with her husband. She accommodated to him, considered him, and was aware of him. It is obvious that she could also go to her personal space. It was some dissatisfied feeling in this space that brought her to therapy, that let her know that she was depressed. Since both these spaces are commonly and frequently experienced by most of us, just as they are by Sarah, why do we so rarely have this longed-for intimate experience of feeling them together? Particularly when most of us are, to some degree, like Sarah, in that we feel both the absence of the experience and the need to search for it.

In our offices, the most common complaint, condition, or hurt felt by people who seek therapy is their alienation from themselves when with others: the lack of intimacy, the lack of the whole gamut of qualities, feelings, and behaviors that are the province of intimacy. The prevalence of the problem simply reflects the difficulty we have in being in these two spaces simultaneously, experiencing both at the same time without one changing the other.

Harry goes outside every morning to get the newspaper. It is only about a hundred feet to the street, but he walks slowly and uses the walk as a quiet time to be easily himself. He returns with the paper, and tries to stay in this place with himself during breakfast. Often whether or not he does so depends on his relations with other members of his family, but his going to get the paper is a time he naturally and comfortably uses for himself. Today, when Harry goes out, his neighbor waves and starts to walk over, saying that he needs to talk. Harry has lost his personal space. He is now in a shared space, and in the transition has instantaneously become less Harry. His awareness is now focused on his neighbor. The comfort of the experience will, of course, depend on the quality of Harry's relationship to his neighbor, but the change in spaces happens regardless. "I know him and he knows me; therefore, we have a relationship, and I have to deal with that relationship": This is the unspoken response inside Harry. Think of the subtle but real ways in which each of us, like Harry, has to move back and forth between these spaces at work, at home, in social situations—even in the simple act of going out to get the newspaper.

Balancing Closeness and Intimacy

In some ways it is paradoxical that we are less likely to give up or move out of our personal space when we meet a stranger. Logically, we should be most ourselves with those we are closest to. But in real life we can be so revealingly honest to someone sitting next to us on an airplane, so astonishingly personal with the gas station attendant we encounter somewhere between El Paso and Flagstaff. Our conversations are not necessarily long, sometimes only a statement or two, but they reveal a reality of us that we seldom let out. Staying who we are becomes more difficult the more involved we are with the other person. Our personal space is in greater jeopardy the more closely related to the other we are. It is more difficult with the in-laws than the stranger, with the original family than the in-laws, and similarly increasingly difficult with our occupational family, our colleagues, and our oldest friends. It is most difficult of all with those to whom we are commonly closest: our parents, our partners, and our children. It is with them that we will have maximum difficulty easily and naturally staying ourselves. This is what we meant when we said that Sarah was not intimate enough to be herself with her husband.

In no way does this mean that these more significant relationships are not close and deeply feeling; they are. Quite the reverse: They are the closest, the most deeply feeling, the lifelong relations. We are loving and loved in them, much more so than with strangers, casual friends, or professional colleagues. With people to whom we are especially committed, we experience at its deepest that shared space. What we experience is closeness. It is profound closeness, but not intimacy. No less important or less meaningful, just different. Having it is essential to our well-being, but not sufficient. *Intimacy* nourishes our being in ways closeness cannot.

One of the ways we can understand Kaye is to see what she does as a never-ending cycle of increasing closeness. She is binding her children to her, worried about being close enough to pass germs, consumed with what she may do to others or they to her. She does this even though she knows that it is not what she wants, it is "driving her kids nuts," and it is pushing her husband away from her. Kaye is not crazy. She does not desire these things. She, like Dick, like Sarah, wants something she has yet to define, yet to identify. Kaye's mistake is that she thinks what she wants is more closeness. Like Sarah reading her self-help books, Kaye is "working on" her problem. But the real problem is that by her work she is simply making it worse—making it worse by not understanding that closeness and intimacy are distinct experiences in a relationship. In therapy, perceiving this difference is an enormous help in dealing with couples or individuals.

Betty is fifty-three, a young fifty-three, a high-energy person who is quite verbal. Born a "southern lady" she started her own small company during her forties and learned that she enjoys the business world. She has been coming in for several sessions along with her husband, Charles, who is fifty-two, a "southern gentleman," a real estate broker, equally intelligent, but less verbal and energetic. At least, that is how they present themselves to the outside world. But in therapy, we do not see "southern ladies and gentlemen." Betty says that she stays angry with Charles all the time because he will not talk to her. As reasonable therapists, we ask Charles, "Why don't you talk to her?" Charles answers that he will not talk to her because she is always angry at him. We suggest that it might be helpful if he would talk to her no matter how angry she is. He shrugs. We turn to her and suggest that she might try talking to him without being angry. She shrugs. They are not staging a performance for us; they do this at home, not just about talking to each other, but in the ways they deal with their children, the neighbors, the house, the cat, and everything else that makes up their life together. They can remember a trip to Mexico nine years ago when for ten days they were somehow different, did not do whatever it is they are doing now, but they have not felt that way in a long time.

There is no question that these two people are close. Their primary awareness is of each other; neither has much of himself or herself. Our therapeutic task is to facilitate their intimacy, their awareness of themselves *while* being aware of the other. We have several options for how we will proceed. We can have Charles and Betty come in separately and, by getting them to share their personal space with us, learn more about them as selves. But this will not change the relationship. The only possible way for that change to happen is the intimate experience. As therapists, we share our own awareness: "You know, this feels crazy to me. You two seem to want to get together, but you both persist in doing exactly those things that will guarantee you never will. Why?" In saying this, we are simply expressing what is present in our personal space, in the context of our presence in a shared space with them. We have been intimate. Remember Henry and Gail, the couple who took each other apart constantly? No one outside them is likely to attempt to be intimate with them. Even with a good therapist, it may take a long while before they can hear anybody else but themselves. They are as yet unaware of their particular interaction, their "dance." Betty and Charles are more aware, more ready to hear. At least once, during that trip to Mexico, they saw something different.

We have no doubt that the majority of interactive impasses encountered in couples come out of the confusion between their closeness and their lack of intimacy. Each is aware of the other, not himself or herself. When they do become aware of themselves, the pendulum swings to the other extreme: they are not related to the other. They move back into their personal space, away from the shared space. In their "dance," there is no touching, much less connecting of spaces or selves. Nothing can change, because of this absence of intimacy. Correcting the imbalance is not just an issue for therapy, for people or couples with problems; it is an invaluable, central need in all of us, as persons, spouses, lovers, parents, children, or friends. The same imbalance exists in most of us.

Closeness, which is what you feel and experience with another in the shared space, is a very intense personal awareness of the relationship you have to that other. In this experience (or dimension of reality), you are as aware of the other person as you are of yourself, and more sensitive to his or her thoughts, feelings, needs, defenses, or dreams than to your own. At that moment the other is slightly more important to you than you are to yourself. If the other is immensely more important, yours is not healthy closeness, and you have a problem. The person who gives away too much of himself or herself in closeness is as out of balance as the person who can give nothing. In the shared space of healthy closeness, you modulate and modify your own feelings, thoughts, and behavior to accommodate the other. You listen gently to your friend's complaints about a mutual acquaintance, even though you do not completely agree. How well you do this is indicative of how sensitively and lovingly you experience the other person's being. For most of us, our capacity varies greatly even with our spouse or lover: Like Dick with his plans for Saturday, we often find ourselves "invaded" by those whom we love most.

Have you ever danced with someone who just seemed to "fit" right, as if both of you knew what you were doing without having to think about it? Healthy closeness is like that kind of dance: a dance in which two people are really caring for and complementing each other. In this psychic dance, you will more often than not gladly give up significant portions of your personal space in order to know the other more deeply, to be more un-self-ishly loving. It is much like giving your dance partner extra room, as you, too, are caught up in his or her movements. But the dance will stay beautiful only while it is balanced by the other dimension of reality. Closeness and its parallel, intimacy, are different parts of the matrix of love, and understanding their differences can change how you see parents, spouses, friends, children, lovers, and yourself. The closer you are to someone, the more intimate you can be, even though the closeness itself makes intimacy more difficult. The opposite is also true: The more intimate you are with someone, the greater the possibility of closeness. Similarly, if you are overbalanced with intimacy (and some few people in our culture are), the intimacy will make that greater possibility of closeness more difficult; they are the push and pull of relationship, different experiences of reality that in balance form a matrix for joyful love.

Healthy closeness means giving up significant parts of yourself to deepen your awareness of the other. It is not at all the same as being dependent. You do not accommodate to placate, please, or manipulate the other. You do it to enhance your own experience in the relationship. We can be defensive with each other, as Betty and Charles were, or angry like Henry and Gail, all fearful in the face of their dependence on each other. Then, like them, we are neither healthfully close nor intimate. We are in our personal space with ghost persons, being neurotic in each other's presence. Nothing happens, nothing changes, no one grows.

Neurosis is a synonym for *nonexperience,* for not being in the world as it is, whereas closeness and intimacy are enhancers of experience. When we choose to give away our personal space, the giving has none of the resentment and anger that always accompany neurotic dependence. The latter comes when, out of our own needs, we modify our own personhoods to "take care of" the other.

John is having more and more difficulty staying with his wife. By the time he comes to therapy, he has been thinking about divorce for a while. It might be more correct to say that he *would* be divorced if he did not feel so guilty. Why? If he gives reasons why he wants to leave, it seems to him as if he is ungrateful, wanting to give up an "ideal" relationship. His wife does everything for him: waits on him, defers to his wishes, anticipates his needs, makes sure that he is always comfortable, and only wants to make him happy. John can no longer stand the burden of being responsible for her personhood. For this is the deal they have made: "I will be anything for you if you will just love me, just tell me I am all right, just need me"; "I will need you if you'll be what I want." He wants to change their contract. He feels her hidden anger; he senses her neediness. It does not feel like love to him. He no longer "needs" to tell her what to be. He wants to be free. So does she; she just does not know it yet.

"Taking care of" others is almost always the opposite of caring for them. Caring enhances and enlivens both; "taking care of" diminishes both. This is, of course, less so in taking care of those who are truly dependent: children, the elderly, the ill. But only if we know that we are making a *choice* to "take care of" can we avoid anger and diminishment. You can care enough to choose to "take care of" children and elderly or ill people. The recipients know how fine this line is, and how difficult it is to walk. Buddha once responded to a seeker, "Why are you so angry with me? I have not been taking care of you." Unwanted children and elderly, infirm parents are frequently abused and/or neglected; this hostile caretaking is one of the saddest failings of our society. For most of us, if we think back, the times we would most like to undo with our children are those when we reluctantly and resentfully took care of them: the forced help with the homework instead of shared learning, the rough bath instead of a playtime in the water. We feel the wrongness of it, how it gives the wrong message. "Taking care of" must be chosen and can never replace caring.

I *(Tom)* remember a very instructive experience that brought me to recognize a personal truth in an unforgettable way. One of my infant children could not sleep. She just cried. My wife had stayed up for hours and was worn out. I took my turn. I remember sitting in the living room, holding the child in my arms. She cried; I tried to soothe and comfort. In reality, I was trying to get her to stop crying so she would sleep. She kept crying; my taking care of her did not seem to matter. About five o'clock in the morning I finally understood something: I realized that she *needed* to cry. I did not know why, but I finally stopped trying to get her to be quiet. I gave up "taking care of" her, and started caring for her. Within minutes she stopped crying and slept. I had the experience of being both close and intimate, and she evidently had the same experience.

"Taking care of" is close, not intimate; it is like providing a service. It is a necessary part of life, and when chosen it can be done healthily (be in the true sense a "service"), but it does not build or change relationship. Closeness affirms and sustains relationship. Intimacy changes relationship.

While creating more closeness, intimacy teaches us about ourselves and makes relationship different by allowing us to become different. Few of us could sit in a closet with another person for any length of time without learning a great deal about that person. This would be even more inevitable if we were sitting there with someone we cared about and had chosen to be closeted with. In the closet, our own awareness is focused on the other while we are close. But in some rare moments, in that shared space of our closet and in the presence of the other, we may experience ourselves in some new, different, and more profound way. This is *intimacy*. When I am close, I know you; when I am intimate, I know myself. When I am close, I know you in your presence; when I am intimate, I know myself in your presence. Intimacy is a remarkable experience. Usually I know myself only in my aloneness, my dreams, my personal space. But to feel and know myself in the presence of another is enlivening, enlightening, joyful, and, most of all, freeing. I can be who I am freely and fully in the presence of another. It is the only true freedom we have as human beings. I can be myself without stopping others from being what they are. The two freedoms go hand in hand. I can be myself as a part of everything else in the universe, finally fully belonging and being. I can be my intimate self.

It is easy to see why we so long for intimacy. What is less easy to understand is why we so seldom have it.

2

Personal Forms . . . Me, Myself, and I

Let there be spaces in your togetherness.

—KAHLIL GIBRAN

I *(Pat)* obviously grew up with a father who was a therapist. At the time this fact was irrelevant to me; my dad went to work every day, just like everyone else's dad. However, his career did provide me with my best friend. At that time, Dad was part of the same Atlanta Psychiatric Clinic where we both practice now. Another member of the original staff was Dr. Carl Whitaker, the prominent family therapist. Carl's son Bruce was my age, and we went from being toddlers to young men together, in and out of each other's lives.

Over the years there developed a tradition among the four of us, the two fathers and two sons, of going off on long weekend camping trips. These might be hiking in the mountains, canoeing a river, or fishing on a lake. The activity did not matter, since these occasions were really just an excuse to be together. When we first started our excursions, they were fun, but usual; that is, everyone's role stayed fairly much what it was at home: the fathers tried to teach the sons, and the sons pretended to listen.

But one particular trip up to the mountains of northern Georgia changed the whole experience. This weekend was marked by a series of fiascoes. Carl put unopened cans of beans in the fire to heat; they exploded from the pressure. I went fishing and cast my whole rod and reel into the lake. Bruce tried to retrieve it by trolling with his rod and dropped his in the lake also. Carl went to sleep on his cot, having forgotten to put in the end slats, and when he rolled over his bed closed up on him. Dad went to sleep that night in his sleeping bag. Waking from a nightmare in which hostile Indians were charging down into the ravine we had camped in, he ran and jumped into the lake.

The happy result of all these disasters was that they freed us from our conventions. In a way that was powerfully felt, we all were allowed to be ourselves as persons, instead of being in the traditional father and son roles. To see your father as a person, not just as a father, is an expanding revelation. Seeing your best friend as a person and a self allows you to know your own self in ways you did not before. This kind of experience is *intimacy*. It is not an accident that intimacy occurs in the midst of foibles and mistakes; in them we are very human—as we can be in the midst of real disasters like floods or wars. That outing was so successful that, from then on, all our trips were filled with fiascoes. The pratfalls, absurdities, and even the injuries became part of the family legends. Our behavior was unconscious but very real. The drive to the experience of *self* is universal. It can make us be silly and playful. However, it can also make us risk much more—risk our careers, our relationships, our marriages, and our families.

To look at this concept of *self* directly will help us to answer the questions of why we are out of balance, and why we experience intimacy so infrequently, for intimacy delineates and illuminates *self*.

Although used extensively in the professional and popular language of psychology, the concept of *self* is always vague and loosely defined. It has no clear connection to any concrete human experience to which the reader can relate. Carl Jung, who wrote volumes on the subject, nevertheless wrote of the *self* as essentially indescribable. Yet we believe that if we can describe the intimate experience, we will also be, experientially, defining the *self*.

I *(Tom)* remember a common expression I often used in my childhood. I reserved it for those times when I felt especially good about something that expressed me in a passionate way. In the fifth grade I had a rather formidable teacher. A classmate, not one to whom I was even particularly close, was waving his hand one day to indicate he needed to go to the bathroom. This teacher, being adamant about finishing what she was doing without interruption, ignored his squirming and obviously frantic urgency. Finally, I got up, walked over to him, took his hand, and led him out of the room. When we returned, the teacher sent us to the principal, who sent us home. My mother asked what in the world had made me do it. I answered, "Me, myself, and I." This did not get me very far with my mother, but years later, when I read Sartre's expression "being in the world in good faith," I had an instant recall of that childhood experience. Right or wrong, I had been myself in good faith. Many times after that incident, as I grew to an adolescent, when someone would ask me what had made me do, be, or say something I felt passionate about, I would reply, "Me, myself, and I."

The I *and the* Me

This expression "Me, myself, and I" implies that there are significant differences between the three. We suggest that the differences are indeed significant. The priest and poet Gerard Manley Hopkins saw these differences clearly: ". . . my self-being, my consciousness and feeling of myself, that taste of myself, of I and *me* above and in all things . . ." If you say or think "*I*," it feels very different from when you say or think "*me*." Just as words do, grammar teaches; it carries natural patterns in it. *I* am the subject and *me* is the object. Are these simply different pronouns for talking about the same person? We think not. *I* am initiating, *I* am intrusive, *I* am the actor, *I* am always relating to the world around me in one way or another. *I* am the exerciser of control, decision, denial, clarification, manipulation, closure, and countless other behaviors aimed at my being in the surrounding world, accommodating to it, dealing with its effects on me. It is no accident that *I* and *eye* are homonyms. *I* is the person inside who looks *out,* the operator, not a past being or future being but a present being.

In contrast, things happen to *me*. Others "let me have it," "appreciate me," "do a number on me," or "make love to me." It would really be more accurate to say things happen within *me*. *I* acts. *Me* feels the hurt or happiness. *Me* is both historically conscious and forward-looking; *me,* as summation of past and projection into future, is the foundation on which *I* stand to look out. *Me* is psychologically planning, deciding, arranging *inner* values, experiencing my self-esteem, and dealing with my motivations with respect to the world around me. *I* looks out; *me* looks in. *Me* decides what should or has to be done; *I* decides how to do it. *Me* is my character; *I* is my personality.

Me, myself, and *I* are not the same as superego, id, and ego. Ego, superego, and id are *structural* components of the individual's psyche. *I, me,* and *self* are *functional* components of relationship. There are *I, me,* and *self* aspects in all of the structural components of the psyche.

Carlos has reached the age of forty-three. He has passed his "mid-life crisis" and become more content with his work as an engineer and a little more personal with his wife, Jan, and their two children. He is driving home, listening to a tape of electronic music that his daughter gave him for his birthday. She, as our children tend to do, thinks he can still change and learn to enjoy new things, such as music that is alien to him, and, in fact, he has almost decided that synthesizers are okay, even enjoyable, when, about three blocks from home, he suddenly turns the music off. Why? He has started to think about the fact that Jan said she wanted to talk tonight about getting the house painted. He has moved from *me* to *I*. He is not in conflict about the issue; he knows that the decision needs to be made and does not feel intruded upon. He chose to turn off the tape. His *I* is processing the hows and whys of discussing the house painting. He parks the car and starts walking to the house, still thinking. Noticing their cat stuck in the fence, he bends over and helps it out. He does not actually stop in his physical activity of walking or mental activity of thinking about painting the house. He assists the cat without thinking. That is his *me*.

I and *me* are generally more describable and identifiable when we write or talk of them in particulars. They are not absolute concepts. We can make them substantive by seeing in ourselves, as in Carlos, the ordinariness of the two states and the ways in which we move back and forth between them. What is much more mysterious and difficult to describe is the *self*.

Selfhood

Jeremy is seventeen. He comes in every two weeks with his family for therapy. Tammy, the oldest child, is twenty and comes in during the summer, when she is home from school. Albert, thirteen, is the youngest of the family and the clown of the group. Ed and Katherine, the parents, have been together for twenty-three years and are now in their mid-forties. Theirs has not been an easy marriage. There have been major conflicts. The parents have grown to realize that they had involved the children in these conflicts, so they decided to enter therapy as an entire family. Today everyone is in a fairly good mood, but Ed seems distant and preoccupied. We say, "Ed, you don't seem like yourself today." His youngest child, Albert, immediately pipes in, "Yeah, aren't we lucky." As she has been doing for years, Tammy comes to her father's defense: "I think Dad's still feeling down because Digby died." We know that Digby was their cat and had been ill for some time. We also know Ed has always claimed not to like cats. "How about the rest of you?" we ask. No reply. "So Dad's the only one who's not himself?" Katherine says, "Well, we were all upset when Digby died, but he was old and very sick so it was for the best." Quiet. The issue is just about to fade when Jeremy says softly, "Dad is the only one who knew Digby himself." How can children know such things? We ask, "What do you mean, Jeremy?" He explains, "To the rest of us Digby was our pet, our friend, but to Dad he was a cat." Jeremy understood on some level that his father saw Digby as a *self*.

Why do we say "I was beside myself," and what does it mean? What is the implication of saying "Sometimes I just don't understand myself"? These expressions suggest that both *I* and *me* are experienced as distinct from *self*. It is not *me* that is beside *myself*. The *me* expression is "That's not really me." These are not merely grammatical usages. They are germane and significant expressions of human experience.*

It is *I* who is beside my *self*. The "seeing" person I am recognizes *self* as just as real and powerful an experience as *I* or *me*. The difficulty is that *self* is left so vague, so undescribable, so mystical. Certainly the descriptions of *self* are more spiritual than those of *I*, the personality, or *me*, the character. Psychological literature, particularly in America, is full of material describing the *I*. Originally Anna Freud and Heinz Hartmann in Europe, and Franz Alexander, Alfred Adler, and others in the United States, began moving psychology from the world of the unconscious to the study of the ego. Examples of this orientation are found in the works of John Watson, B. F. Skinner, Karen Horney, Eric Berne, Ernest Beck, Elliot Aronson, and William Glasser, among many others. Most American analysts, psychiatrists, psychologists, therapists, and behaviorists, with their preoccupation with the *I*—a natural and predictable bias, given our active-doing culture—have, in thousands of studies, explored *I* experiences with detailed descriptions of *I*-oriented behaviors. Their work has tremendously expanded our understanding of the *I*, the personality, the conscious process. In contrast, their European counterparts, as exemplified by Wilhelm Reich, Melanie Klien, Max Wertheimer, Wolfgang Kohler, Kurt Koffka, and Jean Piaget, have provided valuable insights into the *me*, the character, the internal process. This work continued with Lévi-Strauss, Ei, Lacan, Ricoeur, and others who are essentially phenomenologically oriented. In

*Language and grammar in some ways know more about humans than humans do. The semanticist Alfred Korzybski wrote about "maps" and "territory" and the relationship between the two, as well as how the structure of language defined those relationships. Ferdinand de Saussure and Roman Jakobson moved linguistics from a historical orientation to a descriptive-structural recognition of the deeper meanings contained in lauguage's structure. The linguist Noam Chomsky and others brought the science of semantics to transformationalism and generative grammar (demonstrating that we have built-in rules that allow us to acquire language, generate sentences on our own, and so forth). Linguistic work with deep meaning, structural meaning, and polysemous meaning (the multiplicity of meanings assignable to our words) has continued with structural anthropologist Claude Lévi-Strauss, the structural psychoanalyst Jacques Lacan, and the psychoanalytic critic Paul Ricoeur. Most recently the French philosopher Jacques Derrida has brought us deconstructionism, which challenges the concepts of "certainty," "fixed meanings," and "assigned meanings," as well as attempts to separate the philosophical assumptions woven into language from the "text" itself. From all this innovative work, it has become increasingly clear that our language contains far more than simple "rendered meanings." It contains both structural and spiritual meaning about us as persons. There is communication and metacommunication; there is meaning and "meaning" within meaning. It may even be that now we are learning that there are meanings "between" meanings. *I, me,* and *self* are both products and producers of such meanings, wherever found.

America it has been the humanists, structuralists, gestaltists, and others, such as Fritz Perls, Mary Henle, Leo Alexander, Abraham Maslow, William Schutz, Richard Bander, John Grinder, and Nancy Chodorow, who, paralleling their European colleagues, have identified the *me* as the center of our being in the world.

Thus, current psychotherapy in our culture, when it is not behavioral or *I*-oriented, revolves around the opposite preoccupation, and is internal and *me*-oriented. Even further, unfortunately, most of psychotherapy, like all human endeavors, always to some extent reflects the ephemeral fashions of the culture: Current infatuation with "I have to be me" or "I have to do my thing" is reflected in therapeutic emphasis on me. This sense of me (as opposed to characterological *me*) is, sadly, often less concerned with the internal state and character than it is with the idea that "being able to do or have whatever I want" is somehow synonymous with being healthy. This orientation might better be described as pseudo-*me*.

The psychological writings on *self* are sparse and ambiguous. Despite the work of people like Jung, Erwin Straus, Eugene Minkowski, and other theorists mentioned earlier, the writings are mostly philosophical, symbolic, metaphorical, spiritual, and Eastern. This is partly why the construct of *self* seems so obscure to those of us reared in the Western culture. We learn the reality of *self* as experience but still have difficulty "seeing" its face.

Since *self* is much closer to nature than *I* or *me* (it may indeed *be* nature), one would then expect its definitions to be mystical, spiritual, vague, and full of the "inscrutability" that human folklore has always ascribed to nature. *Self* is to psychological literature what the notion of the "inscrutable face of nature" is to natural philosophy and theology. The experiences involving *I* and *me* are concrete and describable. They can much more easily be observed, collected, annotated, or behaviorally challenged. They lend themselves much better to clinical and statistical analysis. What a person did, or even how he or she felt or was thinking, is clearer than how the behavior was affected by and in turn affected that person's experience of the *other*.

Self is this elusive relationship between *I-me* and *other*: the relatedness of, the connection of, Ed and the cat Digby, you and me, or our friend Sarah and her universe. (This *I-me/other* is then synonymous with the *I-other* dyad we spoke of in the Prologue.) *Self* is literally nature, and by its nature, for the most part, unparaphrasable. We see its inscrutability in dreams, nonverbal communication, and true altered states of consciousness, all of which are *self*-including experiences.

Where is the *self*? Does inscrutability translate into invisibility? Jung said *self* was indescribable, yet he was aware of its central importance and worked for years on integrating it into theory and therapy. In *The*

Undiscovered Self, he expressed his concern about human reluctance to develop our awareness:

The underestimation of the psychological factor is likely to take a bitter revenge. It is therefore high time we caught up with ourselves in this matter. For the present this must remain a pious wish, because self-knowledge, as well as being highly unpopular, seems to be an unpleasantly idealistic goal, reeks of morality, and is preoccupied with the psychological shadow, which is normally denied whenever possible or at least not spoken of. The task that faces our age is indeed almost insuperably difficult.

Many writers use the concept *self* either idiomatically or metaphysically, as a synonym for *soul,* a special and beautiful word, but without operative meaning and left undefined; left, as Gregory Bateson said in *Steps to an Ecology of Mind,* "So loosely derived and so mutually irrelevant that they [self and soul] mix together to make a sort of conceptual fog which does much to delay the progress of science."

Poets are much less hesitant to proclaim and describe the value of the *self.* Herman Melville, in *Moby Dick,* wrote that "Delight is to him—a far, far upward, and inward delight—who against the proud gods and commodores of this earth, ever stands forth his inexorable self." Walt Whitman wrote in *Starting from Paumanok,* "I have said that the soul is not more than the body, And I have said that the body is not more than the soul, And nothing, not God, is greater to one than one's self is." William Butler Yeats celebrated the self and soul in his "A Dialogue of Self and Soul":

I am content to follow to its source
Every event in action or in thought;
Measure the lot; forgive myself the lot!

Yeats ended "Among School Children": "How can we know the dancer from the dance?" He saw the individual self as a connected part of the larger process, the process Emerson had called the "Over Soul." We would say: The *self* is a bridge to soul.

Despite these difficulties in identifying and describing the *self* process, we would suggest that the persistent and universal concern of humans with what they call *self* tells us that it is a core part of what it means to be human. That is, it defines a dimension of reality and is not a social construct. It is that same dimension of reality we discussed when describing the intimate experience. *Self* is just as real as the *I* or *me.* It can broadly be defined as the ecological dimension of the human psyche. In an ironic way, then, to us, *self* is precisely what Bateson spent most of his creative life trying to describe. His interest in ecology and especially psychoecology (the study of the *relationships* between organisms and their environment, including other organisms) is, in many ways, the study of *intimacy.*

What exactly is this psychoecology? The Bakers are in family therapy. Hal, the father-husband, "needs everything to work out right," according to his own internal agenda. He is a caring and concerned person, as is Jennifer, his wife. She is emotionally volatile and has strong feelings about everything that happens in the family, but feelings that may change within hours. According to Hal and Jennifer, Suzanne, their nineteen-year-old daughter, is exemplary. Their other daughter, Pam, seventeen, is "incorrigible." It is the "problem" of Pam that "brought the family to therapy." Today the parents are frustrated and distraught by the fact that Pam keeps coming home at three or four in the morning despite a midnight curfew. She does this knowing that the punishment has long been predetermined: She is grounded for two weeks. As their therapists, we have been through this battle before. Pam takes her punishment, then once again violates her parents' repeated and clearly stated rules. What can we do? We could deal with it in an *I* way, by suggesting to the parents some stratagems to alter Pam's behavior. For example, we might suggest that so long as they impose limits only in a crisis, they will get nowhere; they need to begin to impose limits on her ordinary, noncrisis living. This *I* approach would be perfectly legitimate and often is helpful. On the other hand, we could employ a *me* approach, by confronting Pam with the fact that the way she is behaving seems to ensure that she will not get what she wants, or at least not what she says she wants. She states that she wants more freedom, to be able to make more of her own choices, but her behavior appears to ensure that she will be less free and will turn more and more control of her life over to her parents. We can point out that she has clearly arranged this pattern, albeit unconsciously. To suggest that she reexamine her motivations would be the *me* approach.

However, there is a third alternative; let us call it the *self* approach. Many therapists who use it call it "family therapy," although not all family therapy is *self*-oriented, and there does not have to be a physically present family for it to happen. It is based on the notion that people in meaningful relationships are all intimately connected. Hal and Jennifer can do whatever they need to do as parents in an *I* way. Their actions may help. Pam can reexamine her own motivations in a *me* way, and that may help. However, suppose we suggest to them that they are all in this together, but that, while related to each other, they are not honestly being themselves within their relationships. They are fabricating a synthetic family. Is there some way they could stay in relationship with one another and remain who they really are? Can they exist as they really are in the presence of *others* who are doing the same? Can the contained and controlled father, Hal, own up to the fact that he really *enjoys* the chosen, although rebellious, freedom of his daughter Pam? Can Jennifer admit the fact that she would like Hal to help her impose limits on her *own* unpredictable, mercurial feelings and actions? Can Suzanne stop having to be good for everybody else and get to be herself in some ways? Can Pam own up to the fact that she is deeply involved in a need to help her parents with their relationship and that this need is *displacing* her own incentives in life? Psychological ecology is an approach that endeavors to bring the family or the *familiar* person to be able to make these changes in their being in the world. Since, in doing this, we will be dealing with the issue of whether these individuals can be in their own personal spaces while they are in their shared space, we will also be dealing with *intimacy*. As therapists, we will be approaching the problem not from the perspective of *I* or *me,* but from the creative, energizing perspective of *self.* We will be trying to deal with the dilemma described by the psychologist Sydney Jourard in *The Transparent Self,* that "Man, perhaps alone of all living forms, is capable of *being* one thing and *seeming* from his actions and talk to be something else."

Looked at in this way, *self* is not all that indescribable. It is a real, beautifully pragmatic concept. A sense of *self* is probably the most significant and meaningful experience we can have. It is as close as humans will come to consciously experiencing the soul. The *self* is what is experienced when we are being intimate. It is the union of spaces we spoke of earlier: the *I* is experienced when we are in the shared space, the *me* when we are in our personal space, and the *self* when we are able to bring the space that is our own into the space we share with *others* and experience both at the same time. *I* and *me* felt together are *self.* Together *I* and *me* form the matrix of *self,* just as together closeness and intimacy form the matrix of love.

The I *Experience*

Since we are defining the *self-intimate* experience in this way, it is worthwhile to try to understand our usage of *I* and *me* on a somewhat deeper level. Too often, *I* dynamics are thought of as self-serving or even narcissistic: "I think only of what I want." This is a distortion. The *I* simply delineates our experience in the shared space, the experience of closeness. It basically means that we pay as much attention to the *other* as we do to our *me.* The *other* does not have to be a person or persons. We may be paying as much attention to a red light, to a corporate organization, or to a culture. One of the clearest ways to see how the distinction between *I* and *me* is perceived is to ask the child of working parents if their parents are different in their workplace than they are at home. If the child is old enough to articulate it, he or she will let you know that the parent *is* experienced as a different person when working. This perception reflects the fact that the parent is in a different *I* space from the one to which the child is accustomed. The change has nothing to do with attitude, feeling, location, or demeanor; it is a different reality. The *I* learns to live with the reality of the *other*, be that *other* a person, a red light, a corporate ethos, or a systemic culture. Learning to live with the reality of the *other* we have called *closeness*. You may feel closer to your spouse or lover, but, as noted above, you have an equally unique closeness to your work and your cultural mores. Just ask your children or friends. The closeness may not be as profound, but it is just as unique. The *I* is what is close: *I* am close to you, *I* am close to the prejudices of my corporate manager, *I* am close to the symbology of the red lights. The *I* responds in a way that at its best not only maximizes our own aggrandizement but, more important, enhances our relationship so we can go on becoming more real, more mutually *self*-benefiting. At least we will not get arrested for running a red light, or fired by the manager when we really want the job. We do need to be aware of the *other*.

Among Phil and Carrie's various conflicts, one in particular appears over and over in the same form. When Phil gets sick he retreats to the bedroom and wants to be left totally alone. When Carrie is ill she likes to be checked on, helped, and to know someone is there. Obviously, each deals with life differently for individual *me* reasons, but that is not the point here. The problem is in their shared space, their *I*. She feels shut out when he does not want her to help him; she feels that he is being selfish. In turn, he feels that she is manipulating and controlling him when she wants his attention. They have not learned to be in the *I* space healthily. It is a fairly common problem.

Because the *I* experience is so action-oriented, so much a part of the culture of closeness, we tend to forget that basically it is not just your being you, your right to be you, *regardless* of the *other*. This assumption is a sad misunderstanding. The true *I* experience is nearly the opposite: It means that I am willing and even glad to modify my own narcissistic needs in order to increase and enhance my total experience in relationship to the *other*, whether the enhancement comes immediately, tomorrow, or next year. This motivation is not manipulative or sociopathic. If the *other* is, for example, a friend, I am genuinely accommodating to his feelings and needs, not to placate him but to increase his acceptance of me as I really am, and his ability and willingness to be himself with me. Such acceptance enables me to be more myself. This in turn not only facilitates our closeness but, more important, enhances the likelihood of our being intimate. All this progression can begin with the *I* accommodating its own needs to the feelings of the other. Such accommodation is not passivity, nor dependence, narcissism, manipulation, or sociopathy, all of which represent a basic imbalance in the *I, me,* and *self*; they are not natural states. If I manipulate you to get you to care for me, I end up not only undermining my own *self*-respect but also your eventual willingness to care for me.

We sit in a session with a couple. Leonard is a handsome, capable, assertive, and very articulate lawyer who tends to stay in his professional posture. Amanda is an attractive, competent, intelligent, and energetic market analyst. She is less articulate but more sensitive than he is, living more in the world of feelings. He is usually very confrontational, even offensive, during our sessions and spends much of the time telling her what is wrong with her. She is generally more placative, but in a slightly withdrawn way. Inevitably, however, she becomes angry and defensive when he starts his lectures on her "deficiencies." His offense/her defense is their usual crisis stance with each other. They care about each other and are committed to staying together, but both confess that they feel rather lost and hopeless about changing their relationship. The hopelessness arises out of their shared conviction that nothing will change because the other will not change. They have fallen into one of the most destructive myths that we encounter as therapists—the myth that change has to be bilateral: "Unless you change, there is no way our relationship can change." The "bilateral" myth is often presented in its corollary form: "If you change first, then I will change, and then our relationship can change." This couple, like so many others, has lost touch with the unilateral power each has in a relationship, the power and effectiveness of the *I* experience, and the importance of staying in charge of one's *self* in relationship. As succinctly stated by Erich Fromm—"Man must accept responsibility for himself. . . . There is no meaning to life except the meaning man gives his life by the unfolding of his powers"—such *self*-responsibility is the only basis for healthy relationship.

Today Leonard is once again confronting Amanda. She is once again angrily defending herself. Suddenly she stops, looks him directly in the eye for a change, and asks, "Don't you know how afraid of you I am?" He sits back in silence for a moment—also a change—and then in a rather subdued and genuinely puzzled manner replies, "I never knew you felt that way. That's not the way I want to make you feel." Both have had an *I* experience out loud; they have moved from a *me* to an *I* encounter. The generated closeness and, over time, intermittent intimate experiences that will come from this beginning will allow them to change.

The *I* then becomes the main facilitator of closeness, not a vehicle for separateness, as is so often implied in the everyday use of the word. *I* is the gift giver, a concept too little understood in our culture. It is unfortunate that *I* has become confused with persona or mask; it is better described as our capacity for closeness to the world around us. It is our ability to be close to others usefully, to interact outside ourselves. Our personality includes our sensitivity to the *other,* our learned ability to modify our own behaviors and feelings without being dependent, manipulative, or destructive. It healthily modifies our actions and emotions on the basis of our real awareness of the *other.*

The "cult of personality," prominent in lay approaches to human behavior (pop psychology, self-help books) and often seen even among professional experts, has not, for some decades now, presented personality as the part of ourselves that respects and works for closeness to others. Rather, such an approach presents personality as an *instrument* to manipulate others. We simply do not accept the validity or usefulness of this. The true *I* wants to be aware of what the *other* feels, thinks, and wants, because what I find in life and relationship largely depends on my capacity to do just that. This *I* is, or can be, the successful engineer of closeness, of the experience of fully being in the space we share with *others.* Personality stripped of human functionality is a role, and thus belongs to the realm of "personality disorders." I can "be assertive," "say no," "dress right," or "go for it all," but if I can not be my*self* with the *other,* I have not succeeded. Successful evolution moves to functionality, not roles.

We are, of course, describing the ideal *I.* None of us has the ideal available to us all the time; we can only hope to grow toward it. We believe that the basic modality of this growth is play. Play is the realm of the *self,* of intimacy, and the *intimate-self* is the dimension in which change can take place. As we will see, *I* and *me* can grow only through this experience.

The Me *Experience*

I *(Pat)* did not read until the second grade. I am not sure why, since by the fifth grade I had become a voracious reader, but I must have had a good reason. Unfortunately, my teachers were unaware of it, and midway through the first grade my parents were asked to come in for a conference. When they returned, I asked Dad what they had talked about. I was naturally nervous, since no one had told me what this meeting was about or had invited me to attend. Dad said, "They think you're retarded." I asked, "What does that mean?" He smiled at me and said, "They think you're stupid, but I told them you weren't." The subject did not come up again until my high-school years, when another teacher noticed that I could not spell. The school sent me to see a psychologist, who gave me all sorts of tests over a two-day period.

Again, naturally, I was nervous. I did not know what the tests were testing for, although at least this time I did attend the meeting. I had to go in to see the psychologist to get the report. I thought that the quickest way to find out would be to ask directly, so I did. He looked at me and quietly laughed. "The tests show, Pat, that you can't spell worth a damn." The point in relating this story is that, while I was anxious about what the *other* (the teacher, the tests, and the psychologist) thought of me, I never was worried about being stupid. In other words, I had concerns in the *I* experience (my personality), but my *me* had been fairly well formed long before even the first incident, and it was not in my *character* to perceive myself as being mentally deficient. Character, as Paul Ricoeur wrote in *Philosophy of the Will,* "is thus not a destiny which governs my life from without, but the inimitable manner in which I exercise my freedom as man; it is never glimpsed in itself, just as the origin of perception never becomes the object of perception. It is involved in the humanity of my own existence, as the origin zero of my field of motivation. I only discern it by allusion in the feeling of difference which makes me other than every other."

The *I*-personality is the most likely part of our person to be neuroticized, and in most of us to some degree it is neuroticized. Each of us has some insecurities, anxieties, and nonproductive worries. We are not born with our personalities. Character is much closer to genetics. Parents can teach the child to deal with the world manipulatively (hysterically, for example), to make one's way by being seductive or placative, by staying a cute little boy or girl, by compartmentalizing the real world so that one never has to relate to the reality of the *other.* This kind of behavior can be easily taught to an impressionable five- or six-year-old. It is much more difficult, and much more ominous, to teach a nine-month-old that he or she is worthless, or that the world is an overly dangerous place in which to live. These latter distortions are matters of *me,* not of *I. Me* is much more basic than *I,* a more core experience. Nature by and large produces "natural" children. That is, if we watch children as they move into the relating world (meet their parents), we see that they invariably try natural remedies to relational problems first: If Mom or Dad is depressed, the child will smile, sing, dance, and offer love. It is only after many, many failures at this that they will decide their loving is not "good enough," and move off to some distortion like placating or *self*-negating. Nature does not create people that way, but, sadly, both the *me* and *I* can be beset by a multitude of neuroticisms, and sometimes by psychosis. *Me* distortions, such as fear of relationship, fear of experience, are usually the most distressing in a person's overall life, primarily because they are always there. Since *me* experiences have less to do with the world around you and more to do with how you perceive yourself, you cannot escape them. At least, not easily. And they are certainly more difficult to change in psychotherapy.

Me is more germinal than *I*, coming from the deeper recesses of our person, closer to our biological, cultural, and psychological roots; *me* is more integrated, and thus much less modifiable and accommodative. It is always more consistent than *I*. The *me* sits in the bottom well of a person and steadfastly wills that person toward those broad behaviors that will meet some very basic emotional needs, such as feeling accepted, being loved, or feeling worthwhile. These needs are usually few in number and arise out of our biological needs, as modified by our earliest and most primitive experiences. The primary needs have been described by psychologist Abraham Maslow as physiological well-being, assurance of safety, social belonging, esteem, and self-actualization. These *natural* needs can be distorted by early experience and thus manifest themselves in indirect ways. Character, which is *me*, is very different from the personality, *I*. Out of these deeper and earlier memories springs our person: consistent, difficult to change, and energized by the force of the will. *Me* is detached and often arrogantly uncompromising with reality, mobilized by those primitive affects and motivations that persist throughout our lives and enable others to recognize us in other places and later times. *Character* meant originally "to carve, engrave, scratch, scrape, cut in grooves, stamp, or brand." The etymology reflects the qualities that we see in *me*; it comprises the deepest imprints of our persons, those that generate the few but powerful and persistent motivational systems that identify us as unique persons, regardless of variations of our personalities over the years.

Beverly is nearly forty. She is an intelligent and attractive woman, although she does not think so. Actually, we should not even say she does not "think" so: She "knows" she is unintelligent and unattractive and cannot be convinced otherwise by external realities. Her attractive qualities do not need to be divined by her therapist. They are evident: Beverly is active in her career, public affairs, community activities, her church, and all other areas of her life. She is sought out by organizations of her peers and colleagues for her talents and competence. However, even while she is involved in these myriad activities, she "knows" that "she" is not this successful, popular person. Her disclaiming is not coming out of the manipulative *I*, playing games to get something; Beverly is truly in pain. The pain affects her relationships, her career, her ways of caring for herself. We can see how early the distortion developed in her, because it predates even her sexuality. Developmentally, she learned she was a "separate" person but then became very distorted about who and what this person was. Her *me*, or character, is suffering.

The *me* is what I experience when I am in my personal space, dreaming, meditating, walking or running, simply being in the world without the distraction of paying attention to anyone or anything else. The *me* carries my history from the past and projects it into the future. It carries my values, both good and bad. The *I* experience of the world around me—the weather, the flowers, the grocer, someone I love—the *I* that emerges and grows in these experiences, expanding closeness and awareness, can energize the solitary *me* experience. When healthy, they nurture each other.

The fact that we experience *me* when alone, even if we are around others, leads to a very common confusion evident in people who come in for therapy. They confuse the existential aloneness of *me,* a natural and necessary state, with the painful feeling of loneliness or deprivation of the *I* experience. Perhaps in no other place can the necessity for the intimate experience be seen so clearly. In intimacy, the *self* gets to know the difference between being alone and being lonely. Therefore, the person can change.

To live exclusively in one's own personal space is to be psychotic. One does not have to be a doctor to diagnose this. It is what makes the average person uneasy around psychotics; we feel we do not exist to them. There is no *I-other* for the psychotic. Conversely, to live exclusively in the shared space is to be neurotic. There is no *me* for the complete neurotic. This, too, we all recognize in its blatant forms. These are the people who are incessantly checking out *others*: "How do you feel about me?" "How does Jim feel about me?" "How does Sally feel about me?" "How does the dog feel about me?" To live in neither shared or personal space, to have available neither *I* nor *me,* is to be psychopathic. The Manson-like cult leader, the "inhuman" human, the people we cannot relate to at all, are in neither space. We do not know where these people are, are coming from, or are going, since they are not participating in the same realities as we are. Professionally, these people are the most difficult to treat; many say they are untreatable.

Most people do not fall into any of the extremes mentioned above. More often, there are mixtures that create intermediate life positions. For example, some people live primarily in their personal *me* space, making intermittent excursions into the shared *I* space. These efforts are all too often ineffective, unrealistic, problem-producing, or unhappy failures. Then these primarily *me* types scurry back to their own world, reluctant to reappear. Therapists label such behavior as borderline states. On the other side is a much larger group who remain too long in the shared *I* space. Such people are variously described as dependent, addictive, hysterical, compulsive; in general, they display what are called personality and neurotic disorders. They seldom experience their personal *me* space except in their dreams, hopes, and fantasies. They frequently come nearest to their separate space in their *self*-destructive behaviors. In other words, their pathology is an unnatural attempt to rebalance themselves; to escape the *I*. Look at what they are actually doing: The alcoholic or cocaine-dependent escapes from *I* awareness into some internal personal, though distorted, space; the depressed person retreats, however ungratifyingly, into his own space by isolating himself from others by his disinterest, apathy, irritability, and preoccupation with his insides; the phobic literally shuts down her access to significant areas of the *I* space. The agoraphobic literally isolates himself in his *me* space by avoiding *all otherness*.

Len is forty-two years old, with three children and an exasperated wife. His wife is not here to tell us so, but, according to Len, "She's really fed up with me." Why? Len has panic reactions whenever he is around crowds, and to Len a crowd is more than two or three people in addition to his family. Consequently, as a couple or family, they cannot go many places or do many things. This constriction is why she is so "fed up" with him. He knows that she tries to be understanding and that she cares but also knows that she is tired of his panic. Through it, Len is "successfully" diminishing his *I* space. The price is very high.

Dieter seems unable to be around his friends without being high. He slowly, but inevitably, will drive them off. He will "regret it," and even be hurt, but will do it again. Why? Like Len, he has to diminish his *I* space and can do it only *self*-destructively. The *others'* experience of him, when he is *I*-less in his intoxication, is that they are irrelevant; they do not matter.

We see the process occurring in somatizations (making oneself ill), antisocial behavior, obsessions, compulsions, panic disorders, and the large number of other neurotic conditions. The neurotic's effort is to retreat to *me*; the neurotic's need is to reduce his or her exhausting, unrelenting involvement with the *other*. These people have little ability to move in and out of their *me* space by choice, so they lose their capacity for spontaneously being themselves. They are personally imprisoned by their unending need to be aware of and respond to the *other*. It is little wonder that they make such desperate efforts to return to the *me*. These efforts are usually unsuccessful, high in personal cost, and frequently lead to relational disasters. As we see so often in adolescents, the rebel is just as dependent as the conformer. Rebellion makes sense in adolescents, who are attempting to learn an *I-me-self* balance. They *have* to rebel in order to grow and learn. Like the young bicyclist in the film *Breaking Away*, who creates a *self* foreign to his family background, they are in the process of *becoming*. But the adult "rebellion" of having to stay away from the *other* leaves the person essentially in the same neurotic place as the adult who *has* to attend to the *other*. There is no *becoming* in either position. In our neuroticisms we gain nothing and lose much, and in these distorted places too many of us have become ultimately lost. The intimate experience, the knowing of *self,* the being in the two spaces at the same time, is the only reality in which we can find ourselves. The Koran says: "God changes not what is in a people, until they change what is in themselves." Such change takes place only through the *intimate self.*

The majority of people are neither psychotic, psychopathic, nor severely impaired neurotically. Personal and shared spaces overlap in most of us. We can move. We do have some choice. Our experience in each space enhances our capacity for experience in the other. We spend some good time alone and are able to return to close relationships with more warmth and energy. We have a close experience with a loved one and our dreams are more creative, our time in our own space is more peaceful. When the *I* does well, the *me* does equally well. But what of *self*? Now that we have said what we think *self* is and how and why it is that way, how can we be more available to that way of being?

3

Personal Process . . . Being in the World in Good Faith

> The no-mind not-thinks no-thoughts about no-things.
>
> —BUDDHA

How does being yourself and being close to another person at the same time happen? How can you be in your own space and a shared space at the same time? How can you be close and personal simultaneously? The frequency with which you are able to do both will determine the quality of your relationships. The capacity to do both is generated by your *intimate self*.

How much your experience of being in one space energizes and enhances your experience of being in the other depends on the experience of intimacy. On a warm sunny day, as a child, you lie in the grass. You are playing with a dandelion, and for a moment realize how you are like the dandelion and how it is like you. That is an experience of *self-intimacy*. In it you become conscious, in a very real way, of your participation in the greater scheme of things. Such connection is easy to identify as a child, particularly in the nonsocial natural world. It is much more difficult for adults to identify and describe similar intimate experiences either with dandelions or with other people.

Larry is a successful businessman and is assertive, patient, articulate, and decisive at work. With his wife, Liz, however, he is shy and hesitant. Yet, despite his hesitancy, he is aware of and sensitive to her in very subtle ways. Liz is committed, loyal, compulsive, and very confrontive. She makes him uneasy.

He says, "Your mother called Tuesday," and she says, "No, it was Wednesday." Factually, she is usually right. He gets confused and angry without knowing it and feels alternately chastised and patronized. She realizes he is angry and becomes placative. This dialectic is how they live together at home, and is how they are together in therapy. They get nowhere in either environment.

The same charade is occurring in their session today. She confronts, accuses, and is factually real in what she says: "I told you I was very upset. The doctor had just called to tell me that Mother might well die. You just sat there, and then you finally said, 'Well, she is getting on in years.' What the hell does that mean? I needed you, and you talk to me like I'm someone in one of your real estate deals. Don't you understand what I want from you?" He sits quietly for a moment, not fighting back, then says, "I know what you want from me, but I'm not sure I have it to give you. I feel so inadequate and dumb. So scared and young. I have no real feeling that I have the strength and sureness you want and need. I'm even surprised that you expect me to be what you need me to be. I want to be, and if I weren't so scared maybe I could be. I'm really sorry that I have not been what you wanted." Here, for once, he gives up his anger and confusion, and responds in a real way.

She gets out of her chair, leans over, and embraces him. He pulls her onto his lap and holds her. She cries. He caresses her hair and tells her, "I am sorry about your mom." For the moment, they are intimate. He has discovered something about himself: that he really can be as she needs him to be. He shared this intimacy with his embrace and caress, and in his open acceptance of her fear and grief about her mother. She shared it with her movement to his embrace and her crying. They discovered something about themselves together, not alone in cognitive solitude. This was an intimate experience. They both knew what they were and could be with each other. Both discovered something new about themselves; both disclosed something new about themselves to the other. How often I experience my *I* (my relationship) and my *me* (my own person) together is how often I experience my *self*. My *self* comes out of my experiencing *I* and *me* simultaneously. Larry felt something new about himself when he felt close to Liz, and he shared the discovery. Liz felt something new about herself when she felt close to Larry, and she shared it. Both of these newly felt awarenesses, these experiences of personal space, were felt when they were close to each other, as they were in the shared space. This simultaneous awareness is intimacy.

Often in nature two differing qualities join to form a third, entirely different thing. Is not salt, so necessary to life, the joining of a caustic metal and a poisonous gas? Is not water, basic to life, a coming together of two odorless and colorless gases, oxygen and hydrogen? When this connection occurs in humans, we are able to experience ourselves simultaneously in our personal space and in the shared space we have with another. Liz and Larry experienced *self,* which transcends their *I* and *me.* They have raised their relatedness to a higher dimension, the one that energizes and expands relationship. Closeness assures the stability of relationship by constantly reiterating its familiarities. Intimacy makes new experiences available and so increases our breadth of familiarity. Since nothing lives that is not changing and growing, intimacy is an essential, vital ingredient of relationship. Without closeness, intimacy would be chaotic. Without intimacy, closeness would and does insidiously deteriorate into role playing and boredom. If you have a plant in your house that you like just the way it is, and you try to keep it that way, it will die. It must grow, change, and be different to stay alive. So it is with you and me.

Self is experienced *only* in intimacy. This is not always interpersonal. In reality, most of our intimate experiences are not with other people. The essence of intimacy is feeling closer to myself while I am in relationship to something other than me. I can more easily experience this with a flower, a river, music, or a poem than I can with a person. I can more easily experience it with a stranger than with someone to whom I am close. The sadness of human beings is that we can be ourselves more easily with inanimate objects and nonhuman life than we can with the people who matter most to us; we can be ourselves more easily with those who are not so important to us than with those whom we cherish. Personal knowledge seems to interfere with intimacy.

We should really say that knowledge makes us less likely to be intimate. We make ourselves less available to intimacy by using our knowledge to increase closeness. When you "know" the route home from work, you no longer *see* the world you pass through. We push ourselves out of balance. The phenomenon is one we will call *capture by the system.* Actually, it is not the knowledge so much as what we do with it that creates the imbalance. One can have knowledge in intimacy—indeed, as we have discussed, new discovery is one of intimacy's main functions—but intimate knowledge is the knowledge of connection (the dyad); the knowledge whereby systems capture us is knowledge of assimilation (the system). We can deal with system as a concept since "systems" have common characteristics. The biologist Ludwig von Bertalanffy in the 1950s began illuminating a General Systems Theory in which he tried to look at systems as entities that operate by rules different from those of the system's component parts. That is, that systems are comparable regardless of the differing nature of their components. His work, along with work in artificial intelligence (Alan Turing), communications theory (Claude Shannon), and cybernetics (Norbert Wiener), led to a new understanding of systems as "operative wholes" with describable rules. One aspect of all systems, as such, is their ability to capture.

This is most easily seen in the noninterpersonal experiences of life.

The cliché "Take the time to smell the roses" is but a recognition of the fact that we normally do not. Assuming that we know roses, we cease to smell them. In just that way we cease being intimate, or, as e. e. cummings says (in *95 poems by e. e. cummings*):

> but though mankind persuades
> itself that every weed's
> a rose, roses (you feel
> certain) will only smile

That is a microcosmic example of capture by the system. Frequently the difficulty that humans have in experiencing their connectedness to the world in areas other than human relationship is that they do not exist "as they are" in the world "as it is," and therefore do not find connections and grow from them. One of the best popular dramatizations of this is found in the movie *The King of Hearts,* in which the ultimate futility and sadness of our capture by our systems are poignantly portrayed in the hero's experience that the "insane" people were more in touch with reality than those in the "normal" world.

We have lost much in this capture. The artist, the musician, the sculptor, the inventor, the poet in all of us is withered from being out of connection with its creative substrate. Humans try to regain these experiences through work, hobbies, or recreation, and this *would* work if we engaged in these activities intimately; we would then find *self.* But most of us do not. We are captured at work, at jogging or tennis, at our stamp collecting or sewing, and end up engaging in *I* or *me* activities. These may still, in some ways, be healthy and helpful to us as persons, but they are not then intimate, and thus do not illuminate *self. Self* can be experienced in *any* and *all* connections in life. The human-human dyad is our prototype, but it is not special in nature. It is just our metaphor.

We are too accustomed to thinking of *self* as *I.* It is not, nor is it *me.* The difference is a matter of consciousness. When my awareness is that of my *self,* I am aware at the same time both of *me,* my inner experience, and of *I,* the world around me. The mutual experiencing of these two awarenesses creates the most significant and revitalizing experience of which a human being is capable. As we said earlier, *self* experienced is what Sartre meant when he spoke of "being in the world in good faith." In our last case study, Larry (*me*) knows that he is angry, hurt, frustrated, and now afraid. Larry (*I*) knows that Liz is withdrawn, fearful, and angry with him. Larry (*self*) is aware that his feelings are no different from his wife's. Each depends on the other. She has no more desire to hurt him than he has to hurt her. She has the same frustrated confusion about what to do that he has. She wants to bridge the gap between them just as much as he does. None of this awareness is cognitive; they feel it, and their feeling is accompanied by a sad gentleness and compassionate tenderness about each other.

Larry also knows, in a nonthinking way, that this experience is familiar. He has had it with others. He has had it in the past. He has even had it with a lawn mower he worked on, a lawn mower that would not be "fixed," like his wife. With this realization, Larry (*self*) experienced himself "being in the world in good faith." He experienced *self* in intimacy, the simultaneous awareness of *I* and *me*. In being intimate with another human, particularly one to whom he is close, he is experiencing *self* on its prototypical level; the most directly he as a human being can feel what he is.

The experience of *self* arising out of intimacy has three unifying characteristics: connectivity, animation, and creativity. These values, similar to those found in Albert Schweitzer's "reverence for life," the Hindu "universal self," and other philosophies, are often better described by poets than by theorists. John Keats, for example, wrote (in a letter to George and Thomas Keats), "At once it struck me what quality went to form a man of achievement, especially in literature, and which Shakespeare possessed so enormously—I mean *negative capability,* that is, when a man is capable of being in uncertainties, mysteries, doubts, without any irritable reaching after fact and reason." His phrase perfectly describes the prerequisite to intimacy. In intimacy, we feel connection, animation, and creation through *negative capability;* that is, by avoiding the "irritable reaching after fact and reason" we remain available to connection, animation, and creation.

Larry, in his momentary intimate awareness, feels immediately more connected to Liz. He feels, almost as immediately, more connected to the others in his life, and even to his past and future. His sense of connection then animates him. He is enlivened by his awareness that it is not that his wife is frustrating him, but that he and she together—the general way he and she live in the world—are causing the frustration. Out of the connection and subsequent animation comes, again almost immediately, a feeling that he can do something about it. He feels empowered, energized, less helpless. He feels creative. Out of this marvelous momentary awareness of his connectivity, and the animation that comes with that awareness, emerges an assurance that he is capable of gently integrating his new experience of his wife. He feels he can do something in his relationship with her that is new and different. No longer living in his privately defined world, but now participating, through this ordinary moment, in the unified time and space of the nature of all things, Larry experiences his intimate *self*.

Connection, animation, and creation are the gifts of the *self* experience, what intimacy brings about. Each seems to precede the other, no matter which occurs first: you feel the connectivity and it animates you, or you feel animated and so immediately more connected. Your animation makes you creative, or your sense of being creative makes you feel more connected.

Connectivity

I drink milk and strengthen a bone in my foot. Conversely, perhaps I am allergic to it. I look at a deep forest and write a poem about it, or paint a picture of it. Or I may look at the deep forest and feel depressed. The difference is, for example, the connection I experience when the milk I drink reinforces the ankle I walk on. I am part of a universal, natural, organic universe that is coherent. I am part of the sun and vitamin D. I am part of walking on the earth. I am connected in a good way with the animal and plant worlds, the physical and chemical worlds. I am connected to my childhood, as well as my yet-to-be-reached old age. I am part of the continuum of nature's reality. All of these connections are very real and very intimate. This harmonious, endless rippling sense of connection to the whole universe may be totally unconscious, but it is nonetheless exceedingly real, life-expanding, and the essence of intimacy.

It is that sense of connection that the novelist D. H. Lawrence was celebrating in this passage from *Apocalypse:* "I am part of the sun as my eye is part of me. That I am part of the earth my feet know perfectly, and my blood is part of the sea. My soul knows that I am part of the human race, my soul is an organic part of the great human race, as my spirit is part of my nation. In my own very self, I am part of my family."

Contrast this response with my response if I am allergic to the milk. Obviously I am close to the milk, and I am certainly connected to it, but by a singular and idiosyncratic association. There is no rippling flow into other connections. I am not moved into the natural, organic universe of infinite links. As a matter of fact, my allergy may well separate me from the sun and make it more difficult for me to walk easily on this earth. It probably also separates me a little from my past and my future. It is a disparate, very individualistic, and isolating experience. My allergy may reflect a close relationship between me and milk, but it is not an intimate relationship. In a very small way, my allergy moves me out of the wholeness of everything.

Although less concrete, my experience of the deep forest's stimulating me to write a poem or paint a picture produces this same sense of a rippling consciousness of my intimate connection to the whole universe. My sense of belonging is psychologically ecological. I know more about mountains, oceans, cities, stars, and even political systems when I write that poem. I am connected. I have been intimate. In contrast, when I look at the deep forest and feel depressed, the feeling suggests a very idiosyncratic, individual, and separating experience for me. I am not propelled into the experience of belonging to the whole universe. I feel, and am, isolated. I am not animated, and so I cannot possibly be energetically creative. I certainly have a close relationship to the forest, either negatively symbolic or negatively nostalgic (perhaps I was once lost in a deep forest), but it is not an intimate experience. I am not expanding myself through my connection to the forest, but enclosing myself. Enclosure is sometimes more comfortable or secure, but it is not growthful. Quite the opposite: It is the core of the neurotic experience.

Nathan is a college student at a university in town. He comes into our offices episodically, where he works in spurts on a long-term unhappiness with himself. He relates his difficulty in finding dates, his feeling ill at ease if he makes a date, his difficulty in knowing what he feels after a date, and a long list of other difficulties with relationship that make him aware of the lack of relational joy in his life. Whenever he gets the chance, he goes up to the mountains to camp or down to one of the remote coastal islands to hike and sleep out under the stars. When we ask him why he goes, he says, "To find myself." We believe he is speaking a literal truth, not giving a metaphorical answer. It is his alienation from *self* that is preventing him from finding a way joyfully to be himself in relationship. He has retained his awareness of being able to make these connections in a nonhuman intimacy. The experiences sustain him while he continues to struggle with learning how to have them with humans. He can experience and use his intimacy with the ocean, the mountains, the islands to change—since intimacy is universal, all connectivity is the same at heart. But it is most profound, and thus most powerfully changing of us, when we are intimate with another human being. As E. M. Forster said in his novel *Howards End,* "Only connect, and the beast and the monk, robbed of the isolation that is life to either, will die." We change only in connection, only in intimacy.

The *intimate self,* with its accompanying connectivity, animation, and creativity, is not just a metaphorical phrase. The *self* connects with the sun to make vitamin D, and without it you would be an unnatural deformity or not be at all. You breathe air or you die. You smoke and pollute that air, and you sever your connections and compromise your animation in very real ways. These are not metaphors; they are real-life experiences, concrete chemical and physical connections. How real psychological and personal connections also are we apparently have yet fully to comprehend. Even compared to the frightful shambles we have made of physical, chemical, and biological ecology, the mess we seem to be making of our psychological, our sociocultural, and our spiritual ecology is more immediately horrifying. Much more was "defoliated" in Vietnam than just the vegetation. The importance of acid rain or the endangered whale is precisely its intimate connection with the demise of the family, the sexual abuse of children, racism, strident nationalism, and war with its nuclear psychosis. It is an appalling ecology. Nuclear winter would be cold in all senses of the word. Clearly, how well we deal with the unhealthiness of our physical environment will depend primarily on how well we can actualize our connectivity to other human beings, to community, and even to the universe; the universe, not as it is experienced in the abstract but in *concrete* experiences like drinking milk and strengthening a bone or walking in a deep forest and writing a poem. We are not talking about romanticism. Psychological ecology represents our real salvation. The health of *self,* arising out of the intimate experience, will probably determine not only our environmental health but our survival as a species.

Temporal Connectivity

Truman and Natalie are finally "settled" into their marriage of nine years. They have formed many of the routines of life that couples do after that many years of closeness. Some of these are healthy: They can share the financial, parental, and maintenance duties. But some of their "routines" block intimacy, in a way that may seem strange until one realizes what the struggle is actually about. For instance, they fight constantly about her stopping smoking and about his coming home from work so late. Their affect tells us that the quarrel is meaningful, even when the fighting seems ridiculous. What are they really doing? They are struggling with each other about *self*: about the lack of intimacy they both feel but cannot talk about directly. Each is demanding that the other love himself or herself in hopes that then the other will be a *self* in relationship. Ultimately, both will have to learn for *themselves* how to experience intimacy.

As we have suggested above, the *self* experienced in intimacy connects us psychologically, interpersonally, and spiritually—in other words, universally. The psychological connections appear to be both spatial and temporal, providing enormously important ties to our past and our future. The *I* and the *me,* as we have described them in their imbalanced and misunderstood states, operate in the isolation of the present. That constriction is the tragedy of the excesses of what we might call the recent *I* and *me* generations of the last decades. Both the *me* generation of the sixties ("Drop out and do your own thing") and the *I* generation of the eighties ("Jump in and make your way to the top") are but the latest examples of attempts to find "what is missing." Both fail in their formulations for solving the longing inside us because the formulas reveal a lack of *self* experience—a lack of connections, as with the past and the future. It surely requires our awareness of all three, simultaneously, for us to be *balanced* in relationship to *ourselves* and *others*. *Self* relates to past and future even though it derives its energies from the present experience of intimacy. *Self* experienced in intimacy connects the whole person to the womb, to birth, to the great-grandparents, to memory, to primary family experience, to ongoing life experience, to current close relationship with friend, child, parent, lover, spouse, and to last night's experience, including a half-remembered dream. *Self* stays connected to all of that without being bound or imprisoned by any of it, provided that it is nourished by ongoing intimacy. This *self*'s connection to the past and future can be the source of enormous nourishment, enhancing our "aliveness" in the present.

It is easy to see the nourishment we take from the past; to see how remembrance significantly shapes our lives. But, unaltered by the present experience of *self* in intimacy, such remembrances become distorted in the *me* and can easily destroy our lives. We are talking about, for example, the person living in the memory of a past lover who cannot love in the now. Unfortunately, remembrance is often the preoccupation of too many contemporary psychotherapists. Their thinking is all focused on the past, with little interest in the present, not to mention the future. Such therapists leave *self* out of their therapy. The *self*, however, brings time together. Tomorrow's anticipated experience can be as animating as the memory of yesterday's experience or last night's dream. The *self* understands connection; it processes it. *Self* is an experiential expert in connections. The *self* can comprehend death as part of life, separation as part of relationship, failure as part of success, and ending as part of beginning. *Self* operates as we dream. The *I* knows only of the immediate reality, not of its rippling connections to starfish and stars. The *me* knows only one's internal experience. Consequently, *I* and *me* know little of the universal, paradoxical importance of death to life, failure to success, and ending to beginning. But when the *self* is experienced in intimacy, it illuminates the *I* and *me*. Because of the *self* experience, *I* is more aware and *me* is more sensitive. The obverse is equally true: When *I* is more aware and *me* is more sensitive, then *self* can be more connected. Balance is essential, as it is in all of nature. Having an aware *I*, a sensitive *me*, and a connected *self* is crucial to one's ability to "be in the world in good faith." Our capacity to be this way depends on our ability to be intimate.

Lila has been coming to therapy for two years. She is slowly unraveling a large tapestry woven over the many years of her life. In accepting her we have to accept her story as the truth of her experience. It becomes very clear from her story that Lila lives in her past. Her lovers are ghost lovers; there is no one now. Like the barrister in the movie *Love Among the Ruins,* we can spend our lives in memories of the past. Few of us are so lucky to have the happy storybook ending. We ask Lila gently, "Lila, why don't you get out and meet somebody new, have some fun? You don't have to marry him." Her reply is always the same. "I'm not free yet from John [Bill, Jack, Joe]. I've got to understand what happened with him. I don't want to be hurt again." Lila, though perfectly sane, is not living in the real world. She is living in a *me*-defined, past world. If we cannot find a way to get her to experience herself, she will continue, like Penelope, to weave and unweave the same threads again and again. Only the *intimate-self* experience allows her to change, to renew herself in time.

Spatial Connectivity

It is more difficult to describe the spatial than the temporal connectivity of *self,* because we seldom consider nonmaterial things as having space. Recall that we have been talking of personal and shared *spaces,* and of *self's* being a spatial union of the two. A good metaphor for this spatial union is the structure of a pond. The surface, the volume, the area, and the reflexivity of the pond are the *I* aspects; the internal waves and the chemistry of the water are the *me* aspects. The pond's being a part of nature's water cycle is its *"self."* Spatially the pond "knows" all its components (the *others*) and all its intimate connections (the process). *Self* is a space-time experience. The two are inseparable in the experience of *self.* We exist in this way when we are intimate.

The balance among *I, me,* and *self* is crucial to our living healthily. Learning where the imbalance lies would be far more instructive of what is really wrong with people than any esoteric, convoluted, and often debilitating analysis of the dynamics of their infantile development. Is *I* healthy? Is *me* introspectively honest? Is *self* operative? Are we experiencing our connections? These are more real questions than the much satirized "Did you love and/or hate your mother?" More important, what are the balances in these experiences? Am I as much *I* as I can be without making me less than *me* really is, and am I fully my *self*? Are my connections less energizing than usual? Are all in intimate balance? If the balance is there, if *I, me,* and *self* are equally present, then you are most what you can be. You are "living in the world in good faith." Having this awareness does not tell you *who* you will be, since each of us is unique; it just tells you that you will be the most that you can be. These questions may seem esoteric when written on paper, but are very real when you are sitting opposite a person in tremendous emotional pain.

The Imbalanced Self

Sally is a very attractive middle-aged woman. She says she wants to be sexual but that she cannot be, because her lover will not initiate sex. In our terms, Sally wants him to want her more than she wants to be her *self,* to feel what she feels, or to do what she wishes.

Jack and Anne's oldest child has gone off to college for the first time this year. Anne has overprotected the children for years. She tells Jack to write to the child. Jack becomes angry, and after some time he says to her, "You know that your telling me to write her lessens the chances that I will." Anne is hurt and irate, saying that he "doesn't understand." Jack tells her, "You know how you feel when men call you 'honey.' Even if they say they are not being chauvinistic, you know they're lying. They won't give up that one little final bit." She understood his analogy and told him so. They both relaxed and had a good evening together.

These two examples illustrate what we mean by imbalance. Sally is *self* out of balance. Her *me* is so overriding that her *I* has become almost nonexistent. There is simply her internal desire to be wanted. She refuses any awareness of or responsibility for initiative in her relationship to her lover. She wants to be wanted by him, for him to take responsibility for their sexual relationship, more than she wants to experience her own sexuality. Because of this imbalance, her experience of *self* cannot occur. Conversely, Jack and Anne managed to reestablish a balance. Jack had sufficient investment in their closeness to share himself. Anne had sufficient investment to listen and understand. In that balancing of *me* and *I* between them, intimacy momentarily occurred.

The key to balance is *self,* which depends on the experience of being intimate. Without this experience, *self* becomes depleted and consequently depletes *me* and *I*. Seriously diminished in energy, the *I* separates from *me,* and begins considering only the environment that surrounds it. Functional *me* is lost, has too much *I* in it. The consummate neurotic is concerned only with what is going on around the *I,* only with what other people think; he or she says, "*I* will live my life in terms of other people's responses to me. *I* am a response in life. Being who I really am is impossible since how *I* am depends on how others expect me to be." The imbalanced *I* may show itself, whether hysterically (I need to be loved), compulsively (I have to do it), dependently (I need to be taken care of), obsessively (I'll think of something else), or psychopathically (I will neither think nor feel), in a number of common neuroses and personality disorders.

Excessive I. Terry is the "perfect" date. He is always on time, never looks at other women, and never gets drunk. He goes wherever she wants to go and does whatever she asks him to do. He comes in for therapy because he cannot understand why no one wants to go out with him twice.

The *I* person, without the balance of the *me* and the *self,* is the *neurotic.* Their illness is their lack of *me* and *self.* They have an excess of *I,* which is not to say that they are overly egocentric; in fact, it really means the opposite. They are too much concerned about and preoccupied with the *other.* The *other* may be what society thinks, what the members of their country club think, what their boss told them that seemed important, whether they are at work or at home, whether they are twenty-six or forty-six and what is expected of the twenty-six-year-old in contrast to the forty-six-year-old, or even whether they are dressed in tennis shorts or in an elegant outfit. They have become what they think and feel the *other* wants them to be. Moreover, their opinion of that is often wrong. Consequently, they frequently behave as they think the *other* wants them to be, only to discover that they were mistaken: The *other* is not in the least appreciative of their accommodation; on the contrary, is usually either uninterested or rebuffing. Consequently, the *I* person almost always feels misunderstood, unloved, and confused. They are confused, as are most neurotics, as to why their dedication to placative and compromising behaviors engenders little or no positive response in the *other.* The *other,* whether society in general or individuals, continues to treat them (they feel) cruelly, or at least insensitively. Whatever behavior they are placatively searching for in the *other,* they almost always get the opposite. Terry tries to please completely, and ends up pleasing not at all. These people are always surprised to be genuinely loved, to be confirmed as *selves* despite their pseudo-selves. Terry would be shocked if a woman called him. He would not know how to *be.* In the words of the thirteenth-century philosopher Meister Eckhart (from *Work and Being*): "One must not always think so much about what one should do, but rather what one should be. Our works do not ennoble us; but we must ennoble our works." The *I* person does not "ennoble" *self,* through an overconcern with the *other.*

Excessive Me. We have been describing the *neurotic,* the *I* person, the person overwhelmingly concerned with the *other.* Obviously, such a person needs more *me.* We defined *me* earlier, but perhaps it can be more fully understood if, as with *I,* we describe it in its excesses. The *me* is awareness of my inner experience. When I am into the *me,* the *other* disappears; it is of no consequence. What is going on within my person is overriding. The *me* experience is totally personal, nonsocial, and non-*other.* Excess of *me* is psychosis.

Byron is back on the inpatient unit once again. He is in and out frequently. In earlier days, he would probably have been a permanent resident of a large state institution. Today, when I *(Pat)* come in to work, he is curled in the corner, over by one of the plants. He is talking and listening to someone, only no one is there. I go over and sit near him, but as I do, he curls further into a ball. I invite him to come out of himself, to talk with me, to touch something outside, but for now he cannot. By persisting, I only threaten further his already frightening *me* world. With patience, gentleness, and time (and often with medications), Byron will slowly show more *I*. He will start responding to others, to the world around him, to our caring. Progress will be slow—we will have to stay gentle and patient—but for a time at least he will come back to some balance again. If, after leaving the unit, he will come to outpatient therapy (which is a big if), what we will have to work on is keeping him from collapsing totally back into his *me* once again.

A persistent, inordinate *me* experience creates psychosis. The *other* is completely subordinated and defined by the *me*. When *me* predominates in experience, the reality of even stars or barely heard whispers are perceived, and most often misperceived, only in ways that are consonant with the *inner* experience. Such consonant misperceptions can range from subtle social biases to flagrant delusions. It does not help to tell the prejudiced person that not all minority people are lazy, criminal, or on welfare. Nor does it help to tell the paranoid psychotic that his neighbor is really his friend, not a communist agent who has wiretapped his phone. Your facts change nothing. You cannot simply add the *I* experience to a person with an excessive *me* by sharing your reality—your own *I* experience. Most people with an excess of *me* are not, of course, psychotic. They are simply people with character disorders, meaning that their ways of being in the world are determined mostly by their inner reality.

Jake comes to therapy because the high school told his parents he needed to. He does not want to be there, and usually makes this pretty obvious. His parents will not come in: "We don't have any problems. If Jake would just straighten out, everything would be fine." In other words, "You fix it." What is it that needs fixing? Why did the school suggest that Jake needed this help? Asking Jake gets us nowhere: "I've got no problems, they just don't like me. I didn't do anything." What the school tells us is that Jake has no empathy, sympathy, or respect for others' feelings. This has been manifested consistently over many years by his behavior there. He takes other people's belongings, bullies younger children, cannot participate in group activities, and cannot maintain any peer relationships. He is living out of too much *me,* and cannot get beyond it. As we discussed earlier, problems of the *me* are more primitive and more difficult to change. To make it worse, Jake does not even perceive himself as being in need of change. If the family will not deal with their connection to Jake, there may be little we can do. Outward Bound and similar programs can sometimes help the "Jakes" of the world, by helping them start making small *reconnections* to *others*. At first this may be inanimate others, such as the mountains or the forest, but it can grow to include humans.

Balance between the *I* and the *me* is essential to mental and emotional health, to our "being in the world in good faith." That balance can be restored and maintained only when the experience of *self* is added. *Self* provides a viable sense of connection, which in turn is the experiential basis for that necessary balance. In the case, for example, of a bigoted person, some balance is restored if he or she has an intimate experience with someone of another race. Just how simple an experience such as this can be crossed my (*Tom's*) mind while in New York City for a meeting. Riding the subway, I found myself seated next to a black man close to my age. He was reading a book by one of my favorite authors. I began to talk with him about what the writer's thoughts had meant to me. In relationship to this stranger I had an experience in which I was *me.* I was aware of *me* while *I* was aware of him. It was an intimate experience. It was a *self* experience. I felt my connection, not only to him, but to all other "hims." The *self* experience restores balance to the *I* and *me.* The anecdote may sound pretentious and solemn, but the experience was not. It was simple, a passing encounter that I soon forgot, except that in a profound sense I did not forget it, and it did make a difference. It is not really relevant that a racially biased white person might have gotten up and moved to another seat when the black man sat down next to him, or, if he had stayed, would not have spoken to him. The simple fact that he would have noted internally that the man was reading one of his own favorite authors would have established a connection, a mini-*self* experience that would have an effect, however unconsciously. He would have made an association, and even in that microscopic intimacy, he would have become more connected to the world in which both he and black people live—the only world that actually *is.* That is how the *self-intimate* experience works. That is both its beauty and its importance.

We have spoken of imbalances of the *I* and *me* experience, and tried to describe briefly the personal distortions that occur when one or the other predominates in someone's life. We have suggested that the balancing experience is the intimate one. Are there any excesses of *self* experience? Can one be too connected in the ways that we have described intimate connections? We do not think so. We have certainly never seen it in any of the people whom we have treated. Perhaps that is because the *self-intimate* experience automatically and naturally augments the *I* and *me* experiences. Having an excess of *self-intimate* experiences would be like having an excess of ecological balance or an excess of love and understanding. If it is real and authentic, there can be no surplus, as there can never be of justice or beauty.

Animation

Your *self-intimate* experiences increase your connections to the rest of the universe, most important your connections with another human. But by itself connection does not complete your "being in the world in good faith." If connection did not animate, you would simply be more aware, but not more alive. We do not think aliveness comes out of the importance of another person to you. We are convinced that the immediacy of your sense of connection and relationship to a used and discarded plastic cup tumbling randomly in the parking lot of a fast-food restaurant can be as important psychologically as your intimate experience with another person. Both can bring you to the *self* experience, the awareness of connectivity, that *I* and *me* live in a broader context than the foolish, prideful idiosyncrasies of our particular and individuated world. This genuine sense of connectivity does much more: It puts us immediately into the *self-intimate* experience, and so enlivens and animates. We are enhanced by being part of the greater whole.

Mel and Kristy have "magic" weekends; that is what they call them. They take turns in planning surprise outings. Each plans what he or she wants to do; the other's job is to go along and enjoy the leader's enjoyment. It gives each an experience of seeing the other differently, of being different from their usual roles with each other. The "weekend plan" has worked well for four years now. Last month Kristy planned a trip up to the mountains to go skiing. This announcement was enlightening to Mel, not just because they had never skied before—he had never even thought that Kristy liked sports. Now he sees a new part of her, makes a new connection, and it enlivens him.

To use a more contemporary word, the experience of being connected *energizes* the person. *Energy* is a physical and personal word—indeed, a valuable and descriptive one—but we prefer the more classical term *anima,* meaning spirit. To be more animated means to be more spirited, and so more spiritual. Energy is spirit; animation simply means a greater capacity to "be in the world in good faith." When people experience the connectivity of the *self-intimate* moment, they have immediately available to them the energy, animation, and spirit to be different. They have the energy that is inherent in the fabric of space-time; they have become part of that fabric. Evil is, as described by the theologian H. A. Williams, dis-integration, the lack of synthesis. This *dis-integration* is our separation from the fabric.

What do we mean by becoming "different"? Being different means simply that you are able to overcome inertia. You experience connection, and thus feel more energetic or spirited. This energy is then available to overcome the inertia. Psychological inertia is no different from physical inertia. there is a very real and powerful tendency in humans to continue to think, feel, and do what they have always thought, felt, and done. They can disappear and even die in their addiction to familiarity. Studies on how our brain functions suggest that it has a tendency to prefer what it already knows; it seeks information to confirm prior knowledge. Intimacy is what allows us to break out of this cycle, to avoid the danger of searching for the perfection of familiarity.

Perfection is attractive and frighteningly seductive. Death, which is almost synonymous with sameness and familiarity, is in this sense very attractive. As the poet Paul Dunbar said in "Compensation," "the master, in infinite mercy, offers the boon of death." We are constantly amazed in our therapeutic practice at the naiveté of most people about death. Seldom do they seem to be aware of their attraction to death. They have, as do most of us, the spurious and deceptive covering belief that death is to be avoided at all costs. Beneath that cover-up lies our more frightful affinity with death. Rest, peace and quiet, certainty, permanence, predictability, and the absolute assurance of continued perfection are the enticements of death. It is true that when we are dead, we are perfectly dead. No one is less dead or more dead than any other. Death, in this sense of perfection, is unbelievably alluring to us all. It is an astonishing tribute to animation and life that the seductiveness of death is so seldom prematurely actualized.

An elderly couple comes in, both in their late sixties. Their lives have been full: four children grown and doing well, ten grandchildren so far. But he has been ill for the past few years, and finally has gotten depressed and been referred to us by his family doctor. He is quiet and withdrawn, and does not say much. She, on the other hand, is animated enough for both of them. She pushes and pulls him. She says, "Oh, you can't give up now. You can't just lie down. You can't quit during the middle of the game."

In the elderly, the seduction of death becomes overt and must be dealt with. It goes beyond just being tired; it has to do with the desire not to have to struggle, to accept that total perfection we misidentify as death's enticement. This woman has no intention of letting him go without a fight. That is why her animation and energy are so high. She will keep trying until, through making an intimate connection, she can energize and enliven him. Only when she feels his *self* ready to quit will she stop.

Creativity

Animation arising out of our experience of connectivity is the antithesis of psychological inertia. It moves us to be different. The energy and spirit to be different are provided by the *self-intimate* experience. The capacity to be different enables us to be creative, which is the third outcome of the *self-intimate* experience. To be *creative* simply means to think, feel, or do something we have not done before. So to be connected is to be animated, and to be animated is to be creative. To be creative is to be different, and to be different is to be a more sensitive *me,* a more aware *I,* and more my *self.* More *me,* more *I,* and more *self* come out of an increase in our sense of connectivity, an energizing increase in our animation, and an increase in our creativity. These specific personal enhancements occur only when we have been intimate. I am unlikely to change my racial prejudices or my paranoid preoccupations simply in the introspective, meditative experience of my inner feelings and thoughts. I am equally unlikely to change these prejudices and preoccupations in the experience of being close to another person, paradoxical as that may seem. I will very likely alter both when I am being fully *me,* more aware of *me* than the *other* but fully aware of the relationship *I* am in at the time. Alone, awareness of *me* does not do it, nor does the closeness of *I* to another. Only awareness of *me* when *I* am close to another enables me to change.

Here is another way of comparing closeness and intimacy that may help us discriminate between the two. The *I* predominates in closeness. The *self* prevails in intimacy. Both *I* and *self* are, of course, relational. *Me* is not relational. *Me* is both important and vitalizing, but it has little to do with relationship. The *I* experience is that of one human knowing, sensing, hearing, and feeling the *other* in order to modify and modulate behavior and interaction with that *other* and thus maximize his or her own experience. Earlier we called this closeness a *personal* relationship. It is a relationship in which the personality is taken seriously—as well it should be in most instances. We do need to be aware of and attendant on each other. *Me* often has to be subordinated to the relationship, and that too is as it should be. We need to listen to, feel, know, and affirm others, which is what closeness allows us to do. It is the basis of familiarity and one of the twin pillars of relationship. The other pillar is the animated, creative, new, and different experience, intimacy. Familiarity provides us with the security in relationship that allows us the freedom to risk being creatively strange. Both pillars are important if a relationship is to change and grow. Again, as is true of all things organic, unless it changes and grows, it will die.

The Hamiltons started family therapy after several of their teenaged children became involved in drugs. Frank and Wendy, married twenty-seven years, have four children, aged twenty-two to fourteen. The middle two evidently had been using drugs for some years. This fact came as a "complete surprise" to the parents: "But the family is so close." "But we're so familiar with each other." "But I've never seen them that way." "I can't believe they'd do anything like that." What becomes clear in our meetings is reflected in these opening remarks: The Hamilton family is overly close—so close that they have missed the changes, the growth in each other, the realities of each other's persons. They have lived but not grown together, because they have not been intimate together.

Sexuality as the Prototype of Intimacy

Intimacy depends on my ability to experience being *me* and *I* simultaneously: being who I am in relationship, sensitively aware of the other person. The prototype of this experience is, oddly, not personal but sexual. Whereas the prototype of closeness is the personal experience (in which I am more aware of the other person than I am of myself), in the sexual experience both persons are much more aware of themselves than they are of the other. The commonality of intimacy and sexuality is not surprising. If someone asked about your relationship to a particular man or woman, and you responded that you had been intimate with him or her for years, the questioner might assume that you had been sexual with that person. Why is this? Intimacy, of course, may be genital, but genitality is not of its essence. The essence of intimacy is the awareness one has of one's *self* in the immediate presence of another person to whom one is closely related. And that is profoundly sexual.

We have found that describing intimacy as more sexual than personal seems to upset people. It should be reassuring. Exclusively *me* sex would almost certainly be masturbatory. There is nothing wrong with that except that it is not a sexual *relationship. I* sex, in which I am more aware of the *other* than I am of my own feelings and sensations, just does not work. It lacks passion. Nothing is more certain to stop a good sexual experience than the simple question "Are you all right?" Intimacy allows for passion. I can be more aware of *me* while *I* am sensitively aware of the other. Impersonal sex lacks passion because it is not personal. Personal sex lacks passion because it is not sexual. Intimate sexuality is both personal and passionate. In the moments after intimate sex you can experience most clearly the difference between closeness and intimacy. If you have been intimately sexual, most aware of you but sensitively aware of the other, then immediately afterward you will feel poignantly and lovingly close to the other person. Your awareness moves from primarily your own experience to an acute and beautiful awareness of the other person. Your intimacy has enhanced your closeness. The feeling may be only momentary, but it is felt. Backs are turned only when the sex has been focused on *me* or *I*. Intimate sex brings some appreciable increase in your closeness.

So when I am close to you, I nourish you. When I am intimate with you, I nourish my *self*. Nourishing my *self* means simply increasing my capacity to be passionate with you. Intimacy enables me to be more *me* with you. Hence, it lends greater depth and breadth to our closeness. The sexual and the personal intensify each other. Among the couples we have seen in therapy, those who seem to sense the differences between the *me, I,* and *self* experiences seem to be the most fulfilled and growthful. They seem able to be in their own personal space (comfortably separate), able to be in their shared space (comfortably close), and able to be in their own personal space within the space they share with others (comfortably intimate). Perhaps even more important, they seem to have developed the capacity easily and trustingly to phase from one experience to the other. It is astonishing how difficult that movement is for most couples. A couple comes home from work, having been in their separate spaces, and finds it frustratingly difficult to move into the space they share. If they do find that shared space, they then have an equally difficult time moving into the more passionate, sexual, intimate experience, whether genital or not. If they are sexual, but insufficiently intimate, they have a difficult time moving back into their closeness. They roll over, back to back, and try to reclaim their separate spaces, usually unsuccessfully, and with a nagging uneasiness. How much more replenishing if they could return to a shared closeness, with its tender awareness of each other, before leaving the relationship to go to their dreams.

The sexual-intimate experience and the personal-closeness experience appear to be mutually exclusive at any given moment. They are not simultaneous, but phasic. When I am close to you, I pay attention to you. I have more awareness of you than of me. I gladly modify my own personal participation because of my caring for, and awareness of, you. My focus is not dependence, because it is of my own choosing. I am not trying to please you to get you to take care of, or care for, me. I am being close to you, affirming not simply you but our relationship, expressing my love of you. At other times I am more aware of myself with you; my experience is of myself with you. I am then more passionate and less compassionate. This passion is communicative, and highly contagious. That I am passionate does not mean I am unaware of you. Indeed, much of the passion comes from my awareness that I am being *me* with you. My passion, which is my heightened experience of my own feelings, depends on your acceptance of my being as I am. That is intimacy. In contrast, to be passionate when alone in your own space may involve a wonderful fantasy experience, but it is not relational. It is not intimacy. Separateness has its own wonders, but it does not make connections.

4

Personal Freedom . . . Grace and Acceptance

My soul can reach, when feeling out of sight
For the ends of Being and ideal Grace

—ELIZABETH BARRETT BROWNING

Being intimate does not occur by serendipity, particularly with persons to whom we are close. As we have said, it is far more likely to simply happen, without any effort on our part, with the mechanic, the stranger next to us on an airplane, the hairdresser. In close relationships, being intimate requires work. We have to learn, or perhaps relearn, what we have to do to allow it to happen and what we have to avoid doing that prevents it from happening. "The readiness is all," as Shakespeare said. Intimacy is a way of being, not doing, so there is no work in the act; the work is in learning how to make ourselves available to it.

We assume that intimacy is natural, a dimension of nature. The newborn baby is fully intimate with the mother. He or she is completely and passionately himself or herself in relationship with the parent. Babies do not modify their hunger, distress, or discomfort because of how these affect the mother or father, at least not initially. Many infants learn much too soon to accommodate. Those more fortunate have a longer period of pure intimacy, of enjoying bonding, before they begin to learn the modifying of behaviors that is essential to the healthy development of the *me* and the *I.* The original intimacy, however, is natural; the inability to experience it has to be learned. Those who have a more profound experience of intimacy in early life grow into adulthood with an easier capacity for being their intimate *selves.*

What are the necessary conditions for the intimate experience, and how can we help bring it about instead of just painfully waiting for it to happen? What do we need to be careful to avoid in our relationships to be sure that we are not keeping ourselves from being intimate?

Intimacy and Psychotherapy

If intimacy is the energizing experience that facilitates change and growth in personal relationship, then psychotherapy should be a crucible relationship within which we can learn about the conditions that foster intimacy. The primary goal of the psychotherapist is to foster and cultivate the intimate experience in the client: to help the client be himself (or herself), in his own space, with maximal awareness of himself while he is in a close relationship with another (that is to say, while he is in a shared space). Is not the neurotic or psychotic condition, most simply put, the partial or total inability of the person to be himself in the presence of *others?* The task of psychotherapy is most often to help clients redevelop the capacity to be intimate. Take, for example, the neurotically dependent person who is enormously capable of closeness, but incapable of being himself. He can be a psychological virtuoso at accommodating his feelings and behaviors to his sense of the other person's needs, but know little of who he really is. The goal of intimacy in any relationship that involves a significant *other,* be it your lover, spouse, child, parent, or therapist, is to allow the *other* to become fully a *self,* and for you to experience your *self* in a growing, energizing, and creative way. The alternate case, the intimate person who needs to learn closeness, is much more rarely seen in therapy, but the goal of becoming a full *self* remains the same.

In our early professional work, it took us some years to discover the primary condition of intimacy. We knew we were well-trained and knowledgeable about psychopathology, and recognized, we think accurately, what was amiss in the people we saw. We knew also what they needed to do to correct their difficulties. And so we did what was obvious: We helped them understand what was wrong, and patiently tried to help them learn what they needed to do and how they needed to change in order to live more fully and be more joyful. No one really changed. They tried, but they really did not change as persons except in temporary, contrived ways. Many, unfortunately, finally resorted to changing their environments—occupation, location, religion, or even spouse or lover; they *themselves* did not change. Out of desperation, we began gradually to abandon real psychotherapy—which attempts to facilitate the development of *self* in relationship—and moved to more and more counseling; that is, identifying the *me* needs, and instructing the *I* how to better gratify them ("You can get along better with your lover, spouse, friend, or boss if you will deal with them this way . . ."). We had to do something to feel we were worth our fees. These techniques did help people cope better, adjust better to their situations, get along with their friends better; but the people *themselves* did not change.

After a period of years, we became increasingly distressed with these results, and increasingly puzzled by the lack of real change. In our view, counseling does not produce real changes in people. It does bring behavioral change (AA helps people stop drinking, career counseling helps people make better decisions, group counseling helps people get along better with each other), and many of these are very valuable, even lifesaving. Most counseling approaches are essentially instructional and therefore tactical. Your *I* gets smarter; you learn more because you have better instructors. What has not changed is your creative capacity to learn from *your own* experience. That changes only when there is an increased, and continually increasing, experience of *self*. This simply means a more abundant, nourishing experience of your connectiveness to the whole rich world around you, to landscapes or stars, lovers or friends. Ultimately, it seemed to us that personal change of a progressively growthful nature, that was not dependent on tutoring by another, would not be brought about cognitively or rationally. What was lacking?

I *(Tom)* supervise a number of younger psychotherapists in my practice. I was listening to one of them discuss a teenage patient who was in some serious trouble. He was uncertain about how he should most effectively intervene and help. Suddenly he said, "I don't really need to discuss this any further with you. I know exactly what that boy needs to do." Remembering my own struggle, I said, "I suspect that his parents also know exactly what that 'boy' needs to do." I was not being sarcastic. I knew that what this therapist thought the "boy" needed to do was, rationally, exactly what the "boy" did need to do, but that was beside the point. What his parents thought he needed to do was probably just what he did *not* need to do; that too was beside the point. Someone—his therapist, if his parents had not done so—needed to let that "boy" know that he was loved and cared for, *just as he was*. Someone had to tell him that he did not need to be different or better in order to be loved or cared for. But the parents had not told him that, and neither had the therapist. In effect, he, also, was saying to his young patient, "If you were different from what you are, then I would approve of you and love you more." Even though his prescription for how the "boy" should be different was a healthier one, it was still a prescription. As such, it withheld from the "boy" the essential prerequisite to growth:

the acceptance of him as he was despite what both of them recognized as his inadequacies and failings. I am sure that young therapist was well-intentioned and cared for the "boy." He wanted him to become "more," and saw a way for him to do so. *But if you do not care for and love me where I am, I cannot go any further.* I am stuck. My very existence is at issue. If I am not worth loving as I am, then I will never be worth loving. If I am not worth loving as I am, then there is *nothing* to improve. If I improve and you love me more because I have changed to meet your expectations and requirements, then when can I ever be intimately quite at ease, no longer anxious about your expectations and requirements for changing? I become an emotional yo-yo, tied to your string. As Eliza Doolittle discovered in *Pygmalion,* conditional love does not feel like love at all; it feels like studying for exams.

When I *(Pat)* first went into psychiatric practice, I would have people come to see me once or twice and then not return. I could not understand why. I knew that I was a reasonably kind and respectful person, with adequate training. What was I doing wrong? It took me some time struggling with myself, and the help of some of the more senior therapists at the clinic, before I came to understand that my "having to help" my clients, my "wanting them to do better," my "helping them change things," was being experienced by these people as my nonacceptance of them. And, in a sense, they were right. I was gentle, I was close, but I was focused on the goal of "improving them." I was not able to be of any real use to them until I could accept them as they were. It took me some time to learn how to do that. It is a great deal harder than it sounds.

It is vitally and fundamentally important to people that they be accepted as they are, without apologies or ifs, ands, or buts. This is who I am, messed up as I am, but me. Can you care for me? I do not ask you to approve of me, or agree with me, or think I am right, but do you care for me? You do not even have to let me be as I am, so long as you care for me as who I am. You can intrude, shout, be upset, get angry, and unload a ton of advice on me, so long as you care. This is not permissiveness. Permissiveness is not acceptance; if anything, it is its opposite. Contained within permissiveness ("I don't worry about where my teenagers are, they are old enough to take care of themselves, and I think they have a right to do what they want to do") is a real sense of not caring. The freedom to be *self* is the permission needed, not behavioral license. The former is the essence of caring; the latter is simply the renunciation of "taking care of." A dramatic example of such acceptance is seen in the struggle of the teacher played by Sidney Poitier in the film *To Sir, With Love.* He had to accept even the "unacceptable lost causes" in his class as worth his disciplined caring. Acceptance of *self* can come in very demanding forms.

Do you accept me as part of us, or am I outside, an alien? There was a very real reason why psychiatrists were originally called *alienists*. Alien is what the person feels who does not feel accepted. Acceptance is rooted in a human's existing as part of the universe, like a flower, a tree, a river, a pond. Neither kicking the oak tree in the front yard nor pretending, desiring, or wishing it were a pine will change its nature. We are what we are on that most connected level, and must be accepted as such. Not to be accepted prevents us from existing on that fundamental plane and gives us no place to be. An alien, a person who does not feel accepted for who he or she is, cannot change, for he or she cannot exist in the real world, the world in which change is possible. The profound importance of being loved for who I am becomes clear: Unless I am loved and cared for as I really am, however much my being that way distresses you, then I cannot change. *I* and *me* cannot exist in the real world as *self*. Accept me as I am, and perhaps I can be different. Give me the feeling that you do not, and cannot, accept me as I am, and I cannot be different. Your lack of acceptance assures my defiant, self-destructive inertia, my staying just *I* and *me*. If I do not feel that acceptance, then I am going to destroy myself with you. Love and accept me as I am; then I can struggle to be different with you. If you will love me only if I am different from who I am, then you do not love me. If indeed I can change and become whatever it is you want me to be in order for you to love me, then my love of you is a dependent need, not a free love. A dependent need is at best a resentful love, and therefore really no love at all. I will defiantly stay as I am, hoping that you will come to accept me as I am, and all the while resenting you for your nonacceptance. There is nowhere for our relationship to go. We are condemned to my unending resentment of you. I cannot be different, I cannot change, because to change would be to give up my respect for myself, my right to be myself. Accept me, even though you do not like the way I am being, and I can grow, be different, and come to a better relationship with you. Otherwise, we are lost in a quagmire of nonacceptance.

Bill and Marie, in trying to decide in which direction their relationship is to move, come in as a couple. When they reach an impasse in their therapy, they come in separately; it is their way of defining the barrier they feel. Of these occasions, each will frequently and directly state, "I'm not giving in." "I'm not changing just because she wants me to." "I know I'm being stubborn, but he hasn't done anything." Getting them to "be reasonable" would not change their feelings. Acceptance is not an intellectual concept, and is not the same as insight.

A simple and common example of the critical role of acceptance in relationship is the alcoholic and his or her *other*. Nelson has been an alcoholic for years. His wife, Dot, and he eventually get into therapy, and with that help, as well as through AA, he finally comes to a period of sobriety. It lasts long enough for life to become bearable for both of them. They are comfortable with each other. He has become what she always wanted, a sober man. We sit in the session, and Dot says quite lovingly, at least apparently, "He is such a loving and wonderful man *now that he is sober.* Our life together is so different, so much bette than those years of *his drunkenness.* Now I really can be close to him. And he is such a better father now that *he is not drinking.*" Nelson is quiet, seemingly not at all pleased with all this praise. We watch him begin to lick his lips. She is not consciously aware of what is happening, but we know that he has decided to get drunk—not intentionally, almost reluctantly, as if he has no choice. And, indeed, at some level he feels he does not have any choice. It is easy to call it addictiveness, but that does not do full justice to what is really happening. Nelson's having a drink, even getting drunk, has become to him, however inappropriately, sadly, and *self*-defeatingly, a way of establishing his right to be himself. In reality, he is establishing his right to "not be himself," but to him the two have become the same. Like many people with problems with weight, smoking, or other unhealthy life positions, the alcoholic comes to confuse his or her right to *avoid* being a *self* with the right to be one. Often, then, alcoholics are in a dilemma, caught between the reason for their drinking—that is, their mistaken belief that they are establishing their right to be themselves (which, if it were indeed their right to be themselves, would be an uncontestably good thing to fight for, whatever the cost)—and the very real fact that the way they fight for it, their right to continually get drunk, is so devastatingly *self*-destructive and dangerous to others.

The power of true acceptance is like a miracle. It can make things that have been stuck for years change in a moment. Most humans are sustained by small everyday acceptances at work, play, and home. We are usually unaware of these small "miracles," but without them we would be even further removed from our intimate *selves.* Acceptance must happen in therapy for any change to occur. One of the reasons that Alcoholics Anonymous, Narcotics Anonymous, and Cocaine Anonymous can help people change their behavior is that people there feel accepted. Acceptance is even more important in this situation because intoxicated persons cannot be themselves, so they cannot participate in the intimate process, and thus cannot really change in *themselves.*

During the many years that I *(Tom)* have spent trying to get alcoholics to stop being drunks, I have experienced some quite unintentional "miracles"; it seems we cannot plan them. We can learn to allow them to happen but cannot schedule them or produce them on demand. In fact, trying to make them happen almost guarantees that they will not. True acceptance appears to be nonrational and nonvolitional.

I was seeing an alcoholic who frequently came drunk to his sessions. This, of course, was a waste of both of our time. I finally told him that I would not talk to him anymore when he was drunk. As you might anticipate, he arrived at his next session quite intoxicated. I reminded him that I had no intention of talking to him when he was in this condition. He started to waddle out, but I stopped him and suggested that he lie on the sofa and sleep it off for the hour. He lay down and immediately fell asleep. The day was cool, so I covered him with my overcoat. I read in my chair nearby, then awakened him at the hour's end. He looked at me and began to cry. Nothing was said, and he left. He has been sober since, some fifteen years now, and has become an impressive person, as a human being, as a husband, as a father and then as a grandfather, and as a writer. How do such transformations occur? Why did this man change when so many others do not?

Grace and Acceptance

In the language of the Judeo-Christian ethic (as well as others—Confucius, Buddha, and Gandhi all took the same position), we need to love the sinner while we condemn the sin. To be capable of doing that is to be capable of real intimacy. Very few people can consistently do so; most can do so only on occasion. When we suggest to the partners of alcoholics that the real issue is whether or not they can love the other when he or she is drunk, we are very aware that we are asking them to be more godly than most humans usually are. Grace, the love of others regardless of their behavior, is an attribute of God; we do not expect it of humans. Nonetheless, unless we have grace in our personal relationships, there is no intimacy, and without intimacy there is no energizing, no growth, no change. We may not be capable of Grace with a capital G, but we can be grace-ful with a small *g*. Intimate grace comes with *spiritus* and transcends system. God's grace is manifest in transcendentalism in all religions. God transcends behavior, judgmentalism, and need. The same would be true for nature as God, universe as God, or universal spirit as God. The *Godly* attribute is the ability to transcend. In humans this attribute is the ability to accept. Acceptance is the human equivalent of God's grace. As grace is the essence of God's beauty and love, so acceptance is the essence of humanity's beauty and capacity for love. "To love for the sake of being loved is human, but to love for the sake of loving is angelic," as philosopher Alphonse de

Lamartine wrote in *Graziellia.* In acceptance we begin to love for the sake of loving.

It is easy to believe that you are an accepting person. That assumption can, unfortunately, be quite deceptive. Acceptance is not a decision, nor is it an attitude. Acceptance is hard, ongoing, psychological work. It is something you have to struggle with over and over in any close relationship. Part of the difficulty is that acceptance can so often be experienced as a social value. G. K. Chesterton was probably right in suggesting that a humanitarian was a person who loved mankind but hated his next-door neighbor. We can contrast this position with that of Jonathan Swift, who wrote that he hated mankind (the systemic manifestations of man) but loved the individual; that is closer to acceptance as a meaningful concept. Acceptance as we are describing it is not a social posture, but an immediate, delimited, and very concrete experience. As such, it is felt by the person who is being accepted not as tolerance, or acquiescence, or forgiveness ("Now that's over, so let's go on from here"), but as something much more positive. When you have done something wrong or stupid, it helps to feel that you are understood, that you are forgiven, or that you, like the rest of us, are only human, and, so what, you made a mistake. Understanding and forgiveness do help, but they are not acceptance. Toleration is not acceptance. Acquiescence is not acceptance. The feeling that we are all in this together is not acceptance. Tolerance, understanding, acquiescence, and a shared sense of belonging are all wonderful social experiences. Acceptance is a personal experience. When we feel accepted even though disagreed with, we do not feel tolerated; we feel loved. Most of us, for most of our lives, try to earn love. We are good, or caring, or sensitive, or successful, and therefore we are loved. We feel we have earned that love. Then again, perhaps we have not. Such love may be given graciously, but since we have been "good," there is an uneasy uncertainty whether the goodness brought about the loving. In acceptance, there is no uneasy uncertainty. We know that, at least in the eyes of the other person, we have done wrong, but nonetheless we are loved, even in our wrongdoing. Such love is a positive, emotional, and experiential affirmation of our person. If I please you and you love me, I am close to you. If I do not please you and you love me, I am intimate with you. Acceptance, in this sense, is a fundamental condition of intimacy.

Acceptance has nothing to do with judgment. With acceptance, there is no better or worse, healthier or sicker, mature or immature. Acceptance has to do with differences without judgment. You are different from me, but I experience you as neither better nor worse than I am. Just different from me. And that difference does not separate us. This same aspect of acceptance applies to noninterpersonal experience also.

Can you accept the weed as well as the flower, the fly as well as the butterfly? Perhaps more important, do you see their commonality not just with each other, but also with you? If we let difference separate us, we lose intimacy.

Each of us expresses our love differently. You may express your love by being excited when I am with you. I may express my love by cooking the dishes I know you like. I have to understand that these are interchangeable. You are no more loving of me when you are excited by me than I am loving of you when I cook you veal scallopini. Both are loving, since each is an individual way of expressing our caring for the other. The love is no less because it is expressed differently. Much of the difficulty in relationships, particularly in terms of acceptance as the foundation of relationship, arises out of these differences in expressions of love. Each of us tends to identify as *loving* those expressions of love that are similar to our own. I may express my love, because of who I am, most immediately by enjoying you, touching you, being wonderfully careless with you, or simply contentedly sitting near you without speaking. You may express an equally deep love feeling by buying me a gift, cooking the veal, working longer hours to bring us more monetary freedom, or simply fixing the broken faucet. These are obviously starkly different ways of loving, but one expression of love is no less loving than the other. In actual experience, that is often not clear to us. The person sitting next to the contentedly silent partner may not have any sense of that presence as an expression of love. The other, watching a spouse or lover fix the faucet, may have no sense of that act as an expression of love. Indeed, both may completely misinterpret these expressions as not love, but distance. It is vitally important to realize that people love differently, but can be loving just as deeply. Of course, they may not be, but they *can* be. It is only through being intimate that we can tell. It is as the poet Shelley wrote in *Prometheus Unbound:* "Familiar acts are beautiful through love." Without intimacy, the familiar captures and we do not realize the love of *others.*

If we are correct about the intimate dyad—that most of us seem to choose to share our lives with our opposites or shadows; that is, we experientially pair—then this tendency to be blind about other ways of expressing loving becomes even more important. We are apt to see *others* as more loving if they express their love as *we* do, because their *expressions* of love are so readily identified by us as loving. The dissimilar expressions of our opposites then will be so much more difficult to identify as loving, and will often be mistakenly identified as coldness or distance. This misperception is very sad. Sadly, it is also very common.

Niels Bohr, the physicist, made an insightful statement about science that can be as well applied to this dilemma: "The opposite of a correct statement is a false statement. But the opposite of a profound truth may well be another profound truth." The opposite of one expression of love may well be another expression of love.

Loving and Liking

There is an important distinction between loving and liking someone. This distinction is too often blurred over and dismissed as simply a difference in intensity or depth of feeling: "I love you" then means that I am more deeply involved with you than if "I like you." "I like you" means that I care a lot about you but do not "love you." But love and like are not a continuum. You do not move from liking to loving; you do not retreat from loving to liking. They are very different experiences. We have seen many couples in therapy in which one of them deeply loved the other but did not like him or her. We have also seen couples, less frequently, in which one of them liked the other but did not love him or her. Where they love but do not like, the relationship is painful but hopeful. Where they like but do not love, the relationship is happier but more hopeless.

Liking someone means that you enjoy the ways that person loves you. It has to do with the struggle people have about the different ways we have of expressing our love for each other. We often dislike people who are loving us, even *while* they are loving us. We do not enjoy the ways they love us, even though we can feel at the moment that we are being loved.

It is difficult for many people to believe that someone could not enjoy being loved, especially when that person really felt loved. Actually, as we have said, this happens quite frequently. Some of us express our love most fully by physical touching; uncensored, joyful, funny, irrelevant talking; or periods of quiet, comfortable silence with the other. Others express our love more fully through caring, attentive service: making healthy meals for those we love, or tending them in hurt and pain, even when they are irascible and petulant. When they need a particular piece of paper to complete their tax return, we know where it is or bring it to them. Each way can be loving. We say "can be" because the same behaviors—touching, talking easily, quietly sitting with someone, preparing food, tending hurts—can also all be behaviors in the service of other motives. These motives can be placative, dependent, accommodative, or simply habit. "Unhealthy closeness" would be a more appropriate name for such motives than "love." For most of us, the problem is that the lack of intimacy leaves us imprisoned by the illusion that love can be expressed only as we express it. Nothing could be further from the truth. Humans love in a *multitude* of ways, and each of us needs to learn that others may love differently but no less deeply. Yet, from our experience in our relationship with patients, it seems that it is very difficult for humans to accept other ways of loving as being as real and authentic as the ways they love.

A couple comes in for their first session. After listening for some time to their descriptions of their struggling and fighting, we ask how she actually feels about him. She expresses her love for him in a very beautiful way. He responds with real surprise: "You really do love me and care about me." He did not feel at all liked in the relationship but could understand that he was loved. Just for that moment, he understood that the two were not the same thing.

In our different ways of loving, we may "sort of feel loved" by the other but are usually vaguely discontented. We wish that the other could or would love as we love, could or would express love as we do. Our wish has to do with liking. We like another when that person expresses his or her loving as we express ours. It really has nothing to do with the love, but with the ways that the love is *expressed* and *shared*. It has to do with the imprisoning and insidious tendency of human beings to like people who are like themselves, even though they almost always pair with people who are very different. When our partners love us in their own ways, different from our own, we know we are being loved, but we are vaguely irritated. This unhealthy closeness creates enormous confusion in our relationships. It may eventually even destroy them. The only experience that allows both persons' love to be what it is is intimacy-acceptance. We can come to, as the theologian Jacob Needleman describes it in *A Sense of the Cosmos*, "Love . . . which helps us to understand the truth about ourselves and our possibilities." We can both find the truth of *ourselves* in intimacy.

Real love surrounds you with a feeling that allows you, perhaps even requires you, to be everything you are as a human being at that moment. When you are most unreservedly loved, you are most fully yourself. Love is a feeling that creatively and insistently facilitates and energizes your fully "being in the world in good faith." This is love made up of acceptance-intimacy and closeness combined.

"Like" has little to do with the *other*. It is a feeling we have within the confines of our *me*-ness. It is *self*-less, in the sense that when we like, we are not in touch with our connection with the *other*. "Like" is how much I enjoy the ways you love me, particularly if you love me in the ways I love you. If you express your love in different and strange ways, I may feel vaguely loved but I will not like you. It is a constant paradox in relationships, feeling loved but not liked, or loving but not liking. We see this confusion in our offices all the time. It is the imbalance, the lack of the intimate experience, that leaves us in this paradox. Without being your intimate *self,* you cannot accept *others* as they are, accept their love as what it is.

Not liking someone we love, not feeling liked by someone we feel loves us, creates a lot of pain as well as confusion in our experience of closeness. When we are close, we are much more aware of the *other* than in the intimate experience. Being close, we are much more sensitive to the *other's* expressions of love, and so are more prone to feel like or dislike. Intimacy transcends like or dislike, and we experience our own being while with the *other*. In intimacy, it is as if we experience love in its most primitive sense, unconcerned with how it is expressed. We *know* we are loved and are not concerned with how. The power of acceptance makes possible our full, unmonitored, and passionate experience of ourselves. It is possible only because of the "unthoughtful" acceptance of us *by the other loving one.*

Metafeelings

Acceptance is a fundamental precondition to intimacy, the center of the intimate experience. In acceptance, you love someone who expresses love differently from the way you do. That is no small psychological feat. To accomplish it you have to do something rather uncommon: You have to transcend your own ways of loving. You have to love without personal, psychological, or "love" prejudice. You love as your *self* instead of your *I* or your *me.*

In acceptance, you realize the communality (commonality) of humanity, a perception beautifully stated by Hyemeyohsts Storm in *Seven Arrows:*

> Each Man, Woman, and Child Upon the Earth
> Is a Living Fire of Power and Color.
> The Powers I Speak of here are
> Cold, Heat, Light, and Darkness.
> They are a Living, Spinning Fire,
> a Medicine Wheel. And these
> Colors from this Living Wheel of
> Fire can be Seen by all Men,
> and Each can Learn from
> them. It is very Simple to See
> the Colors of the Medicine.
> Any Man, Woman, or even a
> Child can See these Colors.

How do you know when you are indeed accepting of other persons, when you experience your commonality with them? They can, of course, tell you in simply being themselves. That is what we meant by suggesting earlier that you can be mistaken about being loving, but you are seldom if ever mistaken about being healthily loved. But, apart from the response of the other, how can you know subjectively when you are on the right track? There is no sure way, since it is easier to delude ourselves about being accepting than any other feeling we have, but there are some guidelines. Most commonly, acceptance is, as we mentioned earlier, confused with four other feelings: toleration, acquiescence, understanding, and a sense of belonging. Occasionally we confuse acceptance with forgiveness. As we have said, all of these are good and helpful human feelings, but none are acceptance. Each is a different subjective experience, both to the tolerant one and the one tolerated, the one to acquiesce (or put up with unangrily) and the one being put up with, the understanding one and the one being understood, the one who emphathizes and the other who feels that empathy. The metafeelings are very different in each experience. Metafeelings are very important subjective states. They are different from our primary feelings. Primary feelings are feelings of joy, elation, anger, sexuality, curiosity, fear, etc.—feelings we are born with. Metafeelings are the feelings we have in response to our experience of these primary feelings. They are feelings about our feelings. Common metafeelings are guilt, consideration, embarrassment, self-consciousness, modesty, politeness, hostility, and a thousand other finely tuned emotions we have when we are not simply being who and what we are. You can feel guilty about your legitimate anger; you can politely deal with a rude person; you can be embarrassed by your natural sexual desires. Metafeelings are learned feelings. They are an aspect of closeness, of system, and can be either healthy or unhealthy.

In our experience, acceptance has no metafeelings associated with it. You do not even feel good, much less noble or righteous. You simply feel accepting. In contrast, when you are tolerant you are likely to feel at least some twinges of "goodness," pride, or righteousness. Toleration enhances the ego; you feel just a little better than the person you tolerate. It has the quality of *noblesse oblige,* which, of course, suggests our awareness of our nobility. Acquiescence, or putting up with someone, also has significant metafeelings. You usually feel a vague resentment toward the other person. It is also usually accompanied by a sense of having been less than honest; perhaps even a sense of having compromised or possibly betrayed your own values. An underlying pity also colors the experience.

The feeling of "understanding" someone is usually accompanied by a sense of dispassionate distance and some mild condescension, usually not intended consciously. It is not cold, but it is not warm, either. It is often considerate and polite. Something lies between me and the other, which is not there when I feel acceptance. When acceptance is present, the space between us is clear, not cloudy or fogged. The seeing and the hearing, all the experiencing senses are sharp, precise, lucid, and unmistakable.

Confusing acceptance with belonging is quite common but seldom identified as such. It becomes clearer when the feeling of belonging is operationally described as a feeling that "we are in this together" or "we are both just human and frail" or "we have been in this relationship a long time, and this is just another of the downs, one that you brought about, but then, I have often been the culprit myself." "We belong together for better or worse." Hopelessness and gratitude are the usual metafeelings that go with a sense of belonging.

The difference between acceptance and forgiveness is more difficult to describe, but we think it is probably the most important of all. When I forgive you, I am aware of your sin; when I accept you, I am not. Both are loving, but acceptance seems to empower you, whereas forgiveness seems to keep you in the family. Acceptance raises you up; forgiveness lets you stay where you are. Forgiveness has a temporal quality that acceptance does not. Forgiveness is redemptive; acceptance is celebrant and resurrective. Closeness is redemptive and temporal; intimacy is celebrant, resurrective, and timeless. We must have them both to live; together they form the matrix of love.

5

Personal Confinement . . . Prejudgmentalism and Judgmentalism

I shut my eyes in order to see.

—PAUL GAUGUIN

Have you ever driven up to your house, something you have done many times, stepped out of your car, and actually "seen" your front door, or the oak tree that is close to the house, or even the walkway down to the door that goes by the tree? Ever wonder why you had never before noticed that the off-shade of green on the hinges of the door made the brass hardware appear stronger and more permanent, or that the worn-out walkway gave you a momentary feeling of the sweet strength of your family? Have you experienced that distinct, unique feeling you get when you *actually* see something and feel the immediacy, the depth, the texture, the permanence, the uniqueness of this usually familiar environment? As Kundera said, truth lies in details—in the way the weathered board is streaked, in the particularity that makes things alive and real to us, even though we seldom are consciously aware of those qualities.

Even more important is the difference inside you when you are "seeing" this way. You see the door differently, but, much more important, you experience yourself differently—more of your *self,* or at least a different and often a fresh, new, and invigorating sense of you. Even if it lasts only seconds, you feel differently when you see things as if for the first time because it *is* a different experience, an *intimate* experience. This is "being in the world in good faith," being intimately connected to your world. In that intimacy you see the *other* as it really is, and you, for that moment, are as you really are.

Humans have these moments all too infrequently. People will say when asked about experiences like this, "Yes, I've done that." "I occasionally feel that, and it's a great feeling." "I really felt good." "I liked it, wish I could feel like that more often." "I felt so much more alive." "One time I felt that; I talked to her and the kids. I was interested. Like I was not looking for something, or didn't want to get away from something. I *had* something. I was interested. They were more interesting. I didn't know why, and really didn't care. I felt fresh and awake and more alive, more connected."

People remember these moments; they have them not often, but memorably. At least for a short time, they are changed and refreshed by them. Essentially, their response is "I liked it, but I don't know where it came from or where and why it went. I would like to have it again, but I guess that's silly, because it just seemed to come out of nowhere." You listen to them talk and you yourself feel a sort of nostalgic and desperate longing to find more such experience. At the same time, you likely feel slightly sad, a little hopeless, and have a sense of similarly nostalgic helplessness. All you can do is to wait for it to happen, and it may never again. Yet the desperate longing for it can powerfully affect lives and relationships, can end careers, destroy marriages, and distort living.

The provocation for this longing, this desire for "seeing" in a way that makes us more alive and refreshed in ourselves, was, in the preceding example, simply a surface, visual awareness of a particular environment. We "saw" the front door and dwelled momentarily on the way in which the brass hardware was enhanced by the off-green jade color. It was a very transient and superficial experience, but its resonance was not at all superficial, and probably not transient. Remembering, we would likely reexperience the differences in our relationship to our spouse or children or lover that evening, and most deeply reexperience the difference in the way we felt about our *self*.

As the novelist Proust described in *Remembrance of Things Past,* smells can be even more personally pervasive. Hashbrowns cooking on Sunday morning suddenly take you back twenty-five years, not simply in memory, but *in* the experience. You smell your own sweat and are back in the small high-school gym, fifteen years old, not sure you are tall enough to make the team, but keeping up with everyone in the exercises just the same. Sounds are much the same. One morning you wake up a little early, while everyone else is still asleep, walk outside barefoot, and hear a single bird sing. You look up, see it in the tree, and are back in a young world. Back in a child's world, not simply remembering, but once again feeling a personal vibration that you had forgotten was still part of you. Taste and touch do much the same. Physical movement brings even more subtle and profound resurgences of earlier experiences. I *(Tom)* recently found myself walking down a slight incline on a sidewalk. With each step I seemed to grow taller. As a ten-year-old I had that sensation walking to school, growing so tall that I could see for miles around. I was, as an adult, momentarily in the same wonderful space I had been in as a ten-year-old. At times like these we become aware of how far removed our spirits tend to be from our "nature" most of the time. These moments are not a neurotic hanging on to the past or an unhealthy living in some other time. Instead, they are brief reconnections to the entirety of our *selves,* a direct experience of our true reality.

These momentary, revealing, and energizing recontacts with what is actually real in our personal experience, with our "nature" connected to the *other's* "nature," are even more startling when we discard the lenses we have learned to look through in seeing *people.* As we said earlier, the human-to-human connection is the most profound for us, for it is *our* metaphor. You look at your daughter one evening; she is suddenly, instantly, and clearly older, bigger, more adult, and even somewhat of a stranger. You see *her.* You are without your historical spectacles, and so she is a different person. Perhaps more correctly we should say that for that moment, just that moment, she is a *person,* not simply your daughter.

Capture by Knowing

Why do we feel this so rarely? Why does it startle us when it happens? We believe it is because we are so captured by "knowing." We "know" in our personal and shared spaces, in very familiar and historical ways. If we are unable to expand that familiarity and transcend that history, we can "know" only neurotically; that is, in a limited and predefined way. If we can see our daughters only *as* our daughters, we become neurotically confined in that particular relationship with them. We cannot know the evolved and new truth of their reality as brand-new fourteen-year-olds—as curious, sexual, exploring, real persons. We know them only as we have known them earlier, familiar and unchanging, and we hang on to a neurotic closeness so as not to risk losing them. Or, worse, psychotically, we see them *only* in our personal space: as we need them, as we define them out of our own desires and motivations. We are left without even the corrective decency of neurotic closeness, in which at least we are aware of *them* historically, even if we are impervious to who they are today.

Judgmentalism and Prejudgmentalism

Neurotic "knowing," the fixed mind-set that comes with the "fixed set of glasses," goes to the heart of one of our original questions: How can we be ourselves while we are in relationship to another person, or to the world around us, or to the memories of our senses? How can we be in relationship to anything, from a speck of dust to our undying love, without seriously looking at the experience from the perspective of our personal participation in it? Why do we spend so little time feeling and knowing our own experiences, being our real *selves* while still being in direct relationship to what we are actually seeing? The green tinge on the brass knobs, the smell of potatoes, the singing birds, the walking as a giant, even our daughters seem so frequently to be just beyond the grasp of our "normal selves." The sensations, our real connection to our environment, can bring back those moments of our being our *real selves,* and we feel that awareness powerfully. Neurotic "knowing" has to be equally powerful to be able to block our intimate *selves.*

What does it mean to know? It can mean something quite superficial—that we have noticed the bird singing, have simply *recognized* the fact of something. "I know it to be so, I recorded it in both mind and memory, and I can attest to it." "I knew it to be so and could describe it." Two distinct experiences are involved here: perceiving with our senses and being certain that we have done so. Both are knowing, but very different kinds of knowledge. "I know you do not like me" (meaning "I experience you not particularly appreciating me") is not the same as my knowing that you hate me, not just in this particular instance, but now and in many other past experiences, on the basis of which I know quite certainly that you hate me.

The distinction is even more complicated. I can say "I know you hate me" and imply that not only do I experience your hatred, but I understand it and I know why you are so angry with me. Knowing sometimes suggests that I have some very special, secret, and private information that no one else has. I know, I possess knowledge that is privy only to me. "I know" can imply cleverness, privacy, prior information, superiority, or deliberation. Moreover, in the biblical sense, knowing can mean sexual intercourse.

So what do we mean when we say that "knowing" blocks intimacy, stops the direct experience of *self* in reality? This "knowing" most likely includes the whole gamut of the connotations above. It conveys every footprint of its evolution in meaning, and every nuance of changing importance. At least the unconscious must be aware, since it has collected this evolution of meaning; for the unconscious records real human history, while culture tries to escape that natural reality. The beauty of the unconscious is that it not only rightfully pushes around our cultural superciliousness, but also insists on reminding us of our real history. The archetypes of Jung transcend cultural boundaries. The drive to *self* is not culturally defined. As Jung himself said in *Psychology and Alchemy,* "The conscious mind allows itself to be trained like a parrot, but the unconscious does not. Which is why St. Augustine thanked God for not making him responsible for his dreams."

Neurotic "knowing," however, includes more than the natural footprints of the origin of the word; it also includes our struggle for security. Such "knowing" has two major components: as "already knowing," it is prejudgmentalism, the fixed set of lenses; as "knowing," it is judgmentalism, the fixed certainty that our own "way of seeing" is the *only* way of seeing.

So what does it really mean when someone says to me, "I know you are angry with me"? Does it mean that right now I recognize that you are angry with me? Not only do I recognize it, but I am certain that you are angry with me even if other experiences suggest that you are not? Or, more patronizing, does it mean that I understand why you dislike me? I am not involved in it. I simply understand it. Or does it mean that I know what no one else knows; I am privy to a personal secret? Voice inflection would often make the distinction; what we are really trying to point out is that *knowing* is a complicated concept and *neurotic "knowing"* is often what humans mean when they "know." And, more important, "knowing," in all these textures of possible meaning, alienates us from our *intimate self.*

"Knowing" and "already knowing" are the states in which we live most of our lives. Together they form a constructed world in which we are the manipulative or innocent architects. We build a "set," as we do in a play. We build the set to suit the characters, particularly the main character, ourselves. We build the set not only to suit and to justify the character we have been in the past, but also to prepare the most suitable environment for the character we *mean* to be. We plan and arrange the set out of what we are, and, if successful, make it unlikely that we will ever be different. Given this, there is no way we can escape our "character." We prejudge our existence and then are "secure" in our certainty. Our set does not have the substantiality, however momentary, of seeing the brass doorknob, the singing bird, or the daughter as a person. These real connections to the *other* are not constructs; they are *self-other* experiences. Our set, like that in any play, is simply a framework, a map of the territory, something to guide us through the behaviors, while assuring that we will never process it, never really *experience* it. We will never feel the intense energy, animation, or revitalization that experience of the *other* gives. We will simply get through life. We will be safe and effective, although a shade unhappy, never really knowing *ourselves* or the *other.* That is the difference between "knowing" and knowing. It is the difference between living without intimacy and living with it. Prejudgmentalism and judgmentalism are not *knowing,* nor are they *living.*

Righteousness

This "living in a set," an unchanging format, prearranged and accepted as reality, is what is so devilishly dangerous about righteousness. Righteousness is a total, subservient belief in a constructed life set. In so living, you lose the most vital ability you can have as a human being—the ability to be the architect of your life, and to experience your evolution as such. Whether history or mythology, the story of Eden is true. We were given a "set" called the Garden of Eden within which to be happy. We were dissatisfied. We sinned, which simply means we rejected the "set." We wanted more than ease and comfort. We wanted to be more like "God." We demanded free choice, the freedom to be the architects of our own lives. And "God," whatever "God" is, gave us that gift. We were given the mixed blessing of being in charge of our own lives.

The quintessence of being human is the ability to make choices. The fundamental experience in being intimate is the experience of making such a choice. The "set," however secure and comfortable as even Eden may have been, deprives us of that experience. We have become actors, rather than creators. We constantly reseek "Eden," the safe, secure, comfortable, and presumably happy set. If life were only this or that prearranged way, we think, we would be safe and happy. Is not this the promise of so many "systems," religious or secular? But the reconstructed Eden is simply a set, a rationalized construct of judgmentalism and prejudgmentalism. We write a black book, which we constantly carry with us, prescribing how we should be with one another, especially how others should be. The other writes his or her own black book and carries it just as righteously. In relations in life, we find ourselves now in the common, incessant, troubled, and ungrowthful battle between different righteousnesses. Intimacy is impossible. Closeness may be possible if we compromise, but it is an unstable and usually unhappy closeness.

Many people make this choice in their relationships. They would rather "know" than be loving or loved. Covertly, they would rather be "right" than happy. The insistence on "knowing" rather than experiencing love, or loving, plagues most relationships. Some people overtly choose to live their "cause" out as their lives. They directly and openly choose being "right" as a way of living. This is not only *self*-destructive, but usually does damage to others' ability to be *themselves.* Most people, more subtly, simply use it as a defense: "I would rather be sure than be loved." "I would rather be right than give in to her or him." We see again and again in our offices the impasse of the earlier-mentioned couple who sat in appositional chairs: her saying she is angry because he will not talk to her, his saying he will not talk to her because she is always angry. And we between them, wondering why two people of such high intelligence and apparent desire for a good relationship are exchanging such *self*-defeating inanities.

Why can they not "see"? They are two persons who need to touch, need to have one of them walk through the unreality and be what he or she is with the other. The movement does not happen because both are mired in their own personal "knowing" (judgmentalism and prejudgmentalism). Being certain and secure appears to be more important to them than being loving or loved. It seldom occurs to these people how un-*self*-caring their position actually is. They seem to have no awareness of the very real *self*-destructiveness of defensiveness, how it isolates and leaves them lonely. They mistake loneliness for chosen aloneness, and so stay unhappy. They seem to have a sense that they are making some choice, and could choose to love and be loved, but they have shut themselves off from the real experience of choice. People who insist on being certain rather than being loved "*know.*" They "*know*" what is "true" and how it should be. They "*know*" who they are. They "*know*" who the *other* is. In such "knowing" they remain unloved and unloving. They can not hear, touch, see, or feel differently. They cannot be intimate, since they cannot experience themselves.

This kind of "knowing" has certain identifiable qualities. It is a "knowing" almost always about the *other,* the outside, or about *me.* It is never about the connection, the *self.* People who talk to us with this kind of "knowing," the righteousness, the firm complete black book under their arms, talk only of him or her, or of *me,* and are judgmental of both. They have no sense of *self,* the reciprocal experience of the connection between *I-me* and the *other.* The discourse changes little if at all over time or with experience. They "see" the situation the same way, think of it the same way, and generally emotionally drown in their sameness. As the cliché says, "Knowing prevents learning," so all that is available is the sameness. Reexperience is simply more reinforcement of everything that is wrong in their relationships and their belief systems. They never learn what Nietzsche described in *Beyond Good and Evil:* "Whoever fights monsters should see to it that in the process he does not become a monster. And when you look long into an abyss, the abyss also looks into you."

Rudy comes into our office because he cannot maintain a relationship. His last lover suggested that he seek help. He did but still describes things in terms of what the *other,* this last one and all those before, did. Rudy has such fixed notions of who, how, and in what way the *other should* be that there is no way that the other *could* be with him. We too feel this. His sense of what we *should* be overwhelms the reasons he came to us. He is un-*self*-caring in his inability to allow himself *to be.*

This un-*self*-caring behavior leaves people repeatedly experiencing the devastating *self*-destructiveness of their defensiveness. They are sure, but living in a lonely world by themselves. Usually they mistake this self-imposed loneliness as the natural human condition: "It's just the way people are." Lonely, unhappy, and certain of how the world really is, or really should be, they are alone, but "right." On many occasions we see people who, when they feel an intimation of aliveness within them, mistake it for nervousness or anxiety. They are assuring that they will remain in that constructed world, "knowing" only what is "real and true." A world in which, sadly, they are the only resident.

You can never be playful in such a "righteous" world. It is an incessantly serious and oppressive place. It is a world that emotionally creaks, strains, works, wars, and all too frequently screeches to a hateful halt in relationship. It is devoid of playfulness, an essential of all learning, whether about stars or people. *Righteousness* is probably the antonym of *playfulness.* When playful, we always learn something. We so easily forget that humans learn the vast majority of what equips them for life—for example, language and social relating skills—before they go to school, and that they accomplish this learning through play. A colleague of ours once remarked that an adult is a child grown inadequate. Picasso claimed that his great goal was to relearn how to paint like a child. The serious, staunch, stalwart adult, defensively "knowing," is always once removed from the *other* reality. He or she is not a natural part of the group, or activity, or experience, or lovemaking, or relationship, or play.

Most people we see in therapy are vaguely aware of this separating part of themselves. They describe the aloneness, the bleakness of always "knowing" (that is, the isolation of judgmentalism and prejudgmentalism), the "work feeling" as compared to the "play feeling," the boredom of their seriousness, the feeling that the *certainty* of their perceptions separates them and leaves them knowing less. They do not quite understand why they should feel bad about being "right" and "honest." They are unwilling or unable to accept the futility of the outcome as a personal reality that should be listened to, so that they can seek other and better ways of relating. They do not seem to contrast either their confusion or their sense of futility to those vivid moments when they were fully able to see the *other* as it really is, unjudgmentally.

Why can't we do this more often? Most people value, actively support, and defend their "knowing" self for a variety of *me* reasons. Most of these reasons are not particularly convoluted, or irretrievably unconscious (they do not all go back to when we were three years old). People simply make the mistake of believing adamantly that "seeing it as it is" is being adult. "I am an adult because I am able to know the world in which I live. And since, as an adult, I know this world, why should I not simply say it as it is?" They should, when what they know is *their experience.* Describing your *self* experience is connection as opposed to "knowing." It is the connection, the awareness, of intimacy. But how we "see things" is not the way they are; it is just how *we* see things. Our truth can only be the truth of our experience. The French painter Georges Braque said, "Truth exists, only falsehood has to be invented." When we believe our "seeing" to be some special "seeing," to be "adult" seeing, we are inventing falsehoods.

In relationship, we could describe the *other* if we could really know it, really know the world in which we are living, the world of me and thee, *know* without the quotes. But such is not the case. In relationship, we believe that we know the world in which we live, but we do not. Instead, we live in the world which we "know," the world of judgmentalism and prejudgmentalism. These are two very different realities. John believes that he knows his wife is very possessive. Actually, he "knows" it, and it distances him from her. He "knows" he needs space. He appears to know the world he lives in, but is that indeed true? In fact, his wife, with her possessiveness, constantly distances him, and he with his fear of closeness invites her possessiveness. Is that not more exactly the world John lives in, rather than the world he "knows" he lives in? The two realities are eons apart. Would it help him to know the truth of his reality, rather than the untruth of his "knowing"? What he "knows" keeps him a prisoner. In truth, both he and she are terrified of real closeness, much less intimacy. *The truth about knowing is that all we can ever really know is ourselves.* What comes in from the outside, the *other,* be it animate or inanimate, we never really know. We never even completely know the only reality we *can* know, the reality of ourselves. That is why "knowing," the predetermined sets, the surety of righteousness, makes learning impossible. That is why taking something, or someone, into the shared space *as they are,* while you remain in your personal space *as you are,* is the only way that intimacy and therefore learning occur. Truth is found in the process of connection, not static "fact."

What does it really mean to say that we can know only ourselves? It is the foundation of intimacy. "I can know only myself, no matter how hard I try to do otherwise." What a blessed relief from having to "know" the *other,* from sitting in front of the switchboard of the *other,* lights constantly flashing, plugging frantically into each new flashing red, to "know" what is going on around us, so that we can act appropriately. What does he feel, how does she behave, what does he want, what does that mean, what is she going to do next, why does he feel that way? The why, what, when, how of the *other,* until we are finally an emotional prisoner, constantly and unsuccessfully trying to decipher a million messages at once. How much simpler to know our own experiences as the basis for our living. A blue chair to you may be a green chair to another. You may not know that some shades of color, like teal, she sees and describes as green. You have both learned independently to see the same color as either blue or green. Who is right? Neither of you, of course. Yet you are both right, at least in relationship to each other. *In relationship,* what we see and experience as anger, resentment, stubbornness, possessiveness, love, or caring may be called one thing by me and another by you. The point is that neither of us already surely "knows." We never really "know." Actual real knowing of the other is not only not everyday and usual, as we so simplistically assume, it is not even possible. You cannot *know* how someone else really is, feels, thinks, or is going to be; certainly not in the sense of "already knowing." Belief in "already knowing," or knowing beforehand what the other person feels, wants, needs, hurts with, and is anticipating from you, is pure illusion. It is a world we, as safe "ego architects" of relationship, construct to meet our own needs and fantasies. It is not what we know in our own hearts to be true.

"Already knowing" is living a lie, because in it we are living on the basis of personal information that is not only specious but speculative. It forgoes the only certain information we have—not what we "know" *others* want, feel, or think, but what we know we feel. The latter is the only real certainty, however uncertain it may be. It is still far more certain than the switchboard information. I know what I feel, or would if I were not distracted by the stereo mass of information that comes in from the *other* switchboard. My wife says she is thinking about getting a divorce. It sounds real, and we, in our relationship, have reason to think that divorce might be probable. I listen to this. I know the history, and the *other* realities. What I feel inside, however, is that she is very angry with me because I am not with her in a way that she wants me to be with her. Which should I listen to, what she says about a divorce or what I feel inside, that she wants to be intimate with me in a way she cannot so far be? If I assume the former in terms of my "already knowing" her to be some way, we are lost. If I ignore the outside, the "knowing" what she feels and wants and how she is, and stay with the reality of what I feel and want—that she really wants to be more intimate with me than she has been—then my behavior will change. If I am wise, I will then ignore the blue and green differences. I live my blue, that she wants to be intimate with me. I respond to her in terms of my own knowing, rather than my "already knowing" of her.

You cannot "know" how someone is, feels, thinks, or desires. You can "already know" your constructed image of him or her from years of relationship, and therefore be unable to see the person now, at this moment. In so doing, you miss the experience of the seeing, hearing, or touching that is real. You cannot "know" *others* even if they are willing to tell you, even if you are feeling close to them when they are telling you. Only when you are intimate do you know, because you know then what *you* are feeling and experiencing. When that is felt and experienced in close relationship, you are privy to the only personal information that can accurately tell you about the *other:* what you know and experience *in your own person.* If we are sitting quietly together and you are reading, I do not know what you feel. I may surmise, because I feel close to you, but I do not "know." If I feel loved, however, I know what you are feeling. That is intimacy; it makes us knowledgeable about the world around us. We can know only what we create in ourselves. I cannot know what I create in you, or what you create in me, only what I create in me.

This concept is troubling to many people. Like relativity and quantum physics on the one hand, and Buddhism and Taoism on the other, the idea of "created reality" is difficult for the "certain" Western mind. The psychiatrist Alex Comfort, in *I and That,* suggests that this distrust is connected to Western religious concepts in which certainty has replaced revelation, mysticism, and sexuality—and, we would add, intimacy.

The inability to know separately makes people hold steadfastly to their "already knowing." If you finally understand that you cannot really know the *other,* you are forced to your sense of aloneness. This existential aloneness, particularly in our culture, has never been understood, or accepted as natural. We confuse it with loneliness and so want to avoid it. Many people come to our offices with a wonderful capacity for aloneness, but feel as if they should do something about changing it. Confusing being alone with loneliness, humans want to avoid it, defend against it, apologize for it. So they create a world in which they are never alone, never not "knowing." "Knowing" (judgmentalism and prejudgmentalism) becomes the primary prerequisite to security. We hold tenaciously to our need to "know," and so construct our "already knowing." We build on it continually. We end up constructing an "already knowing" of the *other* that becomes the primary obstacle to our own immediate seeing and feeling in the present experience. Our "knowing" of the *other,* whether person or forest, blocks our knowing of ourselves. It blocks intimacy.

This way of living entails the loss of true innocence. People mistakenly believe that "knowing" protects them from their innocence. They are convinced that if you live in the real world as an innocent, you will be hurt. But if you "know," construct, your world, you can protect yourself from that hurt. In fact, the only way you can truly experience the real world is "innocently," as children do so much better than adults. Innocence is being available to truth, or, as we said earlier, "being in the world in good faith." It is a way of being available that frees us to experience our world as it really is. From this experience comes truth. If you live in the real world, you *will* be hurt. You will also hurt others. But you will experience others, their growing and dying, and you will experience growing and dying yourself. All of these events will also happen to you in "knowing," but you will not experience them as they are, and therefore will not learn anything from them. You cannot hide from the real world. You can only turn away, make believe you are looking, and delude yourself. True innocence is knowing that you are not living by yourself. You take in the outside by creating a space in which the *other* (he, she, them, or it) can occur in your present experience, unchanged by you, and unchanging of you. You then understand that if change occurs, it happens to "us," not to the *I* or to the *me* or to the *other* alone. You then know that in the course of your life you will experience hurt, hurting, living, and dying, but you will not be constructing them yourself. They will be real, like the door, the walkway, and your daughter. The value of true innocence is that you do not have to "already know" (to prejudge) or "know" (judge). To "already know" and still have hurt or loss happen brings us to our crippling guilt, and to "know" brings us to our arrogant, grandiose, separate sense that we are in this world alone.

This concept of *innocent knowing* is the real meaning of the Garden of Eden, and the reason for the expulsion of its residents, or, more correctly, the reason that the residents insisted on being expelled. If you can do no wrong, you cannot really do any right. If you cannot say no, your yes is meaningless. Adam and Eve were given enough "godliness" to know that innocence that precluded sin was a false, albeit comfortable, innocence. True innocence knows sin. Given enough godliness, Adam and Eve insisted on sinning, mainly to upgrade their goodness. As opposed to orthodox Christian belief, we would suggest that God was pleased with their rebellion. They wanted desperately to be more godly. They wanted the most precious gift of all, to be able to choose. God gave them that: the gift of really knowing, instead of the uneasy comfort of "already knowing"; the freedom to choose, the singular right to be either good or bad, the godlike dignity of being in charge of their own lives. Free will is frightening, but a million times more enlivening than "already knowing." Acceptance is difficult, but much more creative than "knowing." The "Fall" was not from good to evil, but from fate to humanness. And it was, in that sense, a *felix culpa,* a happy fall. It created the soul, the center of choice, of connectivity, and of intimacy. Prior to the "Fall," grace was not an issue; afterward, it was a reality. After the "Fall," we were risen. We were able to make choices, the essence of godliness. "Already knowing," we are secure, are sure, but condemned to being automatons. In the "Fall," God put us beautifully back into nature. We were put back into the beauty of struggle, choice, and experience. In this way, God put us back into evolution. We could choose the path of our own future growth. In evolution, we have the chance to grow as an expansion of *self,* not as the resolution of conflict in closeness that we so often mistake for growth, but that is really our rejection of choice.

You give up choice when you "already know," when you prejudge the response of the *other.* Prejudgment assures a boring relationship, because you never change. (As Dylan Thomas said, "Somebody's boring me . . . I think it's me.") More often than not, the *other* will meet your prejudged expectations. Sadly, so often we choose our relationships for these reasons. In their own prejudging, our partners never change, either.

Prejudgment erodes and forecloses the intimate experience, much as acceptance assures it. Judgmentalism, on the other hand, expresses a conditional loving. It says, usually implicitly, that were you different, then I would love you more. Judgmentalism is lethal to my experience of being un-*self*-consciously myself, fully, easily, and surely aware of myself when I am related to you. Intimacy and closeness are both damaged by judgmentalism. Remarks like "Just what do you mean by that?" or "I never thought I would ever hear you say something like that" or simply "What?" can separate us. But judgmentalism damages intimacy even more dramatically and totally than it does closeness, for intimacy cannot be negotiated. When I am risking being *me* with you, and am by definition defenseless, and you say, "I never thought I would hear you say something like that," I am more devastated than when I am simply misunderstood by you. To give up judgmentalism (the "I 'know' what is so, so don't try to talk to me" attitude) does not mean that you are permissive or passive. You are not giving up or giving in. If you are not being judgmental, you can be listening, or using other relational options. You can disagree; you can even confront; you can share your own feeling responses to what you might otherwise judge; you can ask and inquire; you can leave and go back to your own space, or take countless other courses. To judge and accuse are the responses we are taught; they are the most reflexive. They are also the most futile and most *self*-defeating. The other responses—from disagreeing to being upset or just inquiring—never suggest that the other person is a "bad" person. They do not immediately convey the feeling that you love *others* less because of how they are being, what they feel, or what they believe. Or that you would love them more if they became, immediately and miraculously, what you were instructing them to be—which is exactly what judgmentalism does.

Acceptance, as we have described earlier, has no metafeelings. It is simply acceptance. Judgmentalism, in contrast, has many metafeelings: righteousness, pride, hostility, arrogance, condescension, self-effacement, guilt, embarrassment, self-consciousness, false modesty, false hurt, and martyrdom. All of these neurotic and defensive postures can be the direct result of judgmentalism.

These defensive emanations of judgmentalism are particularly difficult to transcend, to get beyond. Of all human responses, they evoke little or no acceptance in the other. Righteousness and pathetic defensiveness make acceptance very unlikely. When acceptance occasionally does happen, it feels almost heroic and unbelievable. Such righteous people are usually suspicious of grace and acceptance. They either dependently expect this acceptance, and so defeat its intent, or they arrogantly manipulate the acceptance to get what they "think" they want: to get you to agree with their judgments and prejudgments. They never realize their spiritual peerage with the other person, which is what, by accepting, the other is trying to share with them.

We are, of course, discussing the dynamics of the experience of two people relating in an effort to be closer and more intimate. They are in a shared space. Acceptance is not really an issue when you are not in such a shared space. We are not asking for an acceptance of brutality, indifferent coldness, or psychopathy. Anyone who "accepted" such behavior would be sick. A masochist is not an accepting person.

Judgmentalism is most often experienced by others as righteousness. Righteousness can appear in many disguises. Most often it is quite subtle, masked with an assumed innocence. The usual guise is that, far from judging you, I am either being innocently honest or even tolerantly helping you. I am simply "trying to understand you," "just trying to get the facts straight," "trying to help you see the truth," "helping you see how it really is, so our relationship can move on to better things," "just trying to be honest and share my feelings," or in another way saying that I am not doing what I am clearly doing (judging you). "Just let me help you understand what you need to believe."

Ways of judging *others* are countless. I can listen to you. When you finish, I can simply say "Oh." That syllable can express my surprise, my confusion, my hesitation, my curiosity, or other nonjudgmental feelings. But the same "Oh" can be a paralyzing judgment of you. The way it is said, the point at which it is said, my facial expression, and all of the nonverbal intonations can imply the same message: "You are dumb, bad, wrong, defective, unredeemed, unworthy, mean, cold, insensitive, or unfair." I do not even have to say "Oh." I can be equally judgmental by saying nothing. Most often, judging is done ambiguously: "I can't believe you said that." "How could you possibly believe something like that?" "I was just trying to share my feelings with you, and all I get in return is that kind of crap." "Why can't you be honest?" With such verbal strategies, we relate judgmentally without accepting the responsibility for being so.

Judgmentalism is an attitude. The word comes originally from the Sanskrit *disati,* which means "he points out or shows." From this comes the Latin *dictum,* "to say," as in *dictate.* After numerous semantic turns we arrive at the Latin *judex,* which means "he who points to or shows the law." The judge. A judge is appropriate when a crime has been committed. A judge is a disaster in an intimate or close relationship, in which "being with" another, and not crime, is the issue.

Judgmentalism as an attitude is expressed in blaming. *Blame* comes from the Greek word *blasphemia,* which means "to speak ill of," or, more generally, "evil speaking," as in blasphemy. A judgmental attitude is expressed as "I know the law, the truth, the reality. I am simply pointing this out to you. I am not angry. I have no ulterior motives. I am simply trying, calmly and innocently, to help you see the true and the real." But what is really happening is blaming, speaking evil of, in the relationship. When you blame, you blaspheme the *other*. It does not matter whether the blame is "warranted" or not. You "speak evil" of the *other* regardless. To judge in society is both necessary and justifiable. But banks do not invite bank robbers to rob them, the mugged to not suggest mugging to the muggers, the raped do not seduce the raper, the store clerk does not invite the intruder to blow his head off, and the speeder does not tantalize the patrol officer into ticketing her. Not in the real world. Violators of other persons should be judged. In the intimate or close relationship, however, we do invite, suggest, seduce, tantalize; we are seeking relationship. To judge or blame in such a personal endeavor is as inappropriate as indifference to rape or murder would be.

More insidious than blatant judgmentalism is the creeping prejudgment that captures and immobilizes relationships, the "already known" syndrome: "I know what he's like." "I know what she is going to say before she says it." Prejudgment leads to boredom in relationships, and therefore leads people to seek the unknown, the stranger, the affair, the new spouse, the new lover, the one we have not prejudged only because we have never gotten close enough to do so. We are with the new person playfully, passionately, excitingly, and creatively, but only briefly. The strangeness that allows us to play, explore, and be passionate comes out of our really being strangers. That state is short-lived. In contrast, to find strangeness in someone to whom you are close can be much more passionate and creative. To find the new in the familiar is what intimacy is. Prejudgment, "already knowing" so that you leave no room for experiencing newness and strangeness, precludes intimacy. The passionate strangeness of the unknown is ephemeral; it lasts only until you "know" him or her. The true strangeness of any human being is inexhaustible, provided that you do not "already know" or prejudge. Leave the door open, and it would take a hundred lifetimes of relationship to begin to experience the complete fullness of one other person. The psychiatrist Karl Jaspers said in *Philosophy,* "Man is the knower who is always more than he knows of himself." We would add: Man is also the knower to whom the *other* is always more than he knows of.

Andy comes in with his wife. He has "had an affair" that she has "found out about." Actually, Andy told her in the midst of a fight. They both want to "save their marriage" but neither has the slightest idea how to do this. They as yet do not even comprehend why the marriage is in need of saving. In our office, they go through their judging and blaming, their prejudgments and consequent angers. They are both acting out roles they have played many times. They are also very bored.

This boredom accounts for an increasingly common experience among people: the brief affair. Once you "already know" your spouse or lover, prejudge him or her, your sexuality is limited by your preconstruction. This limits your possible experiences together; you can make love only within the confines of your prejudgment of how he or she, or even you, can or will be with each other. Sex is a rerun, no longer fun, no longer exciting, no longer passionate. You lose interest. The feeling of not knowing that comes with being with a stranger awakens passion. The sadness is that we take the play and passion out of our ongoing relationships and convert them into "already knowing" the *other.* All too quickly, the aliveness and magic are gone, and we "have to" look for it elsewhere.

Others turn to the noninterpersonal world to find this newness, this strangeness. They seek new geography, new activities, new sensations. These increase our *self*-experience only so long as they remain process, *experience.* But most often we solidify them into judgment and prejudgment as quickly as we can. I can go to the Rockies and feel awe and wonder for a few days, but I can move to Denver and soon cease to "see" the mountains at all. We will not let things be *what* they are, any more than we let humans be *who* they are. The price is the same: We do not get to be who and what we are.

Sometimes we attempt to correct our deficit of "strangeness" and "newness" by playing games. Janice has thirty-two wigs, and hopes each time that with a wig on she will be new, and her lover will experience her as different. Arnold calls his wife Saturday noon and says he has to work late. She hears the code and arranges for a baby-sitter while he registers at a local hotel. He sits in the lobby, and his wife comes in and sits near him. He will "pick her up" and, since he registered alone, "sneak" her up to his room. They will have a wonderful personal and sexual experience. Illicit *intimacy!* She will leave early in the morning; he will get home a little later, and she will ask him where he had been all night. He will smile and say, "Working." Why do married couples have more exciting sex in hotels than at home? Sadly, even when they can suspend the prejudgment in the hotel, when they get home they immediately reestablish it. Our attachment to "already knowing" is very, very powerful. It is difficult to understand what we are already sure we "do understand." It is difficult to enjoy what we are already sure we "do not enjoy." These relational games, like wigs and hotels—despite the fact that they momentarily bring us to realize that our prejudgment is incorrect, that our spouse or lover is a much better "intimate partner" than we had prejudged them to be—do not teach us to let go of our judgments and prejudgments, or ensure that we are innocent about ourselves. We go back to our own home and bedroom, and immediately return to the prison of closeness and security. We seem to learn little of intimacy through such staged experiences. We seem no more convinced that we can stand in our own space as *ourselves,* and relate at the same time to that "significant *other*" in our shared space, relate to them as they really are.

It becomes easier to understand why human relationship is both the greatest beauty of human endeavor and at the same time the ultimate substrate for the millions of manifestations of our worst inanities. There are, after all, only so many ways to *not see* that walkway we mentioned earlier, or to see it distortedly. Our "already knowing" construct of what a walkway is confines us to some general and usually superficial notion. The walkway is hard, gray, unchanging, uninteresting, always the same, and something to be walked along. Other people, surprisingly, experience the walkway differently. They say such upsetting things as "That tree beside your walkway has certainly grown a lot. It's really beautiful." We feel then the same confusion we feel when a neighbor describes our wife as attractive, sexy, and interesting when we "know" that she is dumpy, dull, and dead, or says she had a stimulating conversation with our husband when we "know" our husband has neither said nor done anything stimulating in years. Our internal answer ("He/she doesn't really know him/her as well as I do") is a devastating prejudgment that precludes really experiencing the spouse. When, like our neighbor, we can be freed from our judgmental construction of the *other* and get back to the *self* world, the possibilities for experiencing the realities of the *other* are unlimited. Expected and prejudged reality disappears as a barrier to our "being in the world in good faith."

As therapists, we see constantly how "already knowing" is *self*-defeating. Our clients describe at length *others* whom we have not met. We finally meet them; they usually bear no resemblance to what the clients have described. Even when we see a couple together, their descriptions of each other bear little resemblance to how we have been experiencing them. We can see how different their "already knowing" is from the reality of the *other* as we are experiencing them. We understand too that they are different with us; that living in the "constrained construct" of how the *other* sees them, they may indeed be with that *other* just as they have been described. We are not concerned here with fault, with whose description is "right" or "who is to blame," but simply with how people are together. It is a relationship, not a courtroom. Sam may be with her as Jackie has described, but since he is so different with us, obviously he *could* be different with her. In that therapeutic experience, one can feel directly how intimacy is immediately possible when and if the other person gives up the "already known" prejudgment. One sees clearly how abruptly the prejudgment stops touching, play, passion, learning, understanding, and growing.

The paradox is that you can actually know only about yourself, but you think you "already know" about the world, particularly the people in it, and because you "already know," you can never really experience them, or be yourself. *I* can make the world as I want it, *me* can set the rules for the relationship, but *self* cannot exist in the artifice that the *I* or *me* constructs. Intimate relationship cannot subsist with just *I* or *me.* It can exist only when *self* is experienced. When *I* constructs ("already knows" another), we are lost. When *me* precludes any real awareness of the other by its judgments (it "knows"), we are lost. Only when *I-me,* as connected *self,* is involved can we be alive. We can construct play worlds as children, knowing them to be constructed, and enjoy them. We, as adults, cannot construct a world in the belief that it is "the real world" without seriously compromising our ability to be in that world freely, openly, and passionately. Children know that they are playing. Adults, in their uncertainty, perpetuate living charades.

From Emily Dickinson:

> The Soul selects her own Society—
> Then—shuts the door—
> To her divine Majority—
> Present no more—

Our "constructions" of the *other* (whom we then "know") explain why we so seldom see the *other* as they are in reality. We instead see them in "our reality." The fact that *others* do the same explains our anger at friend, child, lover, or spouse, when we feel they see us only in their construct, in the way they need to see us, as against who we know we really are, or when they judge us. If, because of their judgment and prejudgment of us, they decide they cannot live with us, we separate. There seems to be no way I can be my *self* with you, so I decide to be *me* without you. Both our own constructions and theirs are unhealthy, out of touch, both literally and metaphorically, and unhappy, or, more descriptively, unhappening. In them, we are steadfastly righteous and destructively *self*-defeating. The oppositional preconstructions and prejudgments provoke the most common type of fight we see in couples in therapy. They insist on defining each other as a way of defending themselves: "she feels," "he says that because," "he is always," "she never," "he isn't," "she is," and on and on, endlessly. It is impossible to listen when we "already know." Listening comes from *list,* "to lean toward." We cannot list when we "already know." We can only be righteously agitated by the other's blockheaded refusal to acknowledge our preconstructed truth. To us, that usually means "the facts," "what really happened," or "Just ask Lois, she was there, you don't have to believe me." Most often, even if the preconstruction does describe the facts, it has little or nothing to do with the relationship. Frank Lloyd Wright put it succinctly: "The truth is more important than the facts."

People live out their preconstructed, "supposed to be" behaviors at home, on the job, in courtings, relationships, marriages, and, not surprisingly, in their therapists' offices. There is an ongoing, passive, and silent contractual arrangement by which a couple can live this way for years or even a lifetime. Each is set in the emotional concrete of "already knowing," and is never experiencing intimacy with the *other*. Each is judging and thus never getting to be a *self*. Too often, the only change occurs when they learn that they are dying; when, sadly, they finally question their own constructions—but, again sadly, usually only for the short time they have left.

Therapists dispassionately point out that judgmental and prejudgmental behaviors are designed by the "unconscious" to prevent and preclude intimacy. This analysis may be a relational truth, but does not speak to the internal, personal, and beautiful interplay of the *I, me,* and *self within* our individual persons. It is hard to believe that people are willing to give up the wonderful feeling of the child lying in the grass, looking at the dandelion, in order to service things or persons *outside* themselves. If they sacrifice such beauty and life, they must be giving it up for *internal* and primitive reasons.

Greek theater offers us a metaphor for this truth. The setting is communal, and in that setting the protagonist gives up much, but only for reasons *inside* himself. The play is *staged* around his relationship with others, but it is the "fatal flaw" within him that engineers his fate. We no longer speak about people's "fatal flaws," but the loss of *selfhood* we are describing (the imbalance in our *I-me-self*) can be just as fatal to our lives. These imbalances we hopelessly perceive as our fate, and that is the most momentous preconstruction of all.

The hope lies in *knowing*. Instead of constructing our own "knowing" and calling it our manifest individual fate, we can freely create a space to let the *other,* be it a thing or person, occur, be "experienced." Living, dying, hurting, being hurt, loving, not being loved, are all real manifestations of all of our fates. That is a communal reality. If we create such a space, not preconstructing or judging the *other,* but willing to experience *ourselves* when we are related to another, then we can experience intimacy in its original meaning, "innermost." The only knowing available to us in our "being in the world in good faith" is our own *self*-experience.

6

Personal Construction . . . Reciprocity and No-Fault Being

What is moral is what you feel good after.

—ERNEST HEMINGWAY

Judgmentalism and prejudgmentalism both make the intimate experience unlikely, probably impossible. "Mislearned" attitudes impair, erode, and in the end usually destroy our capacity to be intimate. But intimacy, since it is natural, has a recurrent vitality. As with all aspects of evolution, it has an insistent and powerful push to happen. The inherent push to more humanness is in a balanced contention with the "civilized" erosion of it that arises out of our preoccupation with security, closeness, society, and interpersonal law and order. It is not only the unnatural arrogance of the latter attitudes that destroy intimacy; more important, the sense of *separation,* of *disconnection* that accompanies this judgmental arrogance, undermines intimacy. The personal arrogance, the loneliness, and the ensuing feeling of loss of connection in human relationship are all expressed in our blaming others.

Blame is a strong and powerful metafeeling; being unnatural, it arises out of a cultural need for a strong social underpinning for what we call "interpersonal law and order." Statistically, of course, blaming is characteristic of human beings, but that does not mean it is inherent in human nature. Animals do not blame, nor does any of the rest of nature. Leaves falling from the trees in autumn do not blame the increasing cold. Nature is connected in its cycles, in its wholeness. In separating ourselves out, we turn to blaming. Significantly, in times of real tragedy and catastrophe we tend to stop blaming, and are, at least for the moment, more accepting of each other and more "naturally" human.

This blaming—an attitude and "feeling" lethal to intimacy, and so eventually destructive of closeness, too—is based on our mistaken notion that human behavior in relationship is a "cause and effect" event. Person A is angry with person B, so person B becomes distant and defensive; or perhaps person B becomes distant and defensive, so person A becomes angry. Suppose neither sequence is at all what is happening. What if person A and person B have these responses simultaneously? From what we know of nature on "lower levels," this is far more likely. This reciprocity is a potentially useful alternative to the more archaic and static concept of cause and effect.

Human beings generally display a startling arrogance about nature. A corresponding naïveté accompanies the arrogance. We set ourselves apart from nature in thinking, feeling, and behaving as if we transcend the natural and are not an integral part of it. This dangerous assumption is obvious on the large scale in our polluting our own drinking water, poisoning our own food chain, and making our air unbreathable. It is easy to say that we should not do it. It is more difficult to understand why we do do it (and then make excuses to ourselves). We forget that, as the biologist and naturalist René Dubos said in *So Human an Animal,* "Man shapes himself through decisions that shape his environment." We act as if we were observers of these processes and not an active part of them. We will study, watch, and describe nature, almost always with the attitude that we are outside it, having different rules and regulations than nature has. It may be our most *self*-destructive delusion. Just as we arrogantly foul our own nest, we naïvely believe that we can understand nature by standing outside it, merely observing. In a very direct way, this belief demonstrates our lack of reciprocity. We do not perceive ourselves as being acted upon as well as being actors.

In this sense, then, we are *unnaturally* related to nature. We objectively describe the universe from a distance and have the illusion that we understand it. But our distant, disconnected, objective attitude keeps us from being and feeling a part of the matrix of what we are really being and experiencing. We lose our connection to our "real nature." Consequently, we lose all possible opportunity of really knowing what we are in relationship to all of nature, much less to each other.

Examples on the large scale, such as pollution, are frightening, but only symptomatic and reflective of a more basic problem. That problem is a lack of any sense of reciprocity in our person-to-person relationships. The human-to-human relationship is the prototype through which, and on the basis of which, we model the ways we deal with our environment. Fouling our nest externally is simply a projection of our fouling the nest we live in one on one.

At the turn of the century, psychology took readily to the mechanistic, causal, and atomistic physical model. It became the paradigm for "scientific" psychology; thus the proliferation of behaviorism and conditioning. Subsequently, more sophisticated strategic systems arose, such as neurolinguistic programming and the concurrent proliferation of strategic therapies, whether with families, networks, or individuals. Meanwhile, physics had matured into a deeper understanding of random indeterminism, quantum reciprocals, complementarity, relativity, and field theories: the dance of nature. Insightfully, the physicist and philosopher Ernst Mach said, "Physics is experience, arranged in economical order." Experience *must* be the basis of our knowledge of anything, because it is *all* we have. We deeply believe that all understanding of nature, *of which we are a part,* whether it be physical, biological, chemical, sociological, ethnological or psychological, will be congruent. Nature is one wholeness.

If this is true, we must seriously review our "natural models"—models of nature that shape our understanding of our human experience, particularly our human relationships. In *Dismantling the Universe,* physicist Richard Morris speaks to this point: "Models are useful because they show us that hidden connections exist in the universe around us." Similarly, in *Reality and Empathy* Alex Comfort describes various world models and analyzes how each then determines "how we see our world." "How we see our world" will to a large extent then determine how we live in it. Intimacy is that dimension of life in which we can know that "models" are metaphors and reality *is* relationship. We can begin by reexamining our basic concepts of space-time, as well as our constricting conceptions of cause and effect. The two are very much connected. Our rigid preoccupations, particularly with cause and effect in linear time and in human relationships, account for the difficulty people have in seeing their relationships as reciprocal. The resultant blaming, based on these simplistic notions of space-time and cause-effect, becomes a constant barrier to intimacy. If you and I are participating in experiences together, and neither you or I is doing anything to the other (causing each other to hurt), then we can transcend blame. But righteousness makes it very difficult to make things right in relationship.

Most of us do not really think of ourselves as living in space-time. We think of the concepts separately, without the hyphen, in an everyday, simple sort of way. I have my space at the office. I can get a change of space (place) by going on vacation. I am supposed to be at work, at a party, or at my child's basketball game at some particular time. The movie starts at a certain time. We live our lives in these simplistic parameters. Many people intuitively feel trapped in them, and indeed, they are trapped. They correctly perceive the stifling unnaturalness that reflects our arrogant and naïve separation from nature. They feel *unconnected.* We tend to think that we have different rules from the atoms, the deer, the raindrops, the sun, or the oak tree in our front yard. We do not. Nature *is* one; that premise is fundamental to understanding intimacy. The outstanding characteristic of intimacy is the profoundly beautiful connection among all things and beings. Nothing that exists is alone. Things and beings being just what they are, in relation to other things and beings being just what they are: that is intimacy. That is the message of the naturalist John Muir (from *John of the Mountains*): "Most people are on the world, not in it—have no conscious sympathy or relationship to anything about them—undiffused, separate, and rigidly alone like marbles of polished stone, touching but separate." We are *unnatural* in our lack of intimacy.

Ecology, homeostasis, conservation of energy, and human emotional healthiness are all the same thing. They are all intimate balanced interactions. Balance in nature is crucial. Imbalance, as we have seen on the large scale, is unnatural and catastrophic. Look at the ecosystems we have destroyed. We are suggesting that exactly these processes operate on the personal level; in fact, that the personal is the prototype for the larger scale.

Time-and-space in nature is much more encompassing than we normally think. Space-time cannot be separated; it is a continuum, not two separate entities. When we meet our friend at some particular time *and* some particular place, we are closer to understanding that continuity. To get a rocket to Mars, you have to shoot it to where Mars *will* be when the rocket gets there. Here on earth we are unendingly and foolishly locked into our past, our present, our future, and our linearly delineated worlds. We see ourselves as the observer of time moving, or we see things moving in "our" space. This way of "seeing" is not an accurate description of reality; it removes us from reality, and therefore from the *self* experience.

I talk with my wife. I say, "Why didn't you remember to call the bank about that account?" In so saying, I am in the space-time of me (the child) and her (the mother). My wife answers me. She may be in the present space-time, or she may be in the space-time of two years ago in another house, when we had this same discussion. I may be psychologically at home with my wife while physically at the office with my partner. Which is reality? The answer is, neither but both. The close interchangeability of time and space is obvious when looked at this way. In my reality, I may be back twenty years, ahead six months, at home, in my parents' house, or in never-never land, although physically I am now here in my office at 5:30 on a Tuesday afternoon.

Reciprocity

Intimacy as a dimension of reality depends on your being in the space you are really in now, related to whatever and whoever is in that space, as they are now, and at the present moment—not time traveling in the past, or future, or space hopping to other places.

The only reality there is is the experiential reality. The poet Wallace Stevens wrote in *The Necessary Angel,* "The subject matter of poetry is not that 'collection of solid, static objects extended in space' but the life that is lived in the scene that it composes; and so reality is not that external scene but the life that is lived in it. Reality is things as they are." Psychological space and time follow nature; they are no different from physical space and time. The interchangeability is meaningful in both directions, including the concept of multidimensionality. In the intimate experience, time can expand, compress, even stop. Place can be transformed, what was ugly become beautiful, what was small become large. We therefore have to recognize that space-time is not a fixed thing outside us that we observe. Instead, it represents a variable of which we are a part. We are a part as reciprocals. This dyadic relationship, *self-other,* is experienced only in intimacy. When we do not experience intimacy, we do not feel the reciprocity inherent in all of nature, including us. Whether the dyad is you and your lover, you and a fish, or you and the universe, the relationship is reciprocal. If it is not, it is distorted. Space-and-time is just one way to see this, albeit perhaps the most basic.

When we live space-time as fixed nonreciprocal "experiences," we block processes that are part of the reality of experience. This is particularly true since all process involves motion. The stability (security) we get from "stopping to see anything [or anyone]" or "stopping anything [or anyone] so we can see" makes that person, thing, or event *other than what it is.* The same is true of "putting anything [or anyone] somewhere else" or "putting anything [or anyone] in another time." When we change the nature of things for our own needs, we stop being part of that nature and thus stop being *ourselves.*

June sees her husband as uncaring, regardless of his behavior. Her judgment is made clear in their therapy sessions. Why? Because she sees him as the father who in fact lived with her in an uncaring way thirty years ago? To see this much is simply to acknowledge the transference phenomenon of traditional analytical thinking. The actual problem, however, is June's distortion of *self,* not her distortion of her husband. It is her distorted space-time that causes her to perceive him in terms of her past and not as himself, not even as *his* past. Thus, she cannot be herself, and cannot be intimate. This process is much deeper than transference, and is not explained by our saying "She is just seeing her husband as a father figure."

Obviously, June has severely constricted and limited her possible experiences with her husband. She has limited what and how and when she can be with him, and indirectly constricted his experience with her. When confined like this in distorted space-time, we limit the available experiences and realities of the other person, or of anything else in our world. This limiting is grounded in our perception of time and space as fixed linear parameters of experience, and it confuses us in our understanding of relationships. We are reduced to the imprisoning naïveté of thinking of personal interaction as simple subject-object and simple cause and effect: "I did this because you did that, and I am this way because you are that way." We reject reciprocity and turn to blaming. We do not live in the recursive world of *self* that actually is; but, instead, in the preconstructed and prejudged worlds of *I* and *me*.

The implications of liberating our minds from these frozen, static notions of time and space are far-reaching. We should begin to see time and space as always modifying each other, for they are seldom as they appear to be on the surface. They move suddenly in all directions, not as fixed parameters but as threads of the same fabric in which we are woven. We could understand that what we are calling a fight now is a way of touching in some space-time, a way of learning in another, a way of making love in a third, a way of avoiding some other fight in a fourth. Knowing this would allow us free access to our *self,* and enlarge our understanding of human experience in relationship and nature in general. Redefining psychological space-time, as it is actually experienced in relationship, would significantly increase not only our understanding of intimacy, but our capacity for intimacy.

Sandy and Alan spend their hour in our office living selected parts of their existence backward: "I was mad at you because you didn't talk to me about asking your parents over." "Well, I didn't talk to you about it because you were already upset over the kids." "I was upset about the kids because you were so ugly to them last time they were late." And on and on. There is no reciprocity here, only blaming.

Reciprocity does not mean that storms do not inundate rivers and overflow their banks. It does not mean that a brutal husband beats his wife because she wants him to, or that the husband of an alcoholic wife is an accomplice to her drinking. It does not mean that the unresponsive lover is responsible for his partner's sexual affairs. It does not mean that we are all equally, directly responsible for what happens. It *does* mean that we are all responsible in some way. Storms cause floods, but if we paid attention to cutting timber and to grading land and to farming in ways more compatible with nature, then storms would probably be less devastating. Reciprocity does mean that if the righteousness of the wife were less derisive, the beating by the husband might be less severe. Her change might not prevent his brutality, but it would modify it. In staying with him, she participates, and how she participates affects the experience. Reciprocity does not mean that the drunken woman would not have been drunk under any circumstances, but that the husband by his staying participates in her undoing of herself and therefore in their undoing of themselves. It does not mean that the unresponsive lover wants his partner to have an affair, but it does mean that he participates in the fact that she does so, by being out of touch with his own sexual nature.

Reciprocity means that we are all actively involved in what happens to us; no one is the singular and ultimate villain. There is no such simplistic format as cause and effect in relationships. One person does not simply have an affair apart from his or her relationship to his or her "betrayed" partner. To some extent, and granting that the extent is variable, the "wronged" person is also participating in the affair. It may be a minor participation, or it may be an insistent and overwhelming demand that the other have an affair. (Some people are "excited" by their lover's making love to someone else.) Whichever is true, there is some involvement on the part of the "injured" and "innocent" party. Nature knows no unconnected realities. In minor or major ways, everyone is involved. Reciprocity is not either your causing *X* and my being affected by *X*, or the reverse; it is us together. Whatever is happening to us is happening to me; whatever is happening to me is happening to us.

Self-responsibility

What is equally important is our realization that the only part we can do anything about is ourselves. We cannot change other people. We cannot *will* or *force* change in the way our spouses or lovers are; they will be as they will be. We will be as we will be. Or we can be different. That choice is our freedom, our free will. The most important personal realization on our part is that *we are the only person we can change.* By realizing that, we can perhaps assure intimacy. The gift of choice carries the responsibility *and* the joy of *self.* We must first come to realize about ourselves what Lewis Carroll's Alice realized in Wonderland: "'I can't explain *myself,* I'm afraid, sir,' said Alice, 'because I'm not myself, you see.'"

If you explain yourself in terms of something beyond yourself, if you live an arrow of time that goes one to two to three, and deals with each segment as causal to the next, you will miss the greater truth that life is a moving and flowing dance in which there is reciprocity but not causality. I am not who I am because of you. I do not feel what I feel because of you. I do not do what I do because of you. I may dance easily or awkwardly with you in terms of my feelings and actions, but you are not causing me to be, to feel, or to do what I do. What we are saying here does not mean that people or things are never causally related; of course they are. People use guns and bullets to kill, just as tornadoes destroy property and lives. Injustice is perpetrated by actions that have effects. We are speaking of ways of seeing and being, not of doing; we are talking about how you are you, not about what could happen to you. It is clear that you can beat me up and I will feel pain; I may participate in this a lot or a little. I may provoke a violent person; I may choose to live with a person prone to violence. But when you say you do not want to relate to me, my *feeling* "beaten up" comes to a great extent from *my* participation, and is *completely* my responsibility. I reciprocally participate in life with you. I am responsible for my sense of *self* myself. Only I can beat up on my *intima.*

If we insist on seeing life in a one-dimensional, linear, and causal way, we will be out of touch with our experiences. We will miss those expansions and compressions of time, those alternations of space that mark the intimate experience. In our pairings, whether me-you, lovers, spouses, bosses and employees, or parents and children, we will inevitably clash when we shut ourselves off in our own fixed time and space, for invariably they will be different, and thus leave us no way to touch. There will be no dance, none of the rhythmic random movements on which all of nature is based. To be so "out of touch" is unnaturally and biologically arrogant. It is also deadly.

Despite us, nature continues to function. And we are, despite ourselves, part of nature and part of experience. Our rhythms affect the rhythms of others. Our feelings are immediately contagious. Depression breeds depression in others, and anxiety breeds anxiety, just as calmness and gentleness elicit serenity and acceptance in others. Joy, excitement, elation, and happiness are all reciprocal. This is the nature of nature. The golden rule, found in some form in all religions and philosophies, calls us to our nature, not as a judged morality, but as experienced reciprocity. The dance of connection is universal. Only our rigidity limits our choices, confines our experiences and our participation in them. In a sense, all pathology, whether physical, psychological, or social, is based in rigidity, the loss of the ability to move and be with things as they are. We cling to our rigidity as our security. Thus, when our depression meets the rhythm of joy in our spouse or lover, the depression has a powerful, perverse insistence. We insist on *our* rhythm, *our* space and *our* time, and usually to *our* personal and relational detriment. The permutations are endless. Imprisoning our *selves,* we seldom recognize our *self*-destructiveness. We lose our freedom to participate in the experiential dance.

Buckminster Fuller spoke of our difficulty in dancing, our difficulty in participating in *natural* rhythm, *natural* space, *natural* time: "Nature is trying very hard to make us succeed, but nature does not depend on us. We are not the only experiment." The rigidity in most of us comes from our inability to understand and participate in the world in a reciprocal and recursive way. Naturalness includes but is not limited to the nature love glorified by romantics—as here, in Lord Byron's *Childe Harold's Pilgrimage*:

> I live not in myself, but I become
> Portion of that around me; and to me
> High mountains are a feeding, but the hum
> Of human cities torture . . .

Participation in the world (mountains *and* cities) as *self* is connection. It is experiencing the dyad through your being.

Stephanie spends the majority of her time and energy "looking for a relationship." As a result of not "finding one," she is chronically depressed and feels "incomplete." She sees her problem wholly in terms of the inadequacies of the men she dates, that they cannot be what she needs. Her perception may to some degree be true, but Stephanie has yet to ask herself how *she* is, why *she* is as she is with them, or, most significant, why *she* feels the same incompleteness with the rest of her world. The intimate person who has not yet found a primary pairing is not depressed. Such people may be lonely, they may be sad, but usually they are simply "ready." Like Maude, in the movie *Harold and Maude,* who lived life to the fullest, who took joy whenever and wherever she could, the intimate person participates in life as it is presented.

Socialization and Security

How are we taught not to dance in relationship? How are we taught not to know when we *are* experientially dancing? And why are we taught so? Clearly, the historical answer is the primacy humans have placed on the need to assure social stability. The *self* is sacrificed to the system. Socialization revolves around getting the child to accept fixed time and space rules that translate into simple linear notions of cause and effect. But with this "knowledge," sadly, comes judgmentalism, the loss of freedom of *self,* the giving away of the gift of individual choice. We teach these constructs to our children so they will be "secure," as we are, so they will fit into the system. We do this socializing through creating metafeelings. These "feelings about our feelings" (shame, embarrassment, self-consciousness, shyness, guilt, modesty, politeness, consideration, hostility, and all the other socially "useful" controllers) are unnatural, however common to civilized human beings.

How can we say that feelings so common and omnipresent are not natural? Because we can see how they are learned by children; and because too often they express the neurotic imbalance of our persons, our culture, and our society that results when *self* is denied in the service of systemic closeness. The displacement of feelings by metafeelings reflects our abysmal neglect of the *self/intimate* experience. In saying so, we are not advocating anarchy; socialization is not "bad," and metafeelings have useful purpose. As we have pointed out, healthy closeness is as important as intimacy. But unhealthy closeness, the being captured by the system, is destructive to both *self* and system, to intimacy and closeness. The French philosopher Jacques Maritain described unhealthy closeness in *Three Reformers* when he said, "In the modern social order, the *person* is sacrificed to the *individual*." The "individual" is part of the system; the "person" is the *self*.

Couples can spend their years together standing still in their security, and never dancing. Ensuring the perimeters of their own time and space preoccupies them. Their lack of reciprocity and unwillingness to live in nature's space-time, much like their "already knowing," destroys intimacy. When they begin to see both *I-me* and *other* moving in a common universe, intimacy becomes possible. Their experiential dancing may not be graceful at first, but it will bring them, however awkwardly, to a natural beginning.

Bonnie is absolutely convinced that if her husband were less depressed and perfectionistic, they would have an ideal marriage. She and Gene are both committed to stay in their marriage. They have three sons, and much of their troubled and angry relating centers around the children. Gene is angry because the oldest boy, though still an honor student in a good school in the area, has a three-point grade average instead of a four-point. Bonnie feels that the boy has done well and should be congratulated on what he has accomplished, even if he does not work very hard. Gene is just as convinced that if his wife were more "down to earth," more insistent that the children "do what they can and should do," less permissive, and less protective, then the children would all make straight As and everything would be okay. Both positions are right, and both are wrong. The problem is that there is no connection between these two people, no dance; they are not "living in the world in good faith."

Internally, Bonnie feels and believes that her husband is right, that she is basically an irresponsible, overly emotional, overly protective, unrealistic person. Inside, she feels that her husband's depression is a reflection of her lack of support and lovingness toward him, the "proof" that her love is not good enough. Nonetheless, she responds to his depression and angry self-pity with explosive anger of her own. She begins by trying to talk to him with feeling and understanding, but he does not hear her. He feels that she is so emotional and irrational (and ultimately so angry) that he cannot really talk to her. And as he retreats, she grows angrier.

Internally, Gene feels and believes that he is responsible for Bonnie and their sons on every level of their beings, much as he feels responsible for making everything right in the world. Since this responsibility cannot possibly be met, he inevitably feels inadequate. He feels as if he is trying to save everyone but, given his inadequacies, can do so only if they help him. He is always angry, because they will not and cannot help by being as he needs them to be, and he is always returned to his sense of being an inadequate *self.*

Gene and Bonnie can be incessantly angry with each other, both blaming and righteous, and neither capable of transcending their indignation and projections. At the same time, both can be deeply unhappy with themselves. There is no joy in their blaming, their lack of reciprocity. Indeed, this felt lack is precisely what each of them most blames the other for. The substrate of this sad form of relationship lies in the fact that neither one has any real sense of the connected time-space of nature. They each have their own individual time, their own individual space, their own individual guarded borders, so there can be no reciprocity. When they fight, there is no commonality, and certainly no touching. They have no intimate moments to restore them and release them from this unnatural system. Theirs is not a marital problem, but a personal problem.

Bonnie has psychological problems that, at best, are simply expressed in her relationship to Gene. She covertly and insidiously, although not consciously, demands that others be responsible for her well-being and for how she sees herself. She hides her dependence from herself, but behaves in ways that unendingly demand attention, support, and direction. However, as soon as she gets what she is always unconsciously seeking, she becomes angry and distraught. She blames the other for her feeling that her love is not good enough, her worth is inadequate, her being herself is insufficient. Her genuine lovingness, caring, and gentleness are held hostage to these needs.

Gene has his own emotional problems that clearly predate his relationship to Bonnie. He has an insatiable need to control everything and everyone in his environment. He is not mean or power-hungry; he simply needs everything always to be all right. He is convinced that he knows how everything could be all right, if only everyone else would cooperate. He is a good person who with all good intentions manages to keep everyone around him guilty and angry, while he himself, since he constantly fails, is forever depressed and resentful. He hears Bonnie's needs as demands that he will fail to meet, and therefore he grows more depressed and resentful. His hard work, caring, and deep commitment are displaced by these distortions.

Their mistake is making a marriage of these separate struggles. They agree to live as if they share a common time and space, but they do not. That is, they verbally agree to live as if they were reciprocal, to be realistically responsive to the other in the moment. However, neither of them is reciprocal, not within themselves nor with each other. Neither is dealing with the time-space they are actually in when they struggle with each other. They are not just psychologically transferred, but displaced in time and space and, even more destructively, removed from the natural reality in which intimacy takes place. What they are doing amounts to psychological shadowboxing. But shadows have no *self,* and boxing is a desperate way to be married. Bonnie and Gene are not "sick" people. They are "normal." By dissecting and exaggerating them we make them sound disturbed. In reality their disturbance is very much like all of our disturbance: imbalance into closeness, socialization at the cost of *self.* They have lost track of what Margaret Mead discusses in *Some Personal Views*: "Marriage is . . . a reiteration of each individual's development in coming to terms with her or his own temperament, impulses, capacities and gifts." Bonnie and Gene are not coming to terms because they have no common "terms."

Reciprocity, then, is the ability to participate in a common reality. This includes naturally an accepted time-space. I am living with you as I presently am, in this time that we both presently share, in the space that we are presently sharing, with you as you really are now. What happens to us is a product of how well each of us is able to understand our immediate presence. What happens to *me* in that experience is *my* responsibility. What happens to *you* is *your* responsibility. What happens to *us* is both *your* and *my* responsibility. "Life has no meaning except in terms of responsibility," according to Reinhold Niebuhr (in *Faith and History*), and this responsibility is *self*-responsibility.

Oppositional Perceptions of Time-Space

Wally and Jane have lived together for five years. If you were around them for any length of time, you would begin to feel that they do not speak the same language. They use words differently when they relate to each other. Language, as a symbolic system for interacting with the world, has varied meanings for each of them. Their ability to touch, to communicate, to be intimate, is seriously compromised by their awful lack of reciprocity in their symbols, their everyday langauge. Neither can accept the other as just different—not wrong but different. It has always amazed us to see how convinced people are that if one of them is right, then the other is wrong. It surprises couples if we suggest that, more often than not, both of them are right. They simply differ; and difference, connected difference, *is* life. Most humans do not understand this simple fact; they assume that their "way of seeing" or "saying" or "understanding" is universal. Of course, it is not; it is totally individualistic.

The physicist-historian Thomas Kuhn, in *The Structure of Scientific Revolutions,* analyzes the way that paradigm changes cause people to see their world differently: "What a man sees depends both upon what he looks at and also upon what his previous visual-conceptual experience has taught him to see." Not only is our "way of seeing" not universal but the very process of my seeing is defining of *me,* not the *other.*

Jane symbolically lives life as a series of still pictures, one after another. These are usually in black-and-white. Content takes precedence over feeling. Her pictures move in a clearly defined time direction, in search of answers. The qualities of color, motion, and space are controlled. The nuances are relevant only if they clarify and assure her goal. For Jane, space is fragmented pieces. Time ticks steadily on her internal *me* watch. She is time-oriented and synchronized. Her time is consistent and continuous, like clock time. In everyday terms, Jane is an organized, goal-directed, busy person. She takes in information and uses it for decision making.

Wally, on the other hand, lives symbolically in an amorphous world of swirling colors with little time organization. Time is not consistent. Color, motion, and flowing space are more important than direction or goal. There is little sequence; instead, all is now. Wally is "into" process. Jane is "into" goal. He wants to enjoy going to the beach. She wants to get there. Wally is a more relaxed, slow, process-oriented person. He is not very goal-directed and has trouble making decisions.

Jane comes home from work. She is tired and certainly not looking for any more problems. On entering the house she immediately feels tension, and sees it as coming from Wally. Wally, who often gets home from work a little earlier, is sitting at the kitchen table and, if Jane were to describe it, in "one of his moods." She cannot understand that the tension is actually between their ways of being; she has no sense of reciprocity. Experiencing him as the source of tension (blaming him), she retreats into her private world. She impatiently and righteously asks him, "What's wrong?" What she really means is "Explain to me, in some black-and-white, time-oriented way, what it is you have messed up or been unable to handle, so that I can solve it even though I don't want to." It is easy to see that she is not touching him, that her *self* is not available for intimacy. She creates no space where he can exist *as he is*. On the contrary, she demands from him that he exist *as she is*, which is the antithesis of intimacy. She neither sees, hears, nor touches his personhood. She is angry because he is not *as he should be*, and because *others* cannot see the real nature of life as clearly as she believes she can. In no way does this mean that she does not love, care for, and desire to help Wally. But in her inability to be reciprocal, she blames him. She blames him for being who he is. This is what makes healthy closeness unlikely and intimacy impossible. Blaming and righteousness always evoke defensiveness; no one can give up the right to exist, to be who he or she is. No one can let the *other* define him or her.

Wally, naturally, feels attacked by her questions, her attitude. He was looking for something totally different from what has happened. He had been in an argument at work and was looking for someone to listen to him, to give him support. He too wants her to be *as he is* instead of *as she is*, and resents her failure to give him what he wants. Both resent the inability of the other to see what they perceive as the real nature of life. To Wally, Jane interrupts the flow; she stops the colors, the spatial connectivity that is important to him, and so strips him of his existence by coming in oblivious to his real person. But Wally participates in his own undoing, by doing exactly the same with her. Jane secretly thinks Wally is sort of crazy. She feels that when his craziness contaminates her world of ordered realities, it makes everything chaotic. Wally preconsciously feels that Jane is dead; to relate to her as if she were alive and real would kill his internal world. This is a *me* position. He, just as she, is feeling and talking exclusively out of his own feelings and needs. In reality, he is not simply being himself, as he thinks he is, but is being defensive. He feels right and therefore righteous. He has lost touch with the *reciprocity* of his relationship. In doing so, he makes *self/intimacy* impossible. He is behaving the same way she is, for, by her judgmentalism, she is also making *self/intimacy* impossible.

The most important result of living in the reciprocal, rather than the cause-and-effect world, is that we remove blame from relationship. Reciprocity in relationship makes blame superfluous. When, in therapy, a couple accept reciprocity as the reality of nature, change begins. They stop struggling over "the facts." Facts are usually irrelevant in relationship. They often have little to do with the truth of relating, which is its reciprocal nature. The vast majority of our factual explanations are defensive, really apologies. They are useless. When instead we are being ourselves and allowing others to be themselves, life happens. It is not prescribed, and certainly needs no commentary. We interact constantly about what we are, but we talk only about what we do; such behavior is an example of what we mean by capture. The theorist Francisco Varela has written extensively about the way that all dualities are both *it* and *the process of becoming it.* By their very nature, dyads are dualities, and therefore there is no either/or "fact." "Facts" are most often frozen pieces of either space or time. They seldom recognize the process of space-time. They are but a fixed moment of what *is,* and therefore a distortion of the process of reality.

Couples reenact mutual blaming over and over. They not only describe it to us ("He said . . . ," "She said . . ."), but repeatedly act it out in therapy. They seem unaware of the distance between their metaphors, their different personal times, or their different personal spaces. On the other hand, they are painfully aware of the price paid, the lack of touch and contact, the withheld, self-defeating, not-sharing impasses, and the strange unwillingness to communicate. Without reciprocity as the essence of relationship, they are mired in blame, deprived of being *selves.*

The *self* position arises only when we can create a space in our personal world within which the world of the other can exist unchanged. In this intimate space we can taste, touch, watch, hear, smell, listen, and learn. It allows us to know what is knowable, the reality of what is. We exist only as part of, and because of, that experience. It breaks down our isolating arrogance and our lonely naiveté.

Rendezvousing lovers will tell you that time and place in intimacy mean nothing. This is also true of all other intimate experiences. Time-space is free in intimacy. There is no direction, only movement. No specific time-place cuts you off from the connection to the motion of the universal dance of *self* and *other.* You are a "dancer," and part of the dance, not an outside observer.

No-Fault Being

Discovering reciprocity as the fundamental quality of relationship makes change possible because it allows us to get rid of the notion of the "identified patient"—always the other person. Reciprocity allows us to move into seeing *self-other* as a dyad, the basic building block of systems and so to deal with lover, spouse, or family. *We can begin to deal with our systems without being captured by them.* There is no right or wrong in reciprocity, just existence and experience. Neither Wally nor Jane, Bonnie nor Gene is right or wrong. The personal distortions that remove both partners in the pair from the creative possibilities of seeing their relationships as a continuing reciprocal interaction disappear, and intimacy becomes possible. We can, as Carl Rogers taught, care for and love the *other* while allowing them to exist separately; that is, be *themselves* in their relationship to us.

Right and wrong apply to behaviors. Reciprocity applies to being. Can Jane learn to sit and listen, to accept the language and metaphors of Wally, participate in an experience without the need to sequence, schedule, or find an answer? If she can, she might learn something *about herself* and might change. Can Wally learn to accept the language and metaphors of Jane as equally as valid as his own? Can he experience Jane's world without defense or attack? In other words, can they "interface," be in each other's space without changing themselves or the other? For only then can they be intimate. Only in reciprocity, the back and forth, the here and there, the up and down, the in-and-out sharing of our *selves,* is intimacy possible. These, not coincidentally, are sexual metaphors. Sexuality, as we have said, is the prototypical intimate experience. Jane and Wally, like Bonnie and Gene, form an experiential pair. Pairing too, as we shall see, is one of nature's prototypes.

The ravages of relationship that come out of a preoccupation with blame, rather than living in the creative freedom of accepting the real reciprocity of relatedness, are endless. We see hundreds of examples like Richard, who insists that he would not be so distant and aloof were Laurie not so angry and demanding because of his distance and aloofness. Laurie, of course, feels the same way. Both blame and make the other responsible for their unhappiness. In doing so, they abdicate their responsibility for their own joy in life. Neither is "living in the world in good faith."

We are so captured by our systems that it is difficult for people to give up their idiosyncratic perceptions of the world, or of time, or of space, or even of language; to do so feels like giving up what they (mistakenly) perceive as their *selves.* We need to learn that our definitions are only metaphors unique to ourselves. Perhaps useful for the moment, they have no innate reality, no intrinsic truthfulness beyond our persons. They are not expressions of life; they are explications of us as individuals. This is why intimacy is so important. It is how we can change *our persons,* and our persons are all that we can change. We cannot change *others*; we cannot change life. We have to accept, as e. e. cummings said, the "isness" of life.

How powerful, how dangerous these established metaphors can be was addressed by suffragist Elizabeth Cady Stanton in 1888: "Worse still, women had no proper appreciation of themselves as factors in civilization. Believing self-denial a higher virtue than self-development, they ignorantly made ladders of themselves by which fathers, husbands, brothers, and sons reached their highest ambitions, creating an impassable gulf between them and those they loved that no magnetic chords of affection or gratitude could span." The cost of culturally imposed *self*-denial is the personal loss of intimacy, and without intimacy the gulf (personal *and* cultural) expands.

Julie is very upset this evening. She has had a fight with her mother over how she deals with her children. A lot of old feelings have been reexposed. Ged comes home unaware of this fight, and despite the stress gets through dinner, helps get the five- and three-year-old to bed, and then sits down with Julie. Even though he does not understand *her* "reality" of *her* struggle, with *her* mother, he listens. He holds her while she cries and curses. After three hours he still does not understand *her* reality, because it is not possible for anyone to do so. He can know only what he feels. Is he to be blamed for this? No, he is to be praised. He loves, hugs, touches, and stays, without needing to understand from within *her* world. He gives the gift of accepting her symbology, her metaphors, and her immediate definition of her world. He accepts her experience as what it is, and gives it equal validity as his own. In validating *her* reality, he *understands* in his own. That is the only real understanding we can ever have. He can love without knowing, without defining, without purpose. As a result, he will learn and grow, as will Julie. That is reciprocity.

One of the more difficult tasks in therapy is to help people return easily to the *playful* place where they have no fixed notions about their metaphors, their way of seeing. In children, we can watch their playful willingness to try almost anything, while making the experience very real and personally passionate. To the child, a pine cone really is a truck, at least for the moment. He crosses the turbulent river with trepidation, even when that river is a trickle along the curb. Is he not more "living in the world in good faith" than adults who can no longer *be* anything? Would we all not do better to be as Mark Twain (in *Life on the Mississippi)*: "When I'm playful I use the meridians of longitude and parallels of latitude for a seine, and drag the Atlantic Ocean for whales. I scratch my head with the lightning and purr myself to sleep with the thunder." When adults let go and become as children they feel anxious, or lost, or estranged and separated. Why?

Our inability to be as children, to be not childish but *as* children, comes out of our fearful obsession with security. Jesus was most likely speaking to this fear when he said that unless one has the faith of a child, one will not enter the kingdom of heaven. It is a concept also contained in other religions, other belief systems. What is this faith of a child? It is a faith in connection to the whole universe, a faith that you are not alone. Adults collect multiple prescriptions in their search for security. The childlike, free, intimate state of *selfhood* is experienced as unsure; thus, it produces anxiety. We are taught not to dance, but to stand apart and observe. *I* debates with *me,* and in this debate *self* is sacrificed. The natural dance of the child is lost in the very personal spaces and times of the fearful *I* and the obstinate *me*. Our personal history overwhelms us, and our expectations stultify us. We live in our past places and times, or in the ethereal places and times of what we may become. We avoid the present reality of our experience. We are as afraid of our own empowerment as we are of the "power" of the *other*. The reality is that we are being with whom we need to be with, where we need to be, when we need to be, and doing what we need to be doing. This is true despite our protestations, complaints, and denials. We are in our experience, and we must be *fully* in that experience to learn anything or to change anything. Otherwise, we will be captured forever by sameness, familiarity, and system.

The whole issue of growth in relationship depends on the trust we feel in the relationship: "Can I rely on you to accept the equal validity of how I see life, how I feel, who I am?" In other words, "Can I rely on you to live with me reciprocally?" If I can trust you, I can live with you in nonblaming reciprocity—in which, whatever happens to us, we equally participate. We are each responsible for our happiness and unhappiness. If we cannot do this, we will each continue to live in the destructive illusion that the other is responsible for our unhappiness, and we will undo our *selves*. Where there is reciprocal trust, mutuality, we acknowledge each other's authenticity and responsibility: I accept you as really you, in your way, even if I do not understand you. I know you are not controlling me or making me be something that I am not. You are not defining me. That is my responsibility. I know in truth that we both live as part of the real world; we just see it differently. If you can simply *be* with me, we will be reciprocally related. In so doing, we will put blame to rest. Trust is the honest acceptance of our mutuality, our reciprocal responsibility for what happens in our relationship. If you blame, I see you as causal. If you trust, I see you as you and me as me. There is a symmetry between us, as there is in all dyads in nature.

That our living in our own separate worlds precludes intimacy is fairly obvious. How can I trust you if you are not even in my world of experience? But the lack of reciprocity also damages closeness, for it destroys value systems. If we look at closeness as a system with rules, then the values from which the rules derive—such as respect, graciousness, friendliness, and generosity—are extremely important. Simple politeness and courtesy may be among the most important. If there is no acknowlegment of authenticity, no reciprocity of relationship, and no trust, these values are either impossible to maintain or are corrupted. You can see this corruption in all systems: primary relationship, marriage, family, business, church, government, and society. Without values, systems are indescribably dangerous. They abuse and misuse people instead of augmenting and enhancing them. The *self/intimate* experience, grounded in acceptance and reciprocity, provides a natural balance for systemic rules. Antiutopian novels such as *1984* or *Farenheit 451* are both enlightening and frightening because of their dramatic clarity on this point. A social system in which *self* is secondary to the system is a *nonhuman* (inhuman) construct. The two must be in balance, the balance between intimacy and closeness.

Righteously to believe only in our own perspective outrageously denies reciprocity and trust. It leads to blame. It reflects neither an external nor an internal reality, and the very fact that we distinguish between external and internal is part of the distortion such separation produces. While giving up our view of time as linear, and our simplistic notions of cause and effect, we must also give up the dichotomy of external and internal. We must accept *self* as a natural and enduring union of the two.

In *The Ultimate Athlete,* George Leonard speaks to this bifurcation of "inside" and "outside" in terms of Western culture's construct of a duality of mind and body:

> It is only through a heresy in Western thought that we could consider any aspect of life as "nonphysical.". . . it (connecting the realm of the spiritual, the mystical, the abstract, with the world of the physical) would seem perfectly natural to the Greek poet Pindar, for whom athletic contests expressed the highest human aspiration, or to the philosopher Pythagoras, who wrestled in the Olympic Games, or to any one of our ancestors who walked the earth in the centuries before civilization cast its spell over humanity and led us to believe that the body is somehow inferior to the intellect and the spirit.

In intimacy, we feel the connections that allow us to know such splitting as *unnatural,* to learn that there is no internal and external, only internal/external.

When we talked about "already knowing" (prejudgmentalism), we were speaking of the virtual "I," the absurd illusion that there is an observant, knowing "I" who creates and then sees an external special reality. Lack of reciprocity assumes a "me" who defines that reality in terms of time, space, language, symbology, and relationship. It is easy to see how both assumptions remove you from the *reality of nature,* and the *reality of relationship to the other.* With these assumptions, you remove you from your *self.* Like nature, of which it is an explication, *self* is not bound by simple cause and effect, simple linear time, or simple Euclidean space. Without *self,* we are unavailable to the intimate experience. We cannot see the *other* as it is, or be who we are. We cannot experience the tree as it is; we cannot see our daughter as she is; we cannot feel those wonderful changes in time, space, us, or the *other,* that we all so long for. We cannot participate.

7

Personal Responsibility . . . Selfullness and Selfishness

Civilization is the encouragement of difference.

—MOHANDAS GANDHI

Amy is thirty-seven. She has been married to Bob, who is forty-one, for sixteen years. They have three children, all of whom are doing well in school and at home. Physically, Amy comes to therapy alone, but emotionally she brings Bob along with her; she talks mostly about him. She says the same thing over and over, in many different ways: "He's just not there. It's like living by myself. I know he loves me. At least he says he does. But I don't feel anything from him. He's withdrawn into himself all the time. About the only way I can get him to show some feeling is to start a fight or make him angry, and even that isn't easy. It takes a lot to make him fight or be angry. Most of the time he just looks like he doesn't understand. Then if I do get him to be angry, I can't feel very good about myself for being that way. That's not who I really am, that's not what I want. I don't want to fight, but damn it, I do want something. I want to feel some life, some something. I almost had an affair this summer. That's what made me finally come in to see you. I don't want to do that. I know that isn't who I am. I don't believe in affairs, but damn it, I'm desperate! What am I going to do? What are we going to do?"

Amy is a pleasure for a therapist to see. She is honest, open, has not yet betrayed her own sense of values, and wants to move in a healthy direction. Despite the fact that she has not really acknowledged her part in all their difficulties, we get the immediate feeling that she will be able and willing to. She has several options, all of which are based on her being herself with him—staying available to the intimacy she so desperately wants. Perhaps Bob will decide to come with her to therapy, to come in from what appears to be his withdrawal from their relationship and from living in general. He sounds like one of the lonely alone, someone who has not left the relationship to go elsewhere, but who, while he stays physically, is not really there.

We have described the way judgmentalism, prejudgmentalism, and the lack of reciprocity destroy intimacy and damage closeness. A multitude of other life positions do the same. They make intimacy unlikely, and closeness progressively deadening. Like the ways previously described, they represent capture by the system, usually a personal system. Most of these personal postures are, of course, unconscious. Nonetheless, they manifest themselves in conscious and concrete behaviors in our ordinary relationships, and are, therefore, describable. Out of the endless number of such postures, four appear again and again. They consistently manifest themselves as major obstacles to intimacy and serious detriments to healthy closeness.

Personal Postures that Preclude Intimacy

Of these four postures, the broadest and most variegated is *withdrawal.* Withdrawal has a thousand guises, all of which subvert intimacy and infect closeness. Far more subtle, less easy to identify, but perhaps even more extensive is *personal neediness,* wanting to be wanted more than really wanting what you say you want. Similar on the surface, but experientially different, is *overt self-righteousness,* the need to be right overriding our desire to be loved. Finally, and often most difficult to change, is *personal rigidity,* an uncompromising personal posture that makes us unable to let go of our definition of how we are, what we are, and who we are, even in areas that are not meaningful. We define ourselves by our differences and so cut ourselves off from intimacy. These four personal postures in relationship damage intimacy and closeness directly, and destroy the healthy balance between them. Our experience in therapy suggests that these four (along with judgmentalism, prejudgmentalism, and pseudo-reciprocity) are the major disturbers of our ability simply and naturally to be in relationship with each other. They also destroy our ability simply and naturally to be in relationship to nature in general, for withdrawal from life includes renouncing our universality, not just our primary human ties.

Withdrawal

Bob finally comes to our office, but without Amy. Instead, he arrives by himself at one of her scheduled appointments. We spend an hour with him. He is not really present with us, any more than he has been present with his wife. He is withdrawn inside himself. Somewhere inside he has some slight awareness that he is not giving Amy what she wants. This vague disquiet led him to his decision to come in. He feels his own withdrawal, but has no idea why he is so withdrawn, nor does he have any real conscious notion of *how* he is withdrawn. He says he does not want to be this way; we believe him. People, when given the opportunity, want to be *selves*. Whether they have the courage to do so or not, the want is naturally driven. We can be distorted, but few of us are unhuman.

Carl has been in a committed relationship for two years. He finds little joy in it, however, because his lover is more and more preoccupied, turned more and more in other directions. Carl experiences this preoccupation as rejection, and therefore hurts with it. He mistakenly sees the other's own struggle as defining him. It is one of the most common and painful of human life experiences. We internalize *others'* inability to be what and as they are, and thus lose the ability to be what and who we are. Whether the *other* is a friend or a lover makes no difference; we have been captured, and have lost *self*.

Withdrawal from relationship, whatever form it takes, can obviously prevent intimacy. When you remove your*self* from your shared space, there is no way for you to experience that *self*. People withdraw in hundreds of ways, often different on the surface, but with a common result. Some withdraw by shyness, some by depression, and some with alcohol or drugs. Others become incessantly controlling and angry, or righteously judgmental, or simply preoccupied and nonparticipating. Some adopt a mien of condescension, arrogance, pomposity, or passivity. There are many other types of such behavior; the aim of all of them is to retreat from any immediate intimacy or lasting closeness. They all express a fear of intimacy. Why are we so afraid of an experience we so desperately want? Perhaps because we are taught so very well. We thoroughly learn our metafeelings. Most of us are too "socialized." Erich Fromm felt that the needs of the society influenced parents to raise their children to meet those needs. Parenting therefore becomes systematization. We learn to avoid the dance, despite the ongoing music of the child in us. Perhaps we are also afraid because we are concerned that we might get what we want. Often, when we get what we have always wanted, it turns into something else. The dream becomes reality, and we have to live it. Too frequently, our romantic dream of intimacy is a cover for security.

Judy cannot understand why Marty is unable to make a commitment in their relationship. Both have been divorced for several years; they have been seeing each other for the past two. They go to Bermuda, and have joyful fun with each other. Although he is less verbal than she, he has been growing and sharing more. Problems arise only when Judy raises the issue of commitment. Whether she does this directly or indirectly, he immediately moves away from her. He says, "It will be several years before I can think about that," or "I'm not ready," or "Just give me some time." Judy often takes this hesitancy as uncertainty about her. It is not. Fear of intimacy controls Marty's life; Judy just experiences its result.

If Judy chooses to stay, while needing him to change, she participates. If she can accept him as he is, he may or may not grow. But only in accepting him is there a chance, although there can be no guarantee, no security. The risk of intimacy is real. In our offices, we hear both men and women in search of partners say, "The good ones are already taken," or "There are no men/women my age out there who can relate." How true this assumption is, of course, varies with each individual. An unmarried woman over forty reads that demographics show that statistically she has a very small chance of finding a man. But she cannot *live* on the basis of this information without being very unhappy. She can only do something about her, about how she feels, about how she relates, about how she exists with herself in life. That is all nature promises. Not having everything you want in life does not have to change *you,* does not mean that you cannot be joyfully *you.*

Jacques is quiet and shy, and keeps to himself. His anxiety merely at being in the presence of others shuts him out from any personal experience or connection with anyone. At a party he stays off by himself. Usually he does not attend parties at all. He avoids most group experiences because, according to him, "there are too many people." But even more he avoids one-on-one experiences, because "there are too few people." Despite his anxiety, he does want to be connected; his shyness is painful to him. Jacques has many loving qualities, among them respectfulness, caring, generosity, and empathy. He has the potential, if not currently the capacity, for intimacy. He is blocked from experiencing it by his anxiety and fear.

Edith's method of withdrawal is clear to anyone near her. She stays intoxicated most of the time. Not stumbling blind drunk, not blacking out or slurring her speech, just intoxicated enough to never really *be* wherever she actually is. She is not willing or able to participate in the space she is in. She seems incapable of being where she is, doing what she is doing, being with whomever she is presently with. She cannot be here now; she cannot be how she is, because she is drunk. Even those who love her have given up trying to make contact. They still love her, but they do not try to get through anymore. Edith is destroying herself. She has isolated her *self* off to where it will slowly die from neglect and malnourishment. You can be drunk in many ways: on cocaine, marijuana, narcotics, uppers or downers, or "ecstasy." It makes no difference; all artificial states, all pseudo-intimacies, withdraw us from our nature. With some people the *self*-destructiveness is apparent very quickly, with others only over a long period of time, but the damage is always done. With no *self,* one cannot be intimate. Like the deterioration of the alcoholic couple in the film *Days of Wine and Roses,* Edith's *self*-destructiveness is clear to all and painful to those who must deal with it.

Hillary has been depressed for four years. There is no doubt in her or her husband Dylan's mind as to why. They lost an infant son to Sudden Infant Death Syndrome, and Hillary has not been the same since. She does not talk much when they come to therapy; her depression is her existence now. Dylan talks a lot. He has an odd combination of gentleness and anger. He supports her but is also very angry with her. He feels as if he is losing everything: "I know the baby died—" Hillary interrupts, "Robert." He continues, "I know Robert died and I was very sad, but life has to go on. I feel like I lost a child *and* a wife. The other kids have lost their mother. We can't go on this way. There is no joy, no happiness. We're all going to go down unless Hillary comes out of this." He is very animated, almost pleading. In her depression, Hillary has withdrawn her *self* from all of them. She is so afraid of being hurt again, of having another love connection severed, that she is trying to live as if she has no connections. Acting out the fear of intimacy does not ease the pain of the lack of it.

Hillary, Edith, and Jacques are all withdrawing from their shared spaces. Their relatively common ways of withdrawing (shyness, alcohol, depression) are familiar to most of us. We feel the distance, the non-availability. Other forms of withdrawal are less obvious. They involve behaviors that appear normal on the surface. Yet despite their apparent normality, underneath we see the same fear of intimacy that we see so much more overtly in depression or drug abuse.

Have you ever known someone who simply could not refrain from being helpful? At a party, they are always helping the host, getting things for others or cleaning up. They do the same at home. When you visit them, you see all the motions, as they serve you something and try to make you comfortable, but you get no sense of *being* with them. They are just not there as a *self.* This is withdrawal into "taking care of." It is nice and polite but cuts off the intimate experience just as effectively as intoxication or depression. Nick is forty-nine, married for twenty-five years, and the father of two children, who are doing well in college. He is liked by everyone. Nick has withdrawn into being responsible. At any gathering he makes sure that all goes well, everyone is doing all right, all the activities are organized, and that plans are made for the next get-together. If you spend time with Nick, you may either appreciate all his doing or be irritated by it. Either way, you will miss knowing the real him; his behavior ensures that. It is no different for his family. They know his responsible façade; they do not know him. Although Nick will tell you that he enjoys the activity, the party, or the gathering, you can feel his doing and not his being. He does not seem able just joyfully to *be,* and so his *self* is not available to us in the moment.

Nick is one example of the way behavior is often used to withdraw from the intimate experience. People can withdraw in hundreds of other behavioral ways. They can be seductive (busy trying to get someone else to make them a *self*), rebellious (fighting with someone else about being a *self*), religious, rational, or practical. Any behavior that is used in service of the fear of intimacy, in order to stop intimacy from occurring, is a withdrawal. Some forms are merely more obvious than others. Alcoholic withdrawal we can see from across the room; organizational withdrawal (the bureaucratic mind) we may have to live with for years to see clearly.

Withdrawn people have particular difficulty when they come in for therapy. If, as we believe, the intimate experience is what allows people to change, then it must also be the basis of effective and meaningful therapy. A basic, abiding fear of intimacy makes the very help needed difficult to experience, much less to accept. Tolerance of, capacity for, and sensitivity to the intimate experience are the characteristics of the good therapist. How capable he or she is of traveling meaningfully and creatively on the prilgrimage of psychotherapy with the searching person, couple, or family depends fundamentally on a capacity for evoking, sustaining, and shaping the intimate experience. When you allow a surgeon to operate on you, you are, you hope, allowing a healer literally to enter your insides. The two deepest commitments of any physician are preeminent: do no harm and respect the sacred ground to which the allowed intimacy has given him or her access. You have the same hopes, and rights, in psychotherapy, in which you entrust your *personhood* to incursion and exploration. This, too, is your insides.

A therapist may in time be allowed such delicate access to someone's personhood. If he or she is timid or hesitant in the intimate experience, he or she *cannot* be therapeutic. Therapy is experiential; the therapist and the client participate in an experience of intimacy *naturally*. It is the only experiential dimension in which real change can occur. Therapists must be capable of being in such experiences—able to be themselves as they are, while accepting others as they are. If therapists burden the experience with judgmentalism, prejudgmentalism, a lack of reciprocity, or any other anti-intimate posture (including an addiction to closeness or acting out their own needs), they cannot deal intimately with the person seeking change. If they withdraw, they cannot participate in the experience that the other needs in order to be able to change. They cannot help others grow so that they can change *from their own experience.*

Withdrawal is common. It painfully keeps us from seeing our daughters as who they are, the oak tree as what it is, and ourselves for what we have become. Of course, all of us withdraw sometimes, and that can be healthy. Often we return to our personal space to rest, relax, or reflect. Beyond these healthy withdrawals back into ourselves, there are common, ordinary withdrawals from life that are probably not healthy, but are mundane respites from responsibility and relationship. We sleep too little, we are a little ill, we are disappointed that things did not turn out quite as we expected, we are bored—these and thousands of other everyday moods and events can remove us from real experience. Such withdrawals are only temporary respites that do not preclude intimacy in an ongoing way. The latter happens only when withdrawal becomes a way of life, only when withdrawal makes us unavailable to our ordinary lives, even the ordinariness of occasional withdrawals.

Personal Neediness

Ryan lies in bed next to Anita, sexually excited but resentfully doing nothing about it. He resents her lack of sexual initiative. He lies there awake, feeling tortured by frustration and anger. He knows from experience that she makes a wonderfully responsive lover whenever he takes the initiative, but nevertheless he lies there growing more and more uptight, thinking of sarcastic things to say to her, further distorting who she and he actually are. Why? He *wants* to be *wanted* more than he *wants* what *he wants.* He abrogates his responsibility for his own joy, his own pleasure, and his own happiness. The next morning Anita is confused and hurt when Ryan, out of the blue, asks her why she does not fix herself up rather than coming to breakfast looking unattractive. She, for her part, participates in his unhealthiness by maintaining her hurt innocence, her passive unwillingness to accept responsibility for her own sexuality.

Allison is a compulsive, controlling wife who is unendingly angry with her passive, uninitiating, unassertive husband, Mark. She is angry even though the only way he could be active, initiating, and assertive to her satisfaction would be to do things *her* way. They blame each other, she openly and he covertly. He simply says, "What's the use? She is going to have it her way anyhow." He complains of her chronic and frequently heated anger. However, like the sexually frustrated Ryan lying next to the sexually passive and somnolent Anita, Mark does nothing about Allison's angry and compulsive controlling. As a matter of fact, he really does everything he possibly can to provoke what he says he cannot tolerate. He wants her to be less controlling but constantly gives her control. He will not take care of his responsibilities but then feels "controlled" when she "reminds" him. He sets her up. This is not difficult, given her dynamics, but nonetheless, why does he continue to do it? What does he really want? What does she really want? What do they really want in the way of a relationship?

We are convinced from our clinical experience that if you want to see what people really want, ignore what they say they want and look to see what they have actually attained. People get what they want, regardless of what they consciously intend or say they want. If you want to know what it is you really want, look at what you have gotten. Naturally, we do not mean that people want to live in a war zone, that children want to starve, or that our neighbor wants to be assaulted and robbed. We are speaking relationally, and about our ordinary being. What happens to you in a relationship reflects far more accurately what you really want, or can tolerate, than what you keep on verbally insisting you want.

Control is of paramount importance to Allison. She cannot tolerate the uncertain freedom of someone else's even momentarily being in charge. Mark does not want any responsibility in their relationship, even though he complains and berates her for never relinquishing control. He is more secure and comfortable being angry with her in his passive way. Is this what each of them really wants? They certainly have worked diligently to bring it about in their marriage. They avoid doing and being in the relationship in ways that would give them what they *say* they want. They want to be wanted more than they want what they want. They avoid intimacy to maintain the closeness, however unhappy its familiarity, in which they at least "know" how to survive. They want security, and security, sadly, lives on familiarity. Allison and Mark have transformed gratifying closeness into a neurotic and ungratifying struggle. They avoid the intimate experience, which is the only dimension in which they could transform their neurotic closeness into a natural, expanding, and supporting closeness.

Ted is having difficulties with his work that have brought him to an existential dilemma: Is he worthwhile, acceptable, and lovable in himself, even if he does not perform well and fails? He tends to attribute his failing, moreover, to something outside himself, despite the fact that he is even consciously aware that his real problem is his self-doubt. He has the same self-doubts in bed. He cannot perform, and unfortunately, he sees it as performing. He says he wants to succeed. He says he wants to control his sexual prematurity with his partner, Michelle. And, of course, this desire is consciously true. However, more profoundly, he wants to be loved and accepted as a *self, without* having to perform well, and even when failing. He experiences this in his relationship to Michelle, and deals with her as if she has the love and approval to give but withholds it. In reality, it is Ted himself with whom he is having this fight. He is getting what he *really* wants, which is to try to get Michelle to "love him in his failure," at the expense of what he *says* he wants, to be successful and to "perform" sexually.

Because Michelle participates in this way of relating (she will be angry for days after one of his "episodes"), Ted can continue "playing this game" and feel justified and righteous about it. She too is caught up in wanting to be wanted more than she wants to be loved. She says that she wants him to succeed, to make love, to be openly intimate. Yet if we look at her behavior with Ted, we see that is not what she really wants: She gets angry when he cannot perform sexually; she personalizes it. If he tries to talk about his problems or feelings, she points out his failures, shortcomings, mistakes, and his sexual inadequacy. They form a pair; each helps the other continue doing what he or she is really doing. Each helps the other avoid intimacy. As with withdrawal, wanting to be wanted more than you want what you want destroys intimacy.

This pattern is seen clearly in the therapeutic relationship. Mitch comes in depressed. He is twenty-nine, and his second long-term relationship has failed. After we develop a basically trusting rapport with him, we, quite reasonably, given our orientation, ask him why he wants to be depressed. Mitch, startled and obviously irritated, says, "I don't want to be depressed. That's ridiculous. What would I be doing here if I wanted to be depressed? I came to see you because I was depressed and wanted to get over it. Of course I don't want to be depressed!" Is that true? It may be, if Mitch's depression is of the genetic, viral, nutritional, hormonal, or allergic kind—and some depressions are. However, the vast majority are clearly existential or interpersonal. This does not mean they are not concomitantly biochemical. Feelings create biochemistry, just as clearly as biochemistry creates feelings. To separate the two is to take us back to the dead ends of eighteenth-century compartmentalization. Nature is a one, a wholeness, and we are a part of nature. Whatever we experience, we participate in on all levels of our existence, from psychology to physiology.

What can Mitch do? He can, of course, seek extraneous biochemical help, such as medication or nutritional counseling. These may help. But he can also assume more responsibility for the way he is being in this world. He can become his own pharmacy. If he does the latter, he has to assume and then accept the fact that his depression is doing something for him. Since he continues to be depressed, at much expense and distress to himself, he can only assume that whatever the depression is doing in his life must be of primary importance to him. Perhaps it is his way of being angry, his way of seeking help, his way of asking for acceptance, or of forcing himself to reappraise his *self*-image. Perhaps it is all these things.

Looked at in this way, our response to him is clear: "You obviously need to be depressed because it is doing something for you that is very important to you. What we are suggesting is that if you can accept that idea, then maybe we could together find a healthier way to do what you so clearly need to do and insist on doing—probably rightly so, even though you are doing it in a *self*-destructive way. There are better ways than being depressed."

That there are better ways is manifestly true for all of us. Nature is not perverse. Mitch's problem is not much different from that of any of us who find *self*-destructive "solutions" to our life struggles. Destroying ourselves may be our right, but it certainly does nothing healthy for us and is not a natural way to be. Our aim as therapists is not only to stop such behavior but to help people find creative, healthy ways of making their own choices. Similarly, it is not enough to simply "cure" Mitch's depression. We must help him find some way that he himself owns, that is of his nature and allows him to be who and how he wishes: We must help him find a way to intimacy.

All these ways of wanting something else more than we want just to be ourselves are expressions of the fear of intimacy. Whether it is wanting to be right, wanting to be wanted, wanting to be approved of, such forms of avoidance effectively block the intimate experience. It is like saying, "I want someone to want to be intimate with me more than I desire the real experience itself," "I want to be hugged, made love to, and touched, but I'm not going to hug, make love, or touch," "I am more involved with doing than I am with being, with having it done to me than being it myself." All are ways of saying that you are willing to sacrifice the very process that might allow you to experience *in you* the things you want. They trap you in the conviction that the answer always lies outside yourself.

Would you rather I *want* you, *want* to be with you, *want* to touch you; or would you rather I *love* you, *touch* you, *be* with you, take a walk with you, as who I am, and leave you free to be you? The answer is obvious. It would be foolish to choose the desire over the actual experience. Nevertheless, that is what most humans choose. That choice is the finite expression of their capture by the system. Many people trade being themselves for some *other's self*. Since, in reality, this trade is not possible (what you give is your *I* or *me;* what you get is their *I* or *me*), you are *self*-defeating. You give away the most precious thing you own for nothing.

Self cannot be shared for non-*self*. You can never experience intimacy at any level greater than your own ability to be intimate, your own level of *self*-availability. This is why *self*-growth is so crucial, why intimacy as the modality of that growth is so important. It is why *self*-growth is not selfish but expanding, creating, and giving. If you have traded that *self* for wanting something else, you end up like the couple in O'Henry's story "The Gift of the Magi": you sold what you needed to have, in order to have what you sold it to get. Many people look for *self* outside themselves. They never find it; it makes no more natural sense than looking for your skin on someone else.

Overt Self-righteousness

Franz comes into therapy at age fifty-six. He has been married to Tina for thirty-five years and intends to remain married, but his pain with her has reached the level where he feels he has to talk with someone about it. "We went to Europe last month. We had saved for years to go. She wanted to go to Ireland and England. I wanted to go to Germany, where my family originated. She said the weather would be bad there and that the hotel I'd picked looked shabby. It turned out she was right. She would not let go of it. For two weeks we did not have any fun, any peace. She just kept bringing it up. She has always been like that. She just has to be right. I remember years ago I became interested in growing flowers. She would say, 'Don't put those there,' or 'That's not a big enough hole.' Many times she was right. But I just gave up. The garden was no joy to me. It's gotten so I do not really want to do anything with her. She is never happy, no matter what happens. You cannot even buy her a present; she will take it back and buy the 'right thing.' The 'right thing' is always what she chooses, never what the kids, or I, or, for that matter, anyone else gives her."

Tina has chosen a devastating way to avoid intimacy. She would rather be right than be loved. She needs to be right more than she wants to be loved, and everyone relating to her feels it. This particular expression of the fear of intimacy is always very difficult for spouse, child, friend, or lover to deal with. It conveys condescension at best, and more often is experienced as active, uncomfortable hostility. You have to be very understanding, beyond any reasonable ongoing human capacity, to know that this person loves you and to stay with him or her. Since staying requires more patience than the wonder of trying to translate such righteousness into love offers, those who stay do so out of their own needs.

Franz feels that his presence—his person, his *self*—is not important to Tina. He is just a role in a play about righteousness, directed by her. All of these feelings—"I'm not important . . . my presence is immaterial . . . she doesn't even hear me . . . I'm not a person to her"—are but ways he describes the absence of intimacy in their relationship. Tina is unavailable to him. She makes this his fault. He makes it her fault.

Franz has participated for years. He wants to stop, but does not know how. That Tina is often "right" is clear; that she is missing love is even clearer, and certainly more meaningful. She has not consciously chosen the *doing* of rightness over the *being* of love, but in effect that is her choice. She is doing something to her nature, her environment, and her world, instead of being in it. If he wants anything to change, Franz will have to accept responsibility for his *self* and stop blaming Tina.

Intimacy is a gift. As such, it requires free will. There can be no intimacy without free will, and Tina has abdicated hers. She makes no free personal choices. Her need to be right is driven and compelled; she has given up choice. She has given away the gift. The sad thing is that *if* Tina comes in, and *if* we can get through her defenses, she will realize that she knows this, and is probably both sad and in pain from her lack of choice. There is also a good chance, however, that if Tina comes in, she will point out what is wrong with us and what is wrong with what we are doing with Franz. Needing to be right is a very powerful defense against intimacy; righteousness can deflect even the warmest confrontation. Defensiveness is the quintessential manifestation of righteousness. Defensive righteousness eliminates acceptance. Without acceptance, intimacy is impossible. Righteousness grants no freedom to be. John Locke said, "For where is the man that has incontestable evidence of the truth of all that he holds, or of the falsehood of all he condemns?" Voltaire put it more directly: "Doubt is not a pleasant mental state, but certainty is a ridiculous one." Not only ridiculous, but *self*-defeating.

Being right can operate on many levels. Some people need to be right factually, others emotionally, others authoritatively. Having to be right religiously has been one of the most destructive defenses in the history of civilization; humans continue to torture and kill each other in its service. Righteous people usually have to have the last word, the last look, the last feeling, the last action, and even the last understanding: "I can correct what you say, I can concoct or conjure up what you feel, I can know what you think, I can decide and then clearly tell you who and how you are." They are ready to do so, even though they do not know you; worse, they do not know themselves. They will get better and better at being right, and worse and worse at being human. They will miss the whole point of existence. They will sacrifice *selfhood* but, by God, they will be right. Maybe so, but by God—whoever, whatever, however that is—they will be lost, out of touch with their nature.

Personal Rigidity

Patricia wonders whether she will ever have a "permanent" relationship; at least, that worry is why she comes to therapy. Every relationship she enters seems to go wrong; she and her lover end up fighting and struggling. She says, "I don't remember it being that way to start with. I can't understand what keeps happening. It usually starts out with little things, but then just progresses until it includes our whole relationship. Then we break up." This is the history as it seems to Patricia. She looks back and asks herself how they could have been so incompatible without her realizing it from the beginning. "Where did all the differences come from?"

Sidney and Courtney have been coming in every few weeks for about eight months. They have begun some meaningful growth. They have done so by becoming willing to negotiate most of their shared experiences, instead of making every interaction between them a *me* issue. During the first fourteen years of their marriage, and during the first six months of therapy, they spent most of their time struggling with the ways in which they were different. This pattern varied from a chronic awareness of how the other was "not like me" to overt conflict that would arise from time to time. This posture, another way of blocking intimacy, is more subtle and insidious than the others we have looked at. We all "live in our differences" to some degree, because of the ease of seeing the world this way. The ease of so doing, as well as its universality, makes living out of our differences difficult to identify and to label as neurotic. If everyone does it, how can it be anything but normal? But normal does not mean natural, and normality is no warranty of human health or happiness. Naturalness is the sole condition under which the healthy balance of intimacy and closeness exists.

We as humans are more like each other than we are like anything else. Courtney is more like Sidney than a tree is, his car is, his dog is, or a flower is. *He does not know this.* That sounds silly, but in fact he has not lived as if he is aware of this truth, and neither has Courtney. Like Patricia, they had "found" and lived out the differences. Our husband, wife, sibling, parent, child, friend, lover, or even enemy is more like us than anything else in the universe. In the large scheme of nature, there is little difference among humans. Nature is a communality; other humans are our closest neighbors. When we forget this, we miss being joyfully *ourselves*. From William Blake in "Eternity":

> He who bends to himself a joy
> Does the winged life destroy;
> But he who kisses the joy as it flies
> Lives in eternity's sunrise.

We do not, unfortunately, live this way. Not that difference is "bad." On the contrary, we notice difference; we enjoy difference; it gives us variety and adds interest to life. It makes us curious, exciting, and vital. Much of our attraction to difference is an aspect of how our brain functions; to perceive these differences is one of its highest skills. The brain then attempts to fit these "new" things into old categories and minimize differences. So while the brain recognizes difference, it works to shape similarity. If our brains are not to atrophy, we must keep the differences. The trouble begins when we begin to *live* the differences. In our fear of intimacy, we use difference to block the experience of *self*. To the real detriment of intimacy and the slow destruction of genuine closeness, we give up the greater truth, that we are more alike than not, and become fixated on difference. We sometimes fear intimacy as if we would be wholly absorbed by it, and lose our identities. Our mistake is to equate *I* or *me* with identity. You do not lose your identity by being intimate; you lose your *self* by not being available for intimacy.

Do we then give up difference, minimize it, or gloss it over? No. Differences are important, creative, vitalizing, and expanding. Indeed, some slight difference is always a highly significant part of the intimate experience. It is the experience of the *other* as slightly different from us that makes the subsequent closeness deeper, growthful, and likely to foster more intimacy. These differences (between your*self* and the *other*) are to be *experienced,* however, not *lived* (codified into identity). While enormously important, they are no more than a small percentage of our persons. In the vast majority of our thoughts, feelings, and behaviors, we are very much alike. If we include our biochemistry, physiology, and genetic makeup, we are even more alike, despite our slight anatomical differences. To some other species we may be indistinguishable as individuals. Our noses look dissimilar, but they are still largely alike, and certainly do not resemble noses of anteaters or elephants, and even their noses are, like ours, recognizably noses.

The same is true psychologically. Our angers, our sadnesses, our rejections, our joys, and our sexuality are more similar to each other's than they are different. They do vary, however minutely, and these variations are important to recognize in relationship. But it is essential that you remember that the other person is psychologically as well as physiologically far more like you than he or she is different from you. Whatever small percentage the differences are, what is important is deciding when and whether in relationship your differences are worth fighting for. Deciding means choosing. Choosing means that you are not living your differences, only experiencing them. What, among your differences, is worth stopping the flow of the relationship? What should you stand up for or draw the line at? When should you retreat to yourself and simply say, "This is who I am"? When should you, like Martin Luther, take the position "Here I stand; I can do no other"? If agreeing to do something with someone or be something with someone makes you less your *self* in a significant way, makes you like, respect, and love your*self* less, you are better off not doing it. You do not negotiate differences when to do so would change you in some way deeply unacceptable to you. You cannot, for example, compromise your integrity for the *other* and still have it with your *self.* If the *me* in you is to be different, it should be so out of a choice you make from within, not a choice that is determined by the *other.* It should be an action, not a reaction. It should manifest what you are innately, not what you need. Do not do what you can not be. In *Wise Blood,* Flannery O'Connor asks, "Does one's integrity ever lie in what he is not able to do? I think that usually it does, for free will does not mean one will, but many wills conflicting in one man. Freedom cannot be conceived simply." Neither can choice.

Living in faith with your *self* gives rise to an integral morality, an inner morality rather than one dictated from the outside. Make no mistake, it is a much more demanding morality than an external code of ethics or morals. It is not to be confused with "doing your own thing." The sociopath has no outer morality but likewise has no inner morality. Moral feelings are compelling, most compelling when they are felt internally. *Self*-discipline always transcends obedience, just as honor always outlasts fear. The disapproval, dislike, and disrespect of others hurts us, but dislike, disrespect, and disapproval of ourselves depresses us, alienates us, erodes us, and makes us unnatural. It is the basis of what we call *selficide.* As Martin Luther King, Jr., so clearly understood, living in the differences, staying separate over issues that do not matter (such as the color of one's skin or the religion one practices), destroys your internal values, and thus, as we have described, your personality. The resultant destruction of *self* is *selficide.*

Happily, differences that are critical to our inner morality make up only a small fraction of the differences we normally encounter in relationships. Most are acceptable differences, and we need to learn to accept them if we are interested in intimacy and nonneurotic closeness. This realization is what Sidney and Courtney finally came to: "We are not going to live in our differences any longer. That is not why we are married, not what we want to do. There is no joy in it." The capacity to accept difference is what Patricia must learn if she is ever to find a "compatible" partner. It is not easy.

Sacrificing our availability for intimacy for the sake of fighting over needs—that is, nonmeaningful differences—is both foolish and unnatural. The ultimate examples of this folly are prejudice, bigotry, chauvinism, and religious righteousness. It is easy to see how these extremes keep people from being a part of nature, a part of the whole. It is less easy to see the way we all fight over nonmeaningful differences in our everyday relating. We are captured by a great many differences that are not crucial to our being us, but make us lose sight of what we wanted to begin with (for example, that we joined in this relationship to live en-joy with each other). The experience of the *intimate self* is the only one in which we can see that. The acceptable differences, the vast majority, are a constant source of growth, energy, and creativity in life. To choose to live in nonmeaningful difference instead of all these other alternatives is *selficide*.

We repeatedly ask people who come to our office, "Why are you in this relationship?" "Why did you get married in the first place?" "Who do you want to be?" "What are you looking for?" "What do you want from your relationship?" We have never had anyone reply, "I want to fight over the differences, I want to not touch, to not play, to not be myself or ever be intimate." No one says it; but far too many live it.

We have to confront our fear. We have to accept the ways in which we are so much alike, have so much in common, so clearly and repeatedly say we want exactly the same thing. To accept that truth of nature is to learn to live in our healthy *self*, to stay available for intimacy, and to keep our closeness functional. Around 300 B.C., Chuang Tzu wrote, "In the days of perfect nature, man lived together with birds and beasts, and there was no distinction of their kind . . . they were in a state of natural integrity. . . ." We are out of touch with the "perfect nature" of our *selves*, and therefore lose our "natural integrity."

Acceptance of this truth, a return to natural integrity, is basically an acceptance of the ordinariness of life, a realization that you are so much like me that to reject you is to reject me, to invalidate you is to invalidate me. Except for those differences that undo me, I must accept our differences if I am to be able to love me. And in loving me, to love you.

8

Personal Experience . . . Ordinariness and Play

The important thing is not to stop questioning.

—ALBERT EINSTEIN

"Accept the ordinariness of life" is a deceptively simple-sounding personal instruction. As humans, we have a great deal of difficulty following this basic, obvious, and uncomplicated admonition.

Ned comes in about once a month for supervision. He has grown a great deal within himself in the last few years, and for the most part lives life as he wants to. He seems to be in charge of his own existence. He was always an athlete, and still sees life in sports metaphors, even though he is now a minister. "You know, that's how I finally knew I was a baseball player," he says, talking about accepting himself as he is, instead of needing to be whatever others expected of him. "When you're young, when you first start to play ball, and even for years afterward, you say, 'Hey, I want it.' In the tight situation, when the game is on the line, you say, 'Let him hit it to me.' That's what you say out loud. Inside you say, 'Oh, for God's sake let him hit it to Jimmy.' Anybody that tells you different is lying. It took me years and years, and then suddenly one day I found myself out there at second base and I was yelling, 'Hit it to me!' and my insides really meant it. I knew I was a ballplayer then. Maybe not a good one, but I had finally joined the game."

Ned is commenting on the ordinariness of life. We are all anxious. We all have desires to make love to someone we do not even know, fears that no one will like us, secret wishes to be picked first, dread of failure, and questions about whether we are "good enough." We all sometimes feel that we would like to kill our mothers, fathers, brothers, sisters, lovers, husbands, wives, and children. We would also all like to take what is not ours. And we would also all like to go over and hug the person we do not know who looks sad. We would all like to tell *others* we love them. This is humanness, the ordinary. This is why it is ridiculous to tell children, "Do not feel that way." Feelings cannot be mandated; only the expression of them can be controlled. You literally feel things before you know it. You cannot "not think or feel it." It is not ridiculous to talk to children about the meaning of their feelings, the reasons, the behaviors associated with them, or what the feelings tell them about themselves. But you cannot "not feel that," not if you are an ordinary human. In her novel *Middlemarch* George Eliot says, "If we had a keen vision of all that is ordinary in human life, it would be like hearing the grass grow or the squirrel's heart beat, and we should die of that roar which is the other side of silence." Ordinariness, indeed, has that power; it *is* what *is*.

Our ordinariness tends to get lost in our other needs. We behave in terms of what is outside us, instead of behaving out of our *self*. A simple example is commonly seen in families. If we have a child who is very ill, we and everyone else accept and even expect our stress, our fear, and our inability to function normally. We are concerned to the core. However, if it is our relationship to our child, or our spouse or lover, that is sick, neither we nor others accept, much less expect, the same response. This difference is nonordinary. It is extraordinary conditional humanness, which is therefore less than "naturally" human.

It seldom occurs to most of us to think through what we really are as human beings, and thus we proliferate all types of distortions about our *selves*. No one wants to be "common." No one wants to be "average." No one wants to be "ordinary." We are so tied up with our need to be special that we live out of our "special" needs. In *Me: the Narcissistic American,* the psychoanalyst Aaron Stern writes: "Children represent an extension of the unrealistic feelings of specialness parents require. We are living at a time when one cannot help being impressed by the level of aspiration parents project upon their children. . . . Normalcy is no longer adequate; specialness is the uniform of the day." We not only do it to ourselves; we teach it to our children.

This need may be manifest in our wanting to be a hero, a great ballplayer, a famous ballerina, or the president. This form of specialness is fairly benign. Our desires and constructive fantasies or dreams provide us with goals, motivate us, and help determine our lives. Most of the time, such drive is useful. If these desires do not become definitions of us, they will not be *self*-destructive. Those with true gifts, with unique talent, can and do "live them out," in the sense of being dedicated to fulfilling their "dreams." But even they must not allow their *selfhood* to be displaced by the *specialness* of their talent. Talent and specialness are not the same thing. Talent is an aspect of *self;* specialness captures us and displaces *self.* As Faust discovered, one can trade one's soul (*self*) for "specialness." In real life, few of us get the chance to change the contract at the end.

Most of us know inside that we will not realize our fantasies of specialness, and at some point we go forward to be what we ordinarily are. We use our talents in our ordinary lives. Some, those relative few who marry their *self*-esteem to such "fantasies," who cannot give them up and instead live out their fantasies of specialness, end up being destructive to their persons even if they do have unique talent. There is a poem by Chuang Tzu (in *The Way of Chuang Tzu,* by Thomas Merton) that speaks to this:

> "The man of Tao
> remains unknown
> perfect virtue
> produces nothing
> 'No-Self'
> is 'True-Self.'
> and the greatest man
> is Nobody."

This does *not* mean not to pursue all that we can be. It means that we must pursue it without the loss of what we are.

But this form of "specialness " is not the most common danger for us as humans. The distortions that trap most of us are the simple "specialnesses" that remove us from the world as it really is in ways of which we are seldom aware. They are the result of our constructed worlds of judgmentalism and prejudgmentalism, of our lack of reciprocity, of our fear of intimacy and the behaviors that this fear generates. We become "special." We have an insistent, abortive need to be somewhat more than what we really are. We cannot just be "ordinary." Sadly, this translates directly to "we cannot just be our *selves.*" These simple specialnesses come in two general forms: stress and systemization.

The Specialness of Stress

Paula comes to therapy because she feels overstressed and has somatic symptoms. Her internist, after evaluating her stomach pains and assuring her that she did not have something seriously wrong, suggested that she see a therapist to get some help with the stress. She tells us, "I've got too much stress in my life. I just can't deal with it. My stomach feels like it has a hole being burned in it. Dr. Johnson says it's going to, if I don't calm down, but how can I? I have a deadline at work and my boss is pushing me every day. She has no idea of all the things I have going. I'm worried about by dad—he's sick and may have to have surgery. Mick, my husband, is going to have to go to Mobile for *five* days. I just can't deal with it. To top it all off, my damn car is broken again, the same water pump. Nobody can do anything right nowadays. I'm getting stomachaches, and I'm tied up in knots. I just can't deal with it all."

Her complaints sound familiar to most therapists; not only because they hear them so often in their offices, but because they too are human and have their full share of tribulations. We all have particular stresses, and when they accumulate we pass some red line in our ability to cope with them. Is this then Paula's problem? Her dad, her boss, her husband, her car? We think not.

Clearly, the real-life stresses of tragedy, illness, death, war, disaster, and overextension of ourselves on such a scale can undo us. However, catastrophe is not usually normal life; it is not the ordinary. These special pressures that Paula has identified are problems, but are not *the* problem. They are not what is overwhelming her, making her unable to cope, making her ill. What is overwhelming her is her *identifying herself* with her stress. The first type of simple "specialness" in which we as humans get trapped is living in the stress instead of staying ourselves. Perhaps a hypothetical example will make this phenomenon more understandable. You own a business, and 98 percent of it is doing well, while 2 percent is having problems. You have two alternatives. First, you could continue to enjoy and work with the 98 percent, while at the same time doing whatever is possible to change the other 2 percent, in the knowledge that there may be nothing you *can* do. You will remain healthy with this choice. Or you can choose the second alternative: You stop enjoying and working with the 98 percent, and become overinvolved in the 2 percent, which you still may be unable to do anything about. And you will become miserable. Eventually you will end up spending 98 percent of your time and energy on this 2 percent, and be overstressed, unhappy, sick, or any of the other names we have given to the way we mistreat our *selves*. That is what we mean by specialness. We allow the 2 percent to become special, and so lose track of our ordinary *self*, our usual ordinary person.

This imbalance, this distortion of identity, is what has happened to Paula. Her boss, her car, her husband, and her dad have become "special" to her. They are no longer merely real problems in themselves, but have become internalized in her. They now reside in her stomach. They usurp her *self*. She is unable to let the problems be what they actually are. By doing so, she becomes unable to be what she actually is. She cannot learn, grow, and change in the way she needs to for *her* sake. The specialness makes her unavailable to intimacy, *which resides in the ordinary, the natural, the common, and the reality of nature. Self* is experienced only in intimacy; Paula is out of touch with her *self.* She is making her *self* sick. Acceptance is the basis of intimacy; Paula is not accepting *others* as they are, but dealing with them as something within her. She is entrapped by the specialness of these problems in a closeness that not only provides no comfort, but is exacerbating her stress.

This specialness of stress is the 2 percent of Paula's life in which she is mistakenly spending 98 percent of her time. We do not mean that her family, father, husband, and job are only 2 percent important to her, or only 2 percent of her life. We are not talking about their reality; we are talking about her *lack* of reality. By dealing with them as special, she ceases to see them as realities outside herself; instead she reconstructs her *self* around them. She then says, "They are the stress I can't deal with."

The truth of life is much the opposite. The 2 or even 10 percent that is out of the ordinary (*not* special) we usually can do little about. You can be there, feel, and be responsive and available, but *you cannot be more as a person than just being yourself.* You cannot love more than just being yourself. You can not care more than just being yourself. When we are being ourselves, we can know and accept this. And then the stress subsides. It does not go away, but it does become manageable. It becomes ordinary: ordinary worry about a parent's illness, ordinary irritation with a broken car. Not being ourselves, we cannot know this, and make ourselves sick—with ulcers, headaches, depressions, or anxieties.

The Specialness of Systems

What is really *more* stressful to Paula is the second form of simple specialness, which is only the other face of the first. She does not live the 98 percent of her life that is fine, functional, and enjoyable *as it is.* She does not accept her *self,* just as she could not accept the *other.* She has become captured by her system, and deals with her *self* as a *system* instead of a *self.* The distortion is much like that of a teenager with acne: The acne is the 2 percent of his life, but it becomes internalized, and saturates his whole personhood. It distorts the easy, accepting relationships he has with his peers. It overwhelms the fact that two attractive girls in his class are taken with him. It undermines the fact that he is one of the better students in his class. It erodes his person. It is not experienced as ordinary, but as special. As special, it spoils the wonderful, exciting, and beautiful 98 percent of his success as an adolescent—much as the businessman can jeopardize his whole business because of the 2 percent that is not going well. In other words, we cannot let our *selves* be.

Not being ourselves is what actually stresses us, and what made Paula sick. Being, existing in the ordinary, is discarded, and in its place we construct a special world, a world where everything and everybody has some meaning beyond itself and beyond its nature. We construct a world of should, have to, ought to, might, maybe, could, would, I wish, I hope, I need, and on and on. We end up "beside" ourselves, which is a perfect description of being either neurotic or psychotic—being unnatural, not ordinary. If we waste 98 percent of our paycheck at the racetrack, it is ridiculous to claim that the 2 percent we spend to support our family is what is doing us in. That may seem a harsh analogy, but in fact that is exactly what most of us do (and certainly what governments do, or, for that matter, any large system). We do it not so much with our money as with ourselves. We give away our *selves* for all our special needs: dependency, fear, anxiety, greed, lust, being right, being wanted, and so on. Paula is not peacefully in the 98 percent she can do something about. That is the real source of her stress. She insists that the problem is the 2 percent that she cannot change. The intimate experience is the only one in which she has a chance to see and understand this, and thus lower her life stress. In her *self* she can remain healthy; separated from her *self,* she remains ill.

While we most often experience such stress in our lives as a "serious" problem, a short poem by e. e. cummings (from *95 poems by e. e. cummings*) makes this point humorously:

> a total stranger one black day
> knocked living the hell out of me—
>
> who found forgiveness hard because
> my(as it happened)self he was
>
> —but now that fiend and i are such
> immortal friends the other's each

I *(Pat)* had an experience several years ago that, while not graphically pretty, brought the poet's insight home to me very strongly. My wife, our two children, and I went to visit my sister's family for the holidays. Several of my other siblings and their relations were also there, so it was quite close quarters. It was also flu season, and everyone became ill. Instead of the joyous holiday we had anticipated, all over the house there were sick people running to the bathroom and throwing up. In the middle of the night I heard someone vomiting in the hall. I got out of bed to help. There was my young niece, bent over in tears, feeling horrible. I knew just how she felt, for I felt the same way. I found a washcloth, wiped off her face, and took her back to bed. I then got down on the floor to clean up the mess. Being as ill as I was, I felt sorry for myself. I found myself wondering, "Why me? Who is here to take care of me? Where are the grownups?" Suddenly I broke out in a smile. A real *self* smile. I had a *self* realization. Nothing special, just an ordinary experience. I had simply realized that I was the oldest person in that entire house. *I* was one of the "grownups." I was able to take care of my *self,* even when I did not feel like it. This sounds mundane; it is mundane, and that is the point.

To be ourselves in our mundane ordinariness has become one of our most difficult human achievements. It is our lack of the intimate experience that makes this so. We are captured by the system, the closeness in which specialness exists. There is no specialness in nature. As disgusting as it may sound, I was intimate with vomit that night. The experience allowed me to grow, to learn something about myself. The intimate *self* has to come out of the natural and the ordinary.

You come home from work and pull your car into the garage or carport. You are listening to something on the radio that you want to finish hearing. If this takes a few seconds, or even a minute or two, you will be okay. However, if for some reason it goes on for five or ten minutes, you will find something very strange happening. An uneasiness arises inside you, a feeling that you should turn off the radio and go in the house. Why? It is your car, your garage, your radio, your time, your life. *Why can you not do what you want to do?* The answer is, because you will not let your *self* be. We will not let ourselves just exist in the ordinary. We have created expectations of what we *should* be. Our constructed world has captured our *selves.* The system has become more important than our persons.

We usually project this construction out onto the *other:* "My neighbors will think it strange if I just sit here in the car in my garage." "Janet will expect me to come in the door, since she heard the garage door go up and the car pull in." These excuses are not real. They are like Paula saying, "It's my dad, my husband, my boss." It is not. It is me. We do it to ourselves. We make ourselves not ordinary. Not getting to hear what we wanted to on the radio is the smallest of the prices we will pay. But even in this simple example, we see both the constructed world of "I can't be what I want to be and it must be for some reason out there" and the resulting loss of *self* that is the real cost of our systematizing.

What do we do? How do I get to listen to my radio? How does Paula quit making herself sick? Most people live in this perpetual impasse. They have some intuitive sense of what the problem is, and are "working on it." So many people with problems, always "working" on them, and seldom getting anywhere. Why? What does "working on it" mean? It means I am going to be different, something more, stronger, better, and very special. But our problem in the first place was our inability just to let ourselves be. Now we are going to try to solve the problem by again not letting ourselves be. Athletes in a slump press harder to their detriment; in so doing they play even less well. Human beings press as persons, only to be even less personal. It does not work. Like the young therapist who knew what the adolescent boy should do to be "better," we may know what we need to do, but without accepting ourselves as we are, we will change nothing. Accepting ourselves is ordinary. Instead, we feel stress. We work harder to overcome it, only to increase the stress. The cycle is very real and the toll extracted very high.

Play

What are the alternatives? Intimacy, *selfhood,* nonjudgmental acceptance, and living in the ordinary. We could also add the importance of surrendering. You surrender your need for specialness, your special needs, to your ordinary reality, to living ordinarily with the way things and people really are. In our offices every day, people keep asking, "What can I do?" But the problem is one of *being,* not of doing. Perhaps our best answer to them is "You can play."

When we say this to people, most tend politely to listen, to accept it as advice, and then go right on working. Many of them revealingly say, "I'll work on it." Some get very irritated and think we are being silly. It is neither polite advice nor silliness. It is the only thing you can actually *do* to keep on being. Play is the only thing you can *do* and stay ordinary. It is the only thing you can *do* to be intimate. That is very difficult for most of us to accept.

Play is a most misunderstood concept. Most adults neither are able to play nor understand what play is. Gordon Dahl, in *Work, Play, and Worship,* says that play has three essential qualities: it is spiritual rather than economic or social; it is a quality of life, not fragments of a lifetime; and it is man's synthesizing factor in a "component" civilization. We would suggest that this analysis is also a description of intimacy. In *Gods & Games,* David Miller asks why play has become the opposite of seriousness. It did not start out as such; it began as a *natural way of being.* From this perspective the genesis of the other meaning of play (the performance of a natural way of being, which is what theater began as) is much easier to understand. Jürgen Moltmann, in *The Theology of Play,* demonstrates that the religion of ancient humans was a form of playing; that the *doing* man is a later arrival, the man of the world of labor. "Only the innocent, namely children, or those liberated from guilt, namely the beloved, are able to play. . . . When a man sees the meaning of life only in being useful and used, he necessarily gets caught in a crisis of living. . . ." Conversely, "the player is wholly absorbed in the game and takes it seriously, yet at the same time he transcends himself and his game, for it is after all only a game. So he is realizing his freedom without losing it. He steps outside himself without selling himself." In our terms, Moltmann's description suggests how one can avoid capture by the system. The classical description of play is by John Huizinga in *Homo Ludens:* The first and main characteristic of play is that it is free; second, that it is not "real" life; third, that it is limited (it contains its own course and meaning); fourth, that it creates order; and fifth, that a play-community generally tends to become permanent even after the game is over. Again, we would suggest that these are the qualities of the intimate experience, the ordinary, the *self,* and "living in the world in good faith."

If you watch children, you can observe play as an accomplishing activity. Today you are an Indian, I am a cowboy. Tomorrow I will be an Indian and you will be a cowboy. If we are successful in playing, if no adult has ruined it for us by teaching us to feel that it is better to be one or the other, or *how* to be one or the other, then we will have learned to be the best cowboy and the best Indian we can be. You and I, as adults, can also learn how to be the best cowboy and Indian we can be.

It is totally irrelevant if adults watch this play and say, "Those two nitwits have no idea what a cowboy is or what an Indian is, or how cowboys and Indians behave with each other, or that Indians don't have laser pistols." It is not only irrelevant but it will be destructive if they impose their definitions on the players (whether children or adults). We are being all we can be, and that process is the core of being healthy in life. We cannot work on it; we can only play at it. Children do it naturally. Adults do not. We have difficulty doing what we want to do, being the best cowboy we can be, sitting in our car to listen to the radio, simply being our *selves.* We have trouble "being in the world in good faith."

Unfortunately, we adults, instead of learning from children, want to teach them to act "adult." "Grow up," we say. The first time you say to a child, "No, that's not the way a cowboy is," or "That's not the way to draw a mouse," or "The chimney doesn't go on the side of the house," or "Those aren't the right words to that song," or "You shouldn't feel like that," you begin destroying the child's ability to play, the ability to be intimate. Play must be free of judgment and prejudgment. Not to judge even "make-believe" is the epitome of acceptance;

it is the clearest manifestation of reciprocity. Why do adults want to ruin this for children? Why did someone ruin it for us? Adults do not do it to children intentionally to harm them, or because they do not love them, or to stop them from having a good time.

Inability to Play

Children can not understand the antiplay attitudes of adults. They wonder why adults would rather be as they are than play, when "as they are" is depressed, irritable, anxious, sick, resentful of being responsible, always hoping and never being. Why would they prefer that to the ease of play? Puzzled, children try to account for this idiocy in adults. They consequently attribute a variety of motives to adults: for example, adults object to having a good time, they do not love us because they do not enjoy us enjoying ourselves, they think being joyfully yourself is either bad or dangerous. Of course, children's hypotheses of this sort are not usually true (a case can be made for some of them—for example, Puritanism and all its descendants); few adults are that disturbed. Most adults are inadvertently discouraging because they want their children to be "secure." They believe that their children need to be like them, and they mistake this assumption for love. They forget the price they have paid for security. They forget how much they wish that they could play.

The awful reality of this price is apparent in most adults we see. They may have many activities, hobbies, recreations, and interests, but they do not play. Even when they run, they do not run as children do. They are working at running. They spend money, time, and energy *working* at recreation. Consequently, they are not re-created, which is what *recreation* means. They often talk about the play they remember as children, and their eyes come alive. You sense a momentary energy in their voice. However, their talk is all nostalgia, a remembrance of a past that is no more. They believe that play is for children, and in so believing lose their innocence, their ability to live, to be. It is not uncommon for adults to go from activity to activity—tennis, photography, boating, needlepoint—desperately searching for play. They search for the doorway to "being just what I want to be."

The path does not lie in activity. It lies in *being*. Ask the child lying on the grass what she is doing. "Just playing." We have never seen a small child need to search for play. We have never seen small children deliberately play something that made them feel bad. In play, they get hurt, angry, left out, teased, put down, and suffer a gamut of other human traumas, but they do not play something to *make themselves* feel bad. To not do so is ordinary. Animals play in this way even in their "serious" living. That ordinariness is what we have to surrender to. Only in our ordinariness can we be free, can we play, can we recreate, can we be *doing* something about our *selves.*

If indeed adults have any intuitive sense of what play is at all, they consider it foolish. Those appearing at their tennis league game "just to have a good time," to play and enjoy themselves, will be immediately sent home to recover their intensity, their competitive edge. Imagine being cut from the team because you are too serious and competitive, and are not having enough fun, not recreating. Watch two couples "playing" bridge. Are they playing? Does she smile when he trumps her ace? Instead, they behave as if they had four six-shooters taped under the edge of the table, and, so help us, they are as likely to shoot their own partners as the opposition. Is this ordinary? Is it natural? Is it human? No, but it is normal, and considered civilized. "Games" are overcompetitive "contests" to prepare you for the "real struggle."

In too many neighborhoods, you cannot currently find children freely playing. They have been organized to compete by adults who *do not know how to play.* Consequently, we have the "burned-out" eight- or nine-year-old, the "used-up" twelve- or thirteen-year-old. Adults are destroying the playing of children in their own desperation to find play. Movies such as *Stripes, Ghostbusters,* and *Blazing Saddles* are extraordinarily popular not only because they are funny but because they present *playful* adults.

Biological evolution moves very slowly. Whatever its mechanisms, they make changes over long periods of time. Cultural evolution is explosively fast. Biologically, the species *Homo sapiens* has not changed much in the past five or ten thousand years. The incredible cultural changes in that time are obvious. The question then becomes one of human psychology. What is the evolutionary cycle of our psychological being? We suggest that it is natural (of nature), and therefore closer to biological evolution than cultural. If this is so, the ordinary human today is still like the ordinary human of the hunter-gatherer tradition. We do not mean still uneducated, uncivilized, or barbaric. Much of art, education, rules, and codes are cultural changes and social constructions. But so are pollution, consumerism, genocide, religious fanaticism, and countless other evils. Did any tribes hundreds of thousands of years ago deliberately attempt to eradicate a race or ethnic group? Do tigers, zebras, elephants, mice, or butterflies do that? No, it is not natural. Certainly there was violence and strife, but of the kind we see in animals, in the service of growth, not unhealthy closeness. For it to be otherwise would mean that the human being was not part of nature. Civilization is not necessarily synonymous with civility. As culture changed rapidly with the beginning of agriculture and urban living, the stress of the imbalance into closeness escalated. To deal with the culturally imposed stress, we developed more cultural *systems* in order to be "secure," but in this cycle our systems captured us, and undermined our *selves.* We lost the art that is the natural product of humanness, the learning that is the natural quest for knowledge, and the rules that are the natural laws of nature. In return, we got systemic art, systemic education, and systemic government. We also got the behaviors that the systems bring.

Robin Fox theorizes in *Encounter with Anthropology:*

> Repression, alienation, exploitation are the clues. The tragedy is clearly seen: to have the kind of "civilized" society man is now used to and committed to, he has had to turn the society itself into a productive machine in which the people themselves become machines and their relationships mechanical rather than natural. To understand what the natural relationships are that man has lost, it is necessary to look to the primitive: to man reduced to his most natural state—the state that lacks the built-in torture of exploitation. Beyond the savage is the natural world of which man is still, despite his pretensions, a part. . . . Conflict in preclass societies—before the whole society became a productive machine—is simply not of the same order as class conflict.

We do not mean to romanticize the primitive hunter-gatherer man or woman, as filled with Rousseauean "natural" grace and goodness. They surely had some systems of their own. As anthropologist Marvin Harris discusses in *Culture, People, Nature,* systems are the foundation of social structure, economics, politics, and other group phenomena. But without consumptive systems, primitive tribes did survive and carried our evolution forward, when they must have been relatively powerless in their natural surroundings. That they did survive suggests a high degree of intimacy (participation in their nature), an evolved sense of connection with *one another,* as well as with *nature.* Connection must have been a natural reality, and humans must have seen themselves as part of the whole. Creatively playing in nature, as well as gathering and hunting, experiencing all of this as ordinary, they must have had a more intimate sense of *self,* a more natural balance between *I* and *me,* than we do.

This separation of man and nature has long preoccupied philosophers. Spinoza in his *Ethics* concluded: "Most writers on the emotions and on human conduct seem to be treating rather of matters outside of nature than of natural phenomena following nature's general laws. They appear to conceive man to be situated in nature as a kingdom within a kingdom: for they believe . . . that he is determined solely by himself." But only through *self* knowledge can we know ourselves in our nature, in our natures.

How many of us could *sense* which direction home is, where the deer are in the forest, where danger exists? How many of us could survive as *selves?* Not many. Realize what this means: *We are slowly losing the ability to live as a self.* We are not talking about some back-to-the-wilderness, survivalist, "natural man" nonsense. We are talking about a biological reality. Where we are evolutionarily is incongruent with how we are living, and we will probably perish if we do not do something about it. Too many people can not *cope* with the systemic world they live in (and too many others can not *live* in the world the system leaves them to cope with). That they are having to *cope* in the first place means that they are not simply living (or living simply). The healthy meaning of coping—adapting to new circumstances—has been displaced by a grasp for security in a futile attempt to "hold on."

Refinding Play

How do we then, as adults, bring ourselves to play? How do we relearn how to be? How do we set out not to *do,* but to *be* ordinary? First, we cannot *make* play; we have to discover it. The two ways most readily available for adults to rediscover play are surrendering their specialness and indulging in arbitrary spontaneity.

Surrendering our specialness is basically a spiritual activity. In essence, it means "I will give up whatever I do that prevents me from playing, and then maybe, if I am not stopping playfulness from happening, it will come to me." It will. It is natural. This truth was stated passionately by Picasso once in an interview (in Dore Ashton, *Picasso on Art*):

INTERVIEWER: But then, what do you do when the picture is finished?

PICASSO: Have you ever seen a finished picture? A picture or anything else? Woe unto you the day it is said that you are finished! To finish a work? To finish a picture? What nonsense! To finish it means to be through with it, to kill it, to rid it of its soul, to give it its final blow: The most unfortunate one for the painter as well as for the picture.

Picasso was also once asked what had happened to his best paintings. He is purported to have said he had destroyed them. When asked how, he replied, "I finished them." When he found himself overdoing a canvas, he switched the brush to his left hand, the hand with less control, less training, and the fewest techniques, the more natural hand. He painted with the left hand until he had restored the balance. He surrendered his need for perfection to play with the paint, the canvas, the brushes. Out of this surrender came re-creation, the rebirth of his creativity. We can all do this: give up our need to win, and so enjoy the game; give up our need to be first and so enjoy just being; give up our need to be in control, and so enjoy the *other*. But it takes a leap of faith. You have to want what you actually want.

Arbitrary spontaneity is easier for us than surrender. We do not mean foolish or unsafe behavior, just "spontaneous." The "spontaneous" impulse comes from the child that is still alive in all of us, despite what we do to him or her. We have spontaneous thoughts, feelings, and urges that we never act on; we let them go by. Realize that that is *you* going by. You may imagine to yourself, "I think it would be fun to send an anonymous telegram to Jill today saying 'I love you.' . . . Wouldn't it be wild to send Mel and Trish a huge pizza during their formal party? . . . We could go up to the lake tonight just for a swim." These whims do occur to us, but we neither honor nor appreciate them. In calling them arbitrary acts, we mean simply that you must consciously and intentionally assign yourself the job of acting on these whims. Do not process them, think about them, or try to figure them out. Just let yourself be what you are. How about backing your car into the garage instead of pulling it in forward? How about kissing your lover's nose or elbow instead of cheek? How about taking a walk at lunch instead of having a drink? How about lying on the grass instead of mowing it? How about picking a handful of dandelions for your lover, instead of buying roses?

What do these decisions do for us? Is this really play? It is at least a start at breaking up our constructed world. Arbitrary spontaneity destroys specialness and allows ordinariness. The ordinary is new and different, like that weathered old oak tree we never noticed before, and invites us to intimacy. We may, just may, be ourselves for a moment lying there in the grass. If we are, we have regained some of the child in us. We are less habituated and less tied to our constructs and our specialness. Much more insidious than our obvious unhealthy habits, such as smoking and overeating, is the fact that we take our showers the same way, tie our shoes the same way, make love the same way, and relate to our children the same way. We are prisoners of our system. The cost is the lessening of *self*. It is a very poor trade-off. To lose the chance to be ordinary, to be yourself, to be intimate, and to play, is to lose a great deal. To live with someone who will let you be who you are, and someone whom you let be, is a basic dimension and requirement of humanness.

Uniqueness and the Ordinary

People sometimes say, "But I don't want to be just like everyone else." Individuality has nothing to do with what we mean by being ordinary. Being special is not the same as being unique. Each of us is unique; that *is* the *self*. None of us is special, not to nature: not Shakespeare, not Mozart, not Madame Curie, not the wealthy, not the famous, not you, not me. To nature we are all humans, an ordinary part of an ordinary world. A world that in its ordinariness is quite extraordinary. How much we do, or how far we go, or in what way, is up to us; we have the gift of free will. But our nature is not up to us. It is a communal reality.

There is an easy way to see the difference in an example that is both a physical reality and a metaphor at the same time. Each of us stands in some place and looks at the world. Since it is not possible for two people to stand in exactly the same place at exactly the same time, no one else can see the world just as we see it. That is our uniqueness. Yet everybody stands somewhere and sees some world; that is why we are not special. If it frightens us to be alone, we will choose specialness and believe others could, or should, or do, see the way we see, see what we see, see our special world. We pay for our choice by giving up "being in the world in good faith." In other words, doing what we want to do, being *ourselves,* being who we are in relationship while letting *others* be who they are—unique and ordinary together.

Most of us do not live with each other this way. In our relationships and marriages, we end up struggling with our lovers and spouses more than playing with them. Unlike two children who will play, then fight, then return to their play freely, most paired adults end up in chronic low-level struggling that eventually replaces play entirely and destroys intimacy. Why? We have looked at ways we individually diminish our personhood, limit our growth, and undermine our intimate *self.* It also seems clear that we bring about this same diminishment together. That is, we form pairs with some particular *other,* and live out this imbalance into closeness with them. Understanding these experiential pairs may help us find ways to return play to our relationships and in so doing reclaim our ordinary nature.

Pairing does not start out as a diminishment. It usually begins in the expansion we call "falling in love." Dale and Beth walk slowly down the beach; every hundred feet or so they stop and embrace for long moments. They do not see the other people walking, the cottages, the scenery. They feel the warmth of the setting sun, the slight chill of the evening breeze, and the vibration of the pounding surf. They feel these sensations but are not conscious of them. They are connected intimately to each other, and to their world. We cannot ordinarily live our lives walking on the beach, but the real question is why, nevertheless, we cannot ordinarily be with each other in this vibrant, connected way.

9

Personal Pairing . . . Experiential Pairs and Pairing

Everybody wants to be somebody;
Nobody wants to grow.

—GOETHE

What do we mean by *experiential pairing?* Simply that any one person's experience will tend to seek out the reciprocal experience in the other person—reciprocal in the sense that our own experience always seems to seek expansion and clarification in the *other*. We look there for the other face of ourselves. As in Plato's myth, we are constantly searching to find the rest of our persons. The experience that we share with the *other* illuminates, enhances, expands, and clarifies our own. It can move our experience to a new and different level of excitement and consciousness, or it can depress us. Experience runs the entire gamut of our humanness. When we start trying to limit the choices we find, we are not having experiences; instead, we are being close. In *Ways of Seeing,* John Berger writes: "Soon after we can see, we are aware that we can also be seen. The eye of the other combines with our own eye to make it fully credible that we are part of the visible world." If we "hide" from "being seen" in closeness, we lose the "vision" of intimacy.

Donna comes in for her first appointment. She is bright and energetic. Now only thirty-six, she talks about the four marriages she has already been through. What she cannot understand is why all of her husbands turned into alcoholics. The answer is that we find in our unconscious pairing what we do not seek consciously. We then act on our unconscious choice, often repeatedly and to our own detriment. Unhealthy pairing is a search for sameness and security. In healthy experiential pairing, we seek strangeness, newness, and differences with the *other*. We seek an experience different from that of ourselves, a way of growing.

Our brains function by looking to the new, different, and strange, to the future—feelings, knowledge, and experience outside our current boundaries. In this way the brain enhances, clarifies, and becomes conscious of its experience; it fits the new into that which it already knows. We have discussed how intimacy engenders growth in a relationship and how closeness maintains its stability. The two coexist as a matrix; they are equally important and depend upon each other. What we need to address now is the fact that while closeness thrives on familiarity, intimacy thrives on strangeness. Remember how you can really see the tree, the house, your daughter, see them in new ways, see the contrasts, the details, the oddities, the changes. This constant seeking and absorbing aspect of intimacy feeds on strangeness, and we seek and find it mostly with people different from ourselves. We do not mean that Donna is seeking alcoholics. She is seeking an experience that is *apparently* only to be found in those people who are alcoholic. But she seeks it for reasons inside her that have to do with the security of closeness, not the growth of intimacy. She seeks a relationship that is familiar rather than one that is strange and potentially intimate. She has sought the old and familiar and so stayed the same. She pairs unhealthily.

We also can seek this strangeness in the world around us. To see a rose differently, to soar with the bird, or to feel the reality of the deep forest all feed intimacy into us. The creator in each of us can make use of the reality of any newness, be it place, thing, association, or person. Just as with impersonal intimacy, in our pairing we seek another way of seeing ourselves, another type of "vision." All experience is expanding.

Experiential Pairing

If you are with a friend with whom you are close—that is, someone like yourself—you feel familiar, not strange. If for a moment, however, by being yourself in your space, you see and accept the *other* in some new way in the shared space, you will experience something strange, different. You will feel the shift to intimacy. Like the reunited friends in the film *The Big Chill,* you will touch in a new way—a way that allows both you and the *other* to become different with each other. You will experience the shift as a unique change in relatedness, another and very different place to be. Intimacy thrives on the new learning experience for *self*. In intimacy, the strangeness in the *other* allows and even provokes the new and strange we find in ourselves. This is why the intimate experience is so energizing: it changes the relationship, but, more important, it increases our awareness of ourselves. It allows us to change. To realize our search for this difference, this strangeness, helps us to understand experiential pairing, and why in it we seek the other face of ourselves.

Experiential pairing is the basic framework in which the intimate dyad is formed. The *intimate dyad* is our term for the experience between two persons that produces the feelings of intimacy, the greater awareness of *oneself* while feeling close to another. In some ways, *experience* is a better word to describe this dyad than *relationship*. *Relationship* suggests constancy, the known, something ongoing; it is more descriptive of closeness. The intimate experience is usually short-lived, lasting seconds, minutes, or hours, rarely a day. How seldom we have an entire weekend that is felt in such a timeless way, dissociated from the familiar, filled with moments of simple awareness of the flow of our perceptions and experiences. Each perception and experience is sufficient unto itself; the movement from one to the next seems effortless and quite natural. Such weekends are rare, and feel almost like an unreal interlude in our lives. "Lost weekends," but beautifully found. Usually in our relationships, intimate moments are but moments. Relationship brings us closeness and familiarity; experience brings us intimacy and strangeness. That is why people say after something strange or new has happened, "What an experience! . . . You had to experience it! . . . I really had quite an experience!" They have felt intimate. They are energized, animated, and changed.

It should be clear now why it is easier to be intimate with a stranger than with someone closer to you. The strangeness is readily available; the lack of familiarity frees us from our already knowing, our judging and prejudging. The most exciting and powerful intimate experiences, however, occur when we feel the same strangeness with familiar persons. We are most intimate when we are able to be strange with the person to whom we are closest. Think about your close relationships, and you will remember that nothing is as exciting or energizing as experiencing the strangeness of someone who has always been familiar to you. The time at the beach when you saw her walking along the shore, but also saw something new and different and strange about her. You experienced her, and yourself with her, in a way that you had not seen or experienced before. How it excited you, made you want to be with her, to touch, be closer, and share you with her. That is the energy of intimacy. A small surge of intimate energy can be memorable.

Clearly, both relationship and experience, familiarity and strangeness, are necessary and important between lovers or friends. Yet in most of us there is a learned distortion of this balance. The distortion is not natural; it is not nature's way. Our culture and the majority of families in it value familiarity, security, and closeness, and tend to see intimacy as either dangerous or immoral. More often than not, they make experience more difficult and less likely. The old adage "Familiarity breeds contempt" is not necessarily true, but familiarity does too often hinder intimacy. In the absence of intimacy, contempt can grow in relationship and erode both *selves* involved. As Ogden Nash rhymed (in "Family Court") (even if un-*self*-responsibly):

> One would be in less danger
> From the wiles of the stranger
> If one's own kin and kith
> Were more fun to be with

Relationship versus Experience

The most obvious example is the abrupt shift from the intensely intimate and close experience of courtship to the "relationship" after the couple has lived together for some time. The experiences of courtship are rapidly institutionalized into a "marriage" relationship. (The "marriage" does not have to be the traditional legal one. By *marriage* we mean a state of existence between two people who form a pair.) Most couples who come into therapy are individually conscious of the loss of their early intimacy, but seldom openly acknowledge it. Surprisingly, however, some will say that the relationship changed on the honeymoon. The immobilizing seduction of closeness and security must be powerful to warp relationship so quickly, so thoroughly, and so sadly.

Jack comes to therapy once a month. He has been in now five times. He wants his wife "to be like she used to be," by which he means how she was before they got married. He talks about how back then she enjoyed sex, was a "real turn-on," liked watching the ball games with him, and so forth. He does not describe himself to us or talk about how he has changed. He is not really aware of having changed. Early on, he abdicated to his wife his responsibility for the viability of his marriage. He just wants the old days back.

Familiarity and relationship almost immediately become the goal of most pairings. Experience is avoided, because it might jeopardize the relationship by making something change. For all too many pairings, maintaining the relationship becomes, within months or at most a few years, the primary objective. Experience is diminished and avoided as threatening. We believe ourselves to be increasing our security, but nothing could be further from the truth. Keeping the boat steady finally results in the couple sitting silently on opposite seats in a stable but unmoving boat, going nowhere, bored to death, psychologically dead or dying, and usually very sad. In avoiding experience we lose our passion. The simple truth of nature is that what does not grow dies. Nature knows no unchanging states. "It is only by risking our persons from one hour to another that we live at all" (William James, *The Will to Believe*).

Marlene talks to her friends frequently about her feeling that she gets nothing from her relationship. She talks to friends but not to her lover. Nor do her complaints seem to motivate her to change anything, herself or the relationship. Her dissatisfaction is real, but her response is not. She forgoes the passion, the play, the joy, in order to "maintain" the relationship, in order to stay secure. She spends most of her time in our office talking about the relationship, not about herself, and then she wonders why nothing changes. She, like too many humans, lives *in her relationship* instead of *in her self.*

James and Millie have been married eight years. They find themselves spending less and less time together playing, talking, or simply enjoying each other. They converse about their two children, the house, their jobs, or other people, but the conversation does not energize them. It tires them. They have little aliveness or passion together, with others, or even in themselves. Yet their friends often remark on how much they love each other, are a "good couple," and are making a "good family." Even they share in this illusion. Looking more closely, you can quickly discern in each of them a certain disquietude, a marital uneasiness. Something is missing. At this early stage of marriage, the uneasiness is usually still unspoken, and only vaguely conscious. It is occasionally acted out in the angry or petulant moments that invade the "perfect" marriage. Like Jack, like Marlene, neither James nor Millie understands what is wrong, but underneath they have an instinctive sense that *something* is.

When such couples come to therapy, they almost always complain of their lack of "relationship." This is paradoxical, since, if anything, they have an excess of "relationship." In fact, the deficit is really one of experience and intimacy, not "relationship." Without intimacy, energizing is diminished; the aliveness, the play, and the joy are gone. Couples spend months talking about their "relationship," instead of relating. We are reminded of a client who broke through this impasse when approached by his wife, who wanted to talk about their relationship. He said, "I am not interested in talking about our relationship. I would rather have one."

If neurotic behavior is, as we said, an overinvolvement in the *I,* then here we see it in its garden variety. It is possible that James and Millie can, in time, come to realize that the main value of relationship, other than pragmatics like safety (for example, having food and shelter), is that it can allow and even facilitate experience for each of the pair. This realization would make growth, change, and success in life more likely. It would be a return to nature, to the natural. The issue is almost always not the lack of "relationship," but the lack of experience in the relationship. Lack of experience in the relationship means the absence of intimacy.

Accusation

This pattern is so common that we can fairly well predict the therapeutic course. The couple will spend months accusing each other, honestly believing that the other is responsible for their personal misery and the failure of the relationship. Like Jack and his "sexually dead" wife, they simply cannot understand how the other changed so much. The only therapeutic value of these incessant initial accusations is, perhaps, that the inanity and deadness of the approach, done in the presence of an accepting therapist, may become apparent to the couple much more quickly than if they merely continue the same behavior in private. Often, in the latter case, it never becomes apparent to them. Such futile struggling can go on for years, even decades, until someone either literally or figuratively quits. The presence of another adult, impartial yet caring, accepting without being changed, seems to embarrass neuroticism. Sooner or later, the couple usually gives up these futile indictments and begins to negotiate with each other.

Negotiation

In this second stage, James and Millie, for example, go beyond the accusing, until one finally says, "I know that I'm often a controlling person. I like things to go my way. I'm beginning to understand that that does not give you much room to be your own person, and that you often feel put down and misunderstood. I'm going to try to do better about that. I hope I can be more aware of what I am doing with you. Maybe I can back off and give you more room to be who you are. But you need to understand that you never seem to be willing to make a commitment. I need just to know you're staying no matter what. I feel you are always fighting with me. Even when I feel that you agree with me, you don't seem to be willing to say so. Even when I feel that I'm agreeing with you, you seem suspicious, as if I'm manipulating, doing you in, and taking away your freedom to decide. I don't know what to do with that. Is there any way we can each give up something, and maybe get something together in return?" The other replies: "What you say may be true. I know that I'm often defensive, frequently withdrawn, and tend to deal with you by doing nothing and saying even less. I don't know what to do with you. It's true that I feel that agreeing with you has almost always felt like giving in to you. Maybe if you could just back off, learn not to be so controlling, and let me be me, and if I could find more courage to say what I feel, then we could get somewhere."

Both persons are negotiating. It is better than accusing, but still it affects only the closeness relationship, the maintenance part of their living. James and Millie are not different. However, they now *have a chance* to be different; they have made a beginning.

Negotiation can go on for months or years, both in and out of therapy. When we as therapists first realized that the negotiating was almost as futile as the earlier accusing, the fact was confusing and puzzling to us. Why? Everyone is being fair, reasonable, and rational. And, in retrospect, contracts *would* work if people were merely rational, like machines or computers. But, happily, they are not. Negotiation makes relationship more pleasant, fairer, and more sensible, but it does not create significant ongoing change in relatedness. At best, the negotiators become more agreeable robots, settling for a more pleasant security grounded in a new familiarity. At worst, the contract breaks down, and they divorce without ever dealing with their real personal issues. It is difficult to say which is sadder.

The real issue is intimacy. "Can I live with you as I really am? . . . Can I go on loving you if you're able to live with me as you really are? . . . Can we live, not accusing or negotiating, but just being who we are?" How do couples reach this place? Some ask us, "Why not just tell us how to do it, and save us all time? Explain it to us." Again, that would work fine if people were solely rational. But to be a therapist you must be part of an experience, not just a better negotiator. If people were truly entirely rational, they would not have problems. However, they would also not have most of those things that make life meaningful. Making love is not rational; creativity is not rational; awe is not rational. You cannot get to relational meaningfulness, making love, and loving, rationally. Intimacy is not rational, not negotiable; it is natural.

The perceived inanity of the couple's unending accusations finally moves them to negotiate. However futile, the negotiating *experience,* not the negotiations, does provide them and the therapist with an experiential context within which they all can more effectively confront the couple's distorting belief that relationship is more important than experience, or that security is more important than aliveness in relationship. In this context, they are more likely to learn that relationship may be negotiable but experience is not. From there we can begin to examine the parameters of intimacy. Being intimate never occurs when you are accommodating or negotiating in the relationship. Intimacy is beautifully uncompromising, just as closeness is beautifully compromising. Intimacy feeds and energizes closeness. Closeness enriches and expands intimacy. They are powerful reciprocals and form the matrix of love. But intimacy can easily shatter closeness, and closeness can easily cut off and block the intimate experience.

Most of us, like James and Millie, are overbalanced in our closeness, security, and maintenance. We must learn how to be *ourselves* with the *other* healthily. Even when intermittent, intimate experience can assure more closeness. The closeness can make the intimacy indescribably more powerful and energizing than that which we might have with the stranger, the walkway, or the tree. Yet even as intimacy can enhance and expand, it can endanger and engulf relationship. We can be so committed to intimacy that closeness becomes impossible. Closeness can be so important that intimacy becomes impossible. We see both dilemmas in our therapy with people. The prototype for the former (intimacy precluding closeness) is the cowboy, the wanderer, the adventurer. It is no coincidence that our movies and television fare reflect what we in this society so desperately miss, albeit usually reflect it in an extreme and violent metaphor. Shane, Dirty Harry, and Indiana Jones are who they are, do what they want to do, but cannot accommodate healthily into closeness—just as earlier romantic figures (Brontë's Cathy and Heathcliff, Tolstoy's Anna Karenina and Vronsky) cannot. In *Star Wars,* the two heroes symbolically represent the two sides of this imbalance (Luke closeness, Han Solo intimacy). Robert Redford, in *The Electric Horseman,* and Jessica Lange, in *Sweet Dreams,* portrayed the overly intimate person without extreme violence, and therefore portrayed more accurately the relational dilemmas of this life position. The prototype for the latter imbalance (closeness precluding intimacy) is the workaholic businessman, the preoccupied professional, or the self-sacrificing caretaker. Of course, most of us live not on the extremes of the spectrum, but off-center—imbalanced into closeness. Only occasionally do we see the balanced close-intimate experience, sometimes in real life, more often in fantasy or fiction. The films of Spencer Tracy and Katharine Hepburn continue to draw us because they dramatize (suggest the possibility of) a perfectly balanced relationship between equal *selfhoods.*

As therapists, we can often help a couple understand that their preoccupation with relationship diminishes the depth of and joy in that relationship. We can point out that, in our experience with them, each seems to be complaining about the very qualities in the other that attracted them in the first place. He says, "I was originally attracted to her because she was so independent and so very much her own person." She says, "I was attracted to him because he was so willing to listen to me, so accepting of *me*. He never argued." Why then is he so upset now at her being independent? Why is she so angry that he so seldom shares his feelings—irritation, disagreement, and anger included?

The specific qualities that upset and separate the couple are precisely the qualities that could enhance the intimacy in their relationship. He complains of her independence, when indeed her independence was originally what gave him a sense of possible freedom from his unceasing need to take care of *others,* when her not needing to be taken care of was what originally attracted him to her. She, on the other hand, had always felt that *others* had never accepted her independence. They wanted her to be what they wanted her to be, whereas he was excited with her being herself, pleased that she did not need something from him to be herself. She was attracted by his excitement with her independence. Now he is quarreling with her about her "lack of commitment." She is upset over his "possessiveness." The struggle started months after their relationship began, and within a few years became constant confrontation. They were fighting about the very things that had initially brought them together. Why?

It is astonishing how people persist in believing that if they could just have what they wanted, or at least what they think they want, then everything would be wonderful; they would have no further problems. "If I were just loved and cared for, I would be fine." In fact, most people today are much less prepared for being loved than they are for anger and disdain. We forget that the problem is in us, and we insist on seeing it in terms of those outside of *ourselves.* For such people to believe that they immediately and automatically take to love and acceptance is a seductive illusion. They may well have had little experience of such love and acceptance. However wonderful it ultimately may be, love and acceptance are confusing to those of us who are not accustomed to them. They make us more anxious than serene. Real love is confrontive and makes us see ourselves in ways that we have spent years trying to avoid. Familiarity is far more comforting, although it is the "nonloving" and "nonaccepting" experience, conditional on our being some predictable way. Unfortunately, we believe we can depend on that predictability; that being in the familiar will bring us peace. It never does, but we continue to cling to the idea that there is security in sameness. That is one of the therapist's most difficult problems in trying to get the neurotic person to change. Neuroticism has within it a kind of comfort and security. When you are neurotic, you know what to expect, you know how life is. To give up that security is very difficult, even if what replaces it is love and acceptance. The notion that systematized people take easily to emotional health is nonsense. *Self*-responsibility is scary, mostly because it is not the norm—it is not familiar, it is being strange. When we write of intimacy, we write of strangeness and its crucial importance in healthy being, the importance of becoming excited with the strange, the new, and the different. It takes time and learning. If you have seldom been there, it takes *experience* to be there easily. In *The Anti-Christ,* Nietzsche wrote, "Life always gets harder toward the summit—the cold increases, responsibility increases." It is *self*-responsibility.

It may take many people who have been nervous all of their lives months or years before they can distinguish between anxiety and the excitement of being alive and intimate. It is not easy to accustom yourself to being mature. One of the greatest disenchantments of our childhood is that we *were* promised a rose garden, with familiar plots and safe fences. The promise is seldom articulated. It is instead the false, external echo of familiarity. We are promised security, but not aliveness. We end up with neither.

We have been describing couples who confront their relationship initially through mutual accusations, as do most couples. We saw their movement to negotiating, and saw that although negotiating may appear to be progress, more often than not it actually perpetuates the impasse, because the couple will not risk going on. They have found a more comfortable familiarity; it has a powerful ability to capture them.

If the couple and therapist survive these two intransient but seemingly necessary phases, at some point, usually by surprise, something marvelous may happen. One of the couple will experience the therapist being intimate with his or her partner. They will actually experience the experience between the therapist and their *other*. They know, in that moment, the difference between accusing or negotiating in relationship, and having an experience in relatedness. Being a therapist requires patience with the necessarily long-term effort to change people. People come into therapy having had hundreds of thousands of significant emotional interactions with parents, spouses, or lovers. Even if the therapist sees them for years, he or she will have only relatively few experiences in relationship with them to facilitate their changing their lives. The fact that it sometimes happens is in itself a miracle. Humans *do* have a *choice*. As the French writer Léon Blum said in *On Marriage,* "Life does not give itself to one who tries to keep all its advantages at once. I have often thought morality may perhaps consist solely in the courage of making a choice."

How change may happen in the experience of therapy can be seen in a dramatic but not unusual example. Arch and Mary are a couple who have been in therapy for six or seven months. They have been married for twenty-five years. Arch has been alcoholic for the past twenty years, which is what eventually brought them to therapy. He had made at least eight recoveries, with short periods of sobriety, but then would return to drinking. Arch has been sober for the last three or four months. His sobriety now has the same undertones of feeling as his previous sober periods. He is *controlling* his drinking, but he is uneasy and has trouble being himself. He seems like someone waiting for the other shoe to drop. In truth, it is simply a question of time before he begins drinking again.

It is the Christmas season, and holiday punch and cookies are on the table in the waiting room at the office. As they pass the table, the therapist asks Mary if she wants a cup, and then turns to Arch. Mary refuses. Arch looks at his fearful and righteous wife. He looks at the therapist for a moment or two. Then he gets a cup of punch and goes into the office and sits down. He looks at Mary. He looks puzzled. They and the therapist just sit, not speaking. He holds his drink in his hands, turning it around and around in his palms. He does not taste it. Mary just stares. No one talks. After ten or fifteen minutes, Arch begins to cry. Not loudly, but the kind of gentle crying where tears run down your cheeks and drop off your chin without sound. The three continue to sit. The hour finally ends. Arch sets his untouched drink on the table and walks out with his wife. Nothing has been said in the hour. At the door he turns and says, "Thank you very much." They leave.

That was twelve years ago. Arch has not had a drink since. He will tell you that his recovery has not been "willpower." He has not *wanted* to drink since that experience. As a result, his life has changed in many ways. Most important, his relationship with his wife has changed dramatically. Mary had her own experience during that hour: She experienced the interaction between Arch and the therapist in its strangeness, its newness, and its difference. In that intimate experience, she too changed. Since then, she has been content to let him make his own choices without fear of recrimination, and he has made choices that have enhanced his life and relatedness to her.

As was true here, if the couple and the therapist survive the early phases of accusing and negotiating, something different can happen. In this instance, Mary experienced Arch being given a choice. Given that choice, he chose not to drink. He found that he could choose, a different feeling than he had ever discovered in his previous eight "recoveries." She discovered that she could do nothing about that choice. She experienced what she had needed to know for years: his drinking was not who *she* was. She could choose to live with him, or leave him. She finally realized, in her feelings, that judging him was a catastrophe. She chose to stay; he chose to stop drinking.

We are not recommending offering drinks to alcoholics as a treatment for alcoholism. Even though this idea has meaningful implications, it is not the point. The point is that people change only in the moment of intimate experience. This is not a strategy, nor is it something you can consciously do. It is experiential, belonging to the world of being intimate in relationship. Change cannot be *made* to happen this way, but it can and does happen when humans are available to the experience.

Negotiations stop when one or the other of the couple decides and then announces that he or she fully intends to stay in this relationship as of now and as a *self*. The announcement is sometimes very abrupt. Mike and Diane have been in only three times. Diane is quietly and gently talking to the therapist about a real-world problem concerning one of the children. Mike is getting visibly more and more angry. He finally explodes: "You two are wasting time. These things aren't important. I'm here to find out whether we can live with each other and, if we can, how I can do something about it. I'm not interested in that other crap." He falls quiet, and then mumbles an apology. The reality is, however, that the relationship has been moved to a different level. He has announced his presence as a *self* in his marriage.

It often comes as a surprise to couples that they have never previously clearly decided whether they would stay together. It is as if, after the wedding ceremony, be it real or symbolic, the question disappears from their lives. That, of course, is not how any of us exist as a *self*. When one of the couple shares the decision to stay in the relationship as he or she really is, the naïve and disabling notion that it takes two people to change a relationship is challenged. One changes, and in that changing, the relationship immediately becomes different.

Mike and Diane have decided to stay in the relationship but not as before. They now intend to be there as they really are, fully themselves. Being who and what they really and honestly are, sharing feelings out of themselves, regardless of any anticipated responses from the *other*, behaving courageously with those feelings, letting the *other* respond as he or she will, as a *self*. They risk the other's disapproval, anger, and even departure. This is the crucial transition into the intimate experience. It moves them from a concern with "relationship"—closeness, stability, and familiarity—to a concern with experience—intimacy, animation, connection, and creative relatedness. It moves the relationship from a dependent one concerned with either security or control of the *other*, to a relationship that allows and even demands new experience. When done unilaterally, the outcome is usually either a healthy marriage or, perhaps equally as important, a healthy divorce.

Sterling is in pain because he wants to end the relationship he is in, but cannot seem to do it. He does not understand why. After five years he is bored and feels no pleasure in the pairing. He sees this as his partner's fault. He says, "I don't understand how someone can be this or that way, not see this or that, and not change." It has not yet occurred to Sterling to ask himself the same question.

Cindy, thirty-three, has been married for twelve years and is the mother of three. She is intelligent and attractive, but very unhappy and unsettled. She has been in therapy for eight months. She talks about how her marriage needs to change. She usually means by this that her husband, Carl, needs to change. She stays depressed, because she cannot get Carl to come to therapy with her to "save" the marriage or "straighten out" the relationship. Her depression is the result of her feeling that nothing can change until he does. Not even her.

The most important implication of the transition from neurotic accusing or negotiating to courageously being your *self* is the realization that relationships can be changed unilaterally. It does not take both of you. Your life, including your life in your most significant relationships, is in your own hands. You can give up the escapist belief that you are the unwilling and helpless victim of the neurotic actions and feelings of the *other*. This miserable and totally incapacitating misbelief can keep any of us from ever being intimate. Choosing *self*-responsibility puts you back in charge of your own life, especially in those most significant relationships. The simple fact that you feel in charge energizes the relationship and promotes intimacy. Waiting for the *other* is not only personally irresponsible, it is *self*-pitying and hostile. *Self*-responsibility is responsibility to and for your *self*. It is not being in charge of the *other* or the relationship. Albert Camus (in *The Fall*) put this directly: "I shall tell you a great secret, my friend, do not wait for the last judgment, it takes place every day."

You can have what you want in relationship if you are willing to be your *self* without recrimination or judgment of the *other*. It may not come immediately or easily, but it will come. You cannot be different without the other person's becoming different. That is a fact of human relationship; it is an inherent part of relational reciprocity; it is an aspect of nature. It is also a risk. The other may be different in ways that make for a more intimate, honest relationship, or may be different in ways that make it clear to you that this is a relationship you do not choose to be in. But either way, you are free to be more your *self* here, or elsewhere. The belief that relationships change only bilaterally is the most significant reason why relationships are so difficult to change. Acceptance of your unilateral capacity to alter significant relationships is the most powerful step you can take in beginning the process of change in your experience of life. The risk is accepting whatever the resultant change in the *other* may be.

This is precisely what we mean when, as experiential psychotherapists, we suggest that the dynamics of therapy are in the person of the therapist. Intimacy, which is the experience in which people change, can be brought about by the personal participation of the therapist. It is often engendered by the client, but the therapist cannot rely on that, any more than you or I can rely on our spouse or lover for it. If the therapist is concerned only with "relationship" in psychotherapy—with dependent security, maintaining familiarity, or with living as motivated by expectations—then intimacy will be eroded or aborted. The expectations will modify his or her participation in the relationship, and therefore experience and intimacy will be correspondingly diminished. This is no different than it would be in any significant relationship, including marriage. If a therapist needs clients, then he or she will be of small use to them and will lose them, because the need of them will preclude experience and intimacy. If you are caught up in your concern with relationship, you are inevitably impelled toward divorce.

But if your concern is with experience, then intimacy will result. You can choose maintaining familiarity, which, in therapy as well as in primary pairing, can work as the main block to both experience and intimacy and therefore to growth, change, and newness; or you can choose engendering experience and intimacy, which assures change and energy, and so offers a new and healthier closeness. The point is not to get rid of closeness. The point is to balance closeness with intimacy, and to learn what we must experience to keep that closeness viable and growing. A therapist must be able to choose, and must be able to do both.

I *(Pat)* spoke earlier of my difficulty with clients in the beginning of my practice of therapy. I was neither maintaining closeness in a positive way (counseling) nor allowing and nurturing experience (being a therapist). I needed to be able to do both. The goal in psychotherapy is for the client to feel more himself or herself, *while* feeling related to the therapist. It may be comforting to develop a close relationship to the therapist, but unless one goes further and finds a more intimate awareness of *oneself* in that relationship, he or she is simply being comforted, not changing. Comfort may be, and often is, an important and useful experience at difficult times, but it is not the experience that changes us. What is true, and possible, in the therapeutic relationship is even more vitally true, and possible, in our primary pairing.

The intimate dyad then is the experience with another person within which you feel more in touch with your own person while you feel concurrently related to the other. You feel accepted, congruent, integrated, and have little or no need to be anyone other than who you are. There is no need to accommodate to the other's needs, expectations, or previous history. *Sustaining selfhood while you are related to the other person* is the most important ingredient of the intimate experience. The majority of experiences of feeling close to yourself occur outside relationship. Such experiences, however meaningful, are not intimate. They occur in your own personal space. Even impersonal intimacy changes our experience of other *persons* only slowly and indirectly. The *self* experienced in impersonal intimacy may produce great art, but it does not directly deepen personal relationships, except slowly. The unhappy, *self*-destructive lives of so many artists, composers, and writers document this clearly. Similarly, externally stimulated "self" experience (for example, the popular drugs of the last few decades) may have produced some impersonal intimacy, but did nothing to enhance personal relatedness. Tripping is not living. On the contrary, drugs most often make the users lonelier, more isolated, and more alienated. Impersonal intimacy may be experienced in art, music, sculpture, poetry, or literature, but it must be personalized by the viewer or reader to become truly changing of them. Not "personalized" into closeness, but "personalized" into *self,* which may well happen unconsciously. We are most profoundly changed in the intimate experience with those humans to whom we are closest. It is nourishment for the *self* in its most direct state.

Transference and the Intimate Dyad

Is there some predictable, describable, and commonly occurring characteristic of the intimate dyad? As psychiatrists, our initial training was the Freudian psychoanalytical notion that marriage or pairing preferences were primarily dictated by transference. That means that unconsciously we are attracted to persons who are like our mothers or fathers, or even brothers or sisters. Or perhaps our need, out of fear or guilt, to avoid these very people might lead us to find partners who were the exact opposite. In either case, early familial experience determined our mating selection. A few people might be free of such early compulsions and choose a partner freely, but such a person would be rare—someone who, in *personal* choosing, had transcended personal history. We were taught that, more often than not, people paired out of some neurotic repetition compulsion, in order to repair the deficits of their childhoods. Character and personality, as determined by early developmental experiences, dictated the ongoing history and outcome of those significant relationships. Character, as the Greeks insisted, was fate, and inexorably unfolded unless interfered with by some powerful outside force—some experience or relationship occurring outside the parameters of your familial situation: a war, an affair, a critical illness, a religious conversion, therapy, or a magnificent teacher in school. These might move you out of your fate. Usually, however, character, formed in the family, was fate.

Jean is forty years old. She has just finished a fifteen-year marriage. She wonders what has gone wrong. Her husband has turned out to be "unfaithful." She tentatively wonders why she married a man who could do this to her. Within a short time, however, she has carefully selected her next husband, who seems committed, caring, and a "gentleman." She leaves therapy, the real questions unanswered, marries this man, and tries again. Within two years, he is heavily involved with a younger woman at work. She divorces and returns to her therapist, still having only the vaguest idea of how *she* has been involved in what has happened to her marriages. She has not yet discovered that no one is innocent. She chooses a third husband even more carefully. He is in his early fifties, assertive, seems nondependent, was married for twenty-five years prior to the death of his first wife, and never was unfaithful. Again, in a few years he is struggling with his desire to see other women. Jean still cannot understand what she has to do with his infidelity.

She recognizes that it looks as if there is a pattern she is part of, but does not feelingly *know,* in contrast to recognizing, her participation in all these marital failures. She had not made this man unfaithful. He had become unfaithful while with her. But he had not done this with his first wife. Jean was hurt and disconsolate, convinced, as she said, that if she married Saint Francis of Assisi, he would become a gigolo. That, of course, is not true; no one makes someone anything. It takes a special pairing of two people. She had only to pick the "right" person, and had done so, three times. You cannot make someone unfaithful. You can only find a person with that potential and participate in his or her decision to be *self*-deceiving. This is experiential pairing at work. Jean's unfaithfulness was to her *self.* Her unwillingness to see and be her*self,* be her sexuality, be her reality, was her participation. She chose the security of sameness at a frightening price.

Character (our *me,* our ingrained inner qualities) is an awesome determinant of what happens to a person in life. Hope comes from the obvious fact that there are many "Jeans" who marry a second time and find a successful, gratifying relationship. What happens depends on the pairing in each dyad. This pairing is not fortuitous; character is an important factor in our choice of the person with whom we pair. Nonetheless, what happens in that relationship depends on the *pairing,* not simply on the character and personality of either of the two people. It is the experiential pairing that is pivotal. It is not a different Jean or a different next husband, but a different experience between them that allows a change to occur.

Simone comes to therapy wanting to know why "I always end up being mistreated." She does not mean mistreated physically, but that each of her lovers has over time "put me down," "started to criticize me," "started finding things wrong with me." Simone says she has friends who are not critical in this way, but she is never "attracted" to them. She asks, "Why do I love the ones who don't like me?" Simone pairs for her needs. So far she does not know what her needs are. She also does not know why she can be so different with friends as opposed to lovers. She has no sense that she is in control of this difference in herself, or that she is responsible for it.

Jerry was married the first time for eight years. For most of that time he complained about what he called his wife's "hysteria," "impulsiveness," and "stupidity." Two years after his divorce, he remarried. Listening to Jerry, we can hear that this new woman is just as impulsive and feeling-oriented, rather than intellectually oriented (which is probably what Jerry meant by stupid), as his first wife. However, he sees his present wife not as "hysterical" but as fun, playful, surprising, and energetic. What is the difference? It is not in Jerry; he has not grown, and in some senses, the way he sees his second wife is no healthier than the way he saw the first. He sees neither as a real person. But he does see the similar women as different. The difference is in the pairing. The combination is not just the sum of its parts. People powerfully mutate each other, especially in pairing. That Jerry can be different is obvious; whether he can grow up is another question. The psychiatrist Harry Stack Sullivan described this as personality *emerging* in relationship.

Character and personality are not immutable. They are, however, often described as such by behavioral scientists. Character to some extent, and personality to a greater extent, vary, depending on the person with whom you interact. Even with the same person, when (for some reason extraneous to the relationship) that person is for that time discernibly different, then you too will be different. Quitting smoking may alter the personality of one partner; the personality of the other as he or she relates to the first will be clearly different. Personality is relational. It is not inflexible, unchanging, or even predictable. It depends a great deal on the experience in the pairing of the dyad at that moment. It can change significantly in that pairing whenever one of the persons in the pair is even momentarily different. If the change is more permanent, then either the *other* will also change or the couple will separate. These more permanent mutations are changes in character. If I have been afraid of life, closed within myself, and then grow and expand, you will expand with me or the "distance" between us will increase.

This reciprocal nature of pairing underlies our earlier statement that relationships can be changed unilaterally. Change would be easier if both people were working to change, but one, participating in the dyad in a significantly different way, will alter the feelings and behaviors of the other. Experiential pairing therefore must be defined relationally. My experience changes, and with it my personality changes. Most often, the changes are minor. I am more talkative around someone slightly more taciturn than myself. But when the other person in the pairing is radically different from the kinds of persons with whom we usually pair, our own feelings and behaviors can be radically different. Is not this the stuff of our dreams and fantasies, our movies and our romance novels? We meet a tall, dark stranger in a café. We are no longer shy, quiet, asexual, dull, or boring. Instead, we are sensual, witty, and sexually wild. The interaction we are talking about is the manifest base of these fantasies; the problem with the fantasies is that in them we continue to see our *selves* becoming different (freer, more alive, more real) as a function of the *other*. Like those who feel so alive in their affairs while their marriages remain "stagnant," we are still not *self*-responsible.

Feelings and behaviors in us can be even more strangely, vitally changed if the paired person who is being so different with us is, in fact, someone with whom we are very familiar. Here, of course, is the ultimate experience of the reciprocity of closeness and intimacy. It is this experience for which we are searching when we sneak off to rendezvous in hotels with our long-term partners, or wear wigs, or, on a more ordinary level, go off on vacation.

Experiential Pairing and Change

Max consistently "puts down" Tracy in their private life. She is intelligent, sensitive, attractive, and liked by most people who know her, but Max can deal with her only negatively. He undermines her staying fit, trying to grow, or furthering herself professionally. With other women, Max is sensitive, appreciative, and even caring. More bizarre is the way he talks with pride to others about Tracy's accomplishments. His incongruity "irritates the hell" out of Tracy. On a deeper level it hurts her inside in a way she does not understand. She does not see her own involvement in Max's way of relating.

Like Tracy, we cannot begin to understand relationship if we assume that personality is a constant. When we understand that it is relational, dependent upon the paired experience, we suddenly see why in relationships hysterics can become compulsives, schizoids become manic, dependents fiercely independent, neurotics emotionally psychotic, paranoids trusting, and even psychotics sane and real. Remember that those of us who consider ourselves sane and real are frequently at least momentarily neurotic, day in and day out, and may even have our own transient psychotic moments. How we are depends on the experience we have with the *other*. The experience in the pairing determines how we feel and behave as significantly as do our "normal" personality and character. Biology and genetics are powerful and pervasive determinants of human behavior. Personality and character, as they are formed in the crucible of our early family years, are equally so. However, none of these factors are immutable. Were they, they would be totally inconsistent with all the rest of nature, which is characterized by constant change. This phenomenon is not limited to species as a whole, but is equally true of individuals. Change is always determined by experience with our surroundings, including our experience with a single other person. We are part of each other's environment. We exist only in an ecology of life.

The fact that people are able to change radically in relationship may suggest that *selfhood* is constantly mutable. This is certainly true on the cellular and biochemical level, but is obviously not seen macroscopically on the personality and character level. We do after all have "maintained" life positions. In character, in personality, people change reluctantly, resistantly, slowly, and all too often not at all. What is also true is that this inertia in no way means they have any less capacity to change, provided their experiential pairing is significantly "strange" (unfamiliar). That is the key. If we stay in our *I* posture, we will probably never change. If we stay in our *me* posture, we will probably never change. In the first case, we never seem to be sufficiently aware of what is going on inside ourselves, because we are so attentive to our environment. In the latter case, we never seem to be sufficiently aware of what is going on in *others,* because we are so involved with our own personal world. Either way, we have made ourselves unavailable to our capacity to change. We have been captured by system, and will return to the "security" of our maintained position, our established routine, our preset response.

The complicating sadness is that in most relationships the *I* people tend to seek out *others* who allow them to ignore their inner experience, and the *me* people tend to seek out *others* who allow them to remain unaware of what is going on in the world around them, especially the other people in the world around them. That predilection of like-to-like is why people so seldom change. Our personal blindnesses are constantly being reinforced. For friends, we pick those who maintain the blindness that comes with familiarity. As opposed to this, for lovers we correctly choose our "other eyes," but begin immediately to deny them, fight them, and reject them. In doing so, we fight, deny, and reject *ourselves.* We experientially pair, but do not proceed to grow naturally; we are too close, too captured.

The importance of intimacy is that it provides us with experience in our pairing that not only allows us, but usually demands and compels us, to change. Intimacy enables us to bring our *I* and *me* together in a way that brings us to *self*. We become reconnected to the inside and the outside simultaneously. We are back, for however short a time, "living in the world in good faith." This kind of experiential pairing does change people, both people. If it occurs in a whole family, and not simply a dyad, it can change even more people. If it occurred in a neighborhood, a school, a factory, an ethnic group, a town, a political party, a country, it could be awesomely powerful. It might even conceivably occur in a whole society. It is what energizes change and makes more honest, fulfilling relationships possible. Without it, we stay the same, and sameness alone, however stabilizing, inevitably ends in death.

Nature, the beautiful ordering of chaos that connects all living things, has certain built-in assurances against total familiarity. Not insurances, but assurances that growth and life have at least as much change as sameness and death. The struggle of nature is between life and death, order and chaos, growth and stability, pain and comfort, heat and cold, motion and stillness, newness and oldness, sound and silence; it is the difference between a swirling, indescribable pulsating galaxy and a black hole. These are struggles, not choices; pairs, not opposites. Parts of the all, since both sides of each pair are always and inevitably part of a cyclic pattern. What is important is that life always has at least as much power and persuasion as death. No more, but no less. Life is insurgent in some very remarkable if perverse ways. We create smog at a time when we can go to the moon to escape it. As overpopulation begins to exhaust us, we bring forth new, effective contraceptives. Agronomy may be able to catch starvation. Modern medicine is closing in on our culturally driven cancers and viruses. There is a tandem between life and death, the cyclic pattern of nature. A pattern that is clearly of the *self* world. We still participate in this cycle, even though it often seems we are going at it backward. If we do not blow ourselves up, earth may survive for us. It will survive for itself anyway. Life is powerful; not so powerful that we can passively rely on it and abuse it, as if we were outside, but powerful enough to assure those who are part of life—provided they do not confuse assurance with insurance. Nature is evenhanded. Life contains death within it. Nature is about growing and changing.

Stephen Crane, "War Is Kind":

> A man said to the universe:
> "Sir, I exist!"
> "However," replied the universe,
> "The fact has not created in me
> A sense of obligation."

Nature is mainly the texture of living. What does that mean when we are talking about pairing and intimate relationship? It means that nature, life in nature, will in wise and strange ways do everything it can to force us, or at least give us the opportunity, to grow and change. It will not guarantee that growth or change, or ensure that its outcome will be "good" (secure), but it will give us the opportunity. In no other way can evolution be understood. Evolution does not force us to change, grow, or become better and more effective organisms; it simply facilitates the possibilities of this happening. It neither forecloses change nor ensures it, individually. It simply provides us with both the ingredients and the context within which change might happen. Evolution is committed to growth, not change per se. To say so may sound teleological, in that it implies a more goal-oriented process to nature, but we believe that nature simply makes organisms better without in the least ensuring that any change will be "best" or even "for the best." It sets the context so that at least we have the opportunity of growth. "Better" means growth in nature; it is our human "problem" that we think "better" means "more secure." We could say that nature, like God, or as God, gives us the gift of choice, by providing the ingredients of choice. We *can* change, but we may or may not do so. If, as previously mentioned, part of the impetus for the development of the human brain was interpersonal relationship, then our position is not teleological at all, but biological.

What has all this got to do with relationship and intimacy? We assume that evolution does not stop at the generation of species. We imagine that it continues to be a powerful force in the unfolding and upgrading of our consciousness, our culture, and, most important, in the further genesis of our capacity for relatedness, relationship, and connectivity. We assume that evolution is as operative in the permutations of conditions that make intimacy more or less likely as it is in the proliferation of new viruses and the organisms that might one day contain them, even those that are most destructive. We are not Pollyannas or Panglosses about evolution; all may not be for the best in this perhaps not best of all possible worlds. Evolution has no more "investment" in constructive outcome than in destructive outcome. Those are specifically human "ways of seeing." Nature is invested in providing the ingredients and context for the process of change to happen. This assumption reflects our deep and sustaining belief that although nature offers no solace, comfort, or guarantee, it is fair. It knows life and death are part of the same process. It provides growth; it does not define it.

In terms of human beings, the crucial ingredient that nature seems to have provided for us is our insistent, driven, tropic need to complete our being, to search for strangeness. The context it provides for this opportunity is the intimate experience. The expression of this opportunity for growth in intimate experience is experiential pairing.

Our impulse toward pairing is not really so different from the light tropisms of plants in the context of photosynthesis, or the difficult transition of the caterpillar to the butterfly. There are millions of metaphors for evolving change and growth in nature, except that they are not metaphors. They are examples of the process: for example, you could say that the caterpillar is existentially on a par with the butterfly; somehow, however, one has the feeling that even when a butterfly is a caterpillar, it is a caterpillar waiting to be a butterfly. In this sense, all human beings have an existential equivalence. It is equally true that we are all humans waiting to be more successfully human.

Pairing with Our Shadows

It has often occurred to both of us as therapists, when sitting with a couple (at least with most couples who are struggling to find a close and intimate relationship), that if we could magically fuse and merge their personalities and characters, the composite would be a nearly complete human being. Members of such couples seem to seek a relationship with another who has those traits and capacitites that they themselves lack. Using Jungian concepts, we all seem to seek out our "shadows." The shadow part of our person is the part that we do not consciously know, the part we desire but are afraid of, the part we need to integrate within ourselves. Too often we see this part as alien, and keep it alien, out of a plethora of anxieties that we know little or nothing about. Nonetheless, we are attracted to the *other* who has these very traits, and the fact that the source of the attraction is not conscious makes it all the more compelling. We are close, pleased, and gratified with those who are like us, but seldom pair with them. Our "puppy love" pairing (infatuation) is based on our own projected fantasies. As we grow to real love, we begin to have encounters with *others,* many of whom initially irritate us. But these are the people with whom we go on to develop enduring and committed relationships. This is the experiential pairing of humans. These are the persons to whom we are attracted, with whom we get permanently involved. And then we struggle with and against them for decades, aggravated by and confronting the very traits that unconsciously attracted us to them in the first place. We forgo in our relating what Freud admonished: "Being entirely honest with oneself is a good exercise."

We tend to pair with people who are essentially different from ourselves, and to have brief affairs with people who are essentially like ourselves. The pattern of such pairing seems universal and shows few exceptions. The exceptions do not seem to last. Some few that do are purposefully childless marriages. Others are the "companionships" of like-minded friends. Understanding experiential pairing involves seeing that humans are basically motivated in a primitive way to complete themselves, driven unconsciously to become more fully human and so to seek a relationship that will force them to deal experientially with those human qualities and experiences that are outside their consciousness. They unconsciously pair themselves experientially with *others* who will force them to complete their *selves.* Judging by the current 50 percent mortality rate of marriages, experiential pairing does not always, or even more often than not, succeed. As we are more captured by closeness, there is less and less intimate experience in which this growth toward *selfhood* can occur. With the diminishment of *selfhood,* the persistent drive to find it leads to further "looking elsewhere." The lack of *self*-responsibility, the lack of understanding that we can unilaterally be a *self* and change our relationship, leads to these "searches." Experiential pairing is a difficult taskmaster; a *working* relationship takes a great deal of *work.*

There does seem to be an insistent drive, a part of nature, that leads most persons, even when they have failed in such a relationship, to seek out another that is essentially like it, despite superficial differences. Some few others in a second or third marriage instead find a friend, and settle for a companionable relationship. They settle for the stability of closeness along with its attendant comforts. In our experience as therapists, people who so settle give up the possibility of intimacy, and thus of growth and change.

10

Personal Relativity . . . Personality and Relatedness

> The more "other" they become in conjunction,
> the more they find themselves as "self."
>
> —TEILHARD DE CHARDIN

How does Donna come to marry four times, much less marry four alcoholics? We have looked at the drive to pair experientially and some of the dynamics behind it. Now let us look at its form and its effects. Experiential pairing is not simply a psychological construct, a metaphor to understand nature. It is an aspect of nature that pushes our lives in particular directions. These directions do not take away free will, but instead provide a framework within which our choosing occurs.

There is currently debate as to just how much of human behavior is "biologically or genetically" determined, as opposed to "culturally" determined. In *Promethean Fire,* Charles Lumsden and Edward Wilson write:

> All of our behavior is indeed predestined to the degree that we have deeply ingrained goals and principles that organize our daily lives. The free choices made are for the most part thoughts and actions put to the service of these internal guides. Some scholars believe that goals and principles are acquired almost wholly from the surrounding culture, with no genetic biasing. But even if this were true, the individuals would still be determined by forces external to themselves. In this case they would be programed by their culture. Cultural determinism can be as much of a straightjacket as genetic determinism.

We feel that this debate is a pointless argument. The concept of man in nature, connected as a *self, is* our free will. It contains all of what we are, genes, culture, and *spiritus*. Our choosing can exist only in such a context; it is the context in which we exist.

How did you come to be married to your husband or wife? What made you pick the person with whom you are living? How did you come to select Tony or Charlotte as a best friend? Obviously, you met them somewhere, at some particular time, in some particular mood, while feeling some need inside you, and the relationship slowly developed. But why? There are thousands of other human beings out there with whom you might easily have developed a relationship. Why this particular person? Your moods and feelings vary from day to day, month to month, year to year. Why does this particular connection occur? Perhaps the choice is far more limited than we think. It is most likely that, given the thousand possible relationships, *and* given your unconscious needs, only two or three choices were really likely. Despite your varying moods, emotional states, and life stages, there is some individual ongoing process at work that guides your selection.

Tony has come to therapy once a week for four months. He is thirty-two, has never married, but feels very strongly that it is time he did. This urgency seems to be coming from inside him, not from his parents, friends, or peers. The problem that he presents to us is that he does not know which of the two women whom he has been dating for the past three years he should marry. Clearly, this dilemma troubles him, but just as clearly, it is a source of pride. It becomes clear to us as therapists that Tony is not likely to marry either of these women. Neither is a completion of him. They are more like him than different from him. Tony is not ready to hear this, but he is avoiding his growth. He has dated both to avoid having to confront his shadow: the part of him he needs to know but will not acknowledge. On some level he *knows* that to choose either would be to shortchange himself. If he were willing to settle for a companion in life he easily could, and would have already done so. Tony's choices are being narrowed by his own internal drive to find the other part of himself and his concurrent fear of doing exactly that. He comes into therapy to resolve this dilemma. Both parts of him are in the room with the therapist—the part that wants the ease and comfort of being close to someone much like himself, and the more nagging part that wants to be different and grow. He may well marry one of the companionable women, but it is unlikely—not while he has a healthy discontent pushing him to grow, and a vague but powerful awareness that to marry either of them would stultify his own evolution.

Relationships, once they are formed, change constantly, provided there is a gradient of creative difference. It is as we have discussed earlier: sameness in excess assures psychic stagnation and the unnatural, comfortable calm of no creative turmoil, whereas our differences can lead to creative change. You are naturally varied in mood and feeling all the time. The varied combinations of the particular you at one moment experiencing the particular *other* as he or she might be at any given moment are infinite. This is our nature. People are more alike than they are different, but the differences provide the zest, the flavor, and the interest in relationship. The differences certainly energize the relationship and are the substrate of growth. The differences between you and the other are what make your relationship unique. They power the myriad changes that emerge in your aliveness as you are at a different place from moment to moment.

You will also be different with friends, lovers, siblings, spouses, and strangers, because each of them has *his* or *her* own special set of moods, attitudes, and ways of seeing and being at any given moment. Relationships are not so preset and predictable as some of our professional colleagues would have us believe. With each change in you *or* the *other,* relationship will be different in some way. Different but natural. Personality is relational and depends on your experience of the other. How you will be with given individuals is dependent on how they are, and in particular on how they are with you at any given moment.

It may seem that if this is so, life will be very confusing and chaotic, even in our one-to-one relationships. Our primary relationships might shift and change so capriciously that we could not function meaningfully and steadfastly and no closeness would be possible. But, obviously, this is not what happens. Why? First and most important, people are much more alike than different. We all share in cultural personalities (our common experience of the culture), status personalities (our common experience in our own particular part of the culture), and social personalities (our common experience in what we have been taught). Thus, strangeness in experience is not our "maintained" position. It is vitally energizing but intermittent, and is interspersed in our natural stability only enough to assure life and continual change. The similarities provide a basis for relating, and enough consistency to make the differences meaningful but not overwhelming. Moreover, there are reassuring recurrent patterns in life, in seasons, weather, trees, dogs, flowers, rocks, and, of course, in human beings. Our brain naturally sees patterns and in many ways *functions* through the use of them. As part of the universal fabric, we have the same constancy as do rocks and redwoods. The constancy is in continual motion on the lower levels (trees, like the cells in our bodies, change every day) but present themselves as patterns to our ordinary perspectives. Our brains recognize and use these patterns, which may indeed be resonances of the same patterns in the brain itself. We can enjoy and thrive on our chaotic, surging differences while resting in the certainty of the ongoing stability of our patterned similarities.

Moreover, predictable and recurrent patterns obviously occur in relationships even in the tension of experiential pairing. However much strangeness and creative chaos the intimate experience brings to the close relationship, the closeness is almost always sufficient to contain the new and energizing experiences. We cannot be just anybody or anything, psychic chameleons with radically shifting personae; but through the intimate experience, we can be all of the *self* we naturally are. In the somewhat awesome words of Albert Einstein: "There are moments when one feels free from one's own identification with human limitations and inadequacies. At such moments one imagines that one stands on some spot of a small planet, gazing in amazement at the cold yet profoundly moving beauty of the eternal, the unfathomable: life and death flow into one, and there is neither evolution nor destiny; only Being." In intimacy, the person we are is the being we can be.

Experiential pairing can, in fact, be described in terms of some of its more common patterns of relationship. The interfaces of relational patterns, though subjectively unique, fall into easily recognizable categories. Most of the time we become consciously aware of these categories because the pair we are observing seems an exaggerated caricature of a common pattern. When people say, "Now there's a couple! David and Patty!" they are most likely describing one of these patterns made plain. Nonetheless, even when not as obvious or blatant, some form of paired patterning is there in all close relationships. It operates out of our unconscious.

Feelers and Behavers

Rachel and Barry are in their thirties. They have been married for seventeen years, have three children, and are functional, "normal" people. She is a successful lawyer. He is a successful accountant. They exist as a middle-class family without disturbing their neighborhood, colleagues, friends, or in-laws. But Rachel and Barry themselves have been engaging in a chronic, low-grade warfare for all these years. She wants the house clean and structured; he wants it left casually cluttered. She has a budget, which he ignores not with hostility, but with disregard. She worries about the house, the cars, and the kids' schooling. He lets tasks build up to the point where they have to be done. She wants him to "grow up." He wants her to be more romantic.

Sometimes Rachel and Barry nevertheless really enjoy each other. They go to the mountains with two other couples and in some quiet moments rediscover why they married. They probably would not still be together were it not for these few moments. But they continually return to their basic stances in life: she to her responsible concern with the real and practical, and he to his fanciful and playful concern with feeling. They, as you and I, are easily trapped in their closeness and familiarity, their need for security. They defend their individual forts even when they are tired and weary of trying, even when they do not really want to, and even when they know what they are doing is futile and crazy. Over the years, they have come to know their lines (the judgments and prejudgments) like actors in a too-long-running play; they can play their roles without really thinking, without really being there.

The pattern that Rachel and Barry live is the most common of all experiential pairs; the most common way in which people relate to each other. Their pairing is one of *feelers* and *behavers*. Other descriptive words could be used, but the terms *feelers* and *behavers* are both succinct and down to earth. Most people easily recognize someone who is "into feelings" and, conversely, someone who is "into behaving." When a child is hurt playing, one parent automatically asks, "Where does it hurt?" and the other asks, "What happened?" The first is a feeler. The second is a behaver. We take this pattern as the basic type of experiential pairing simply because it is far and away the most common. There are many other pairings, and even basic feelers and behavers also can and do pair in other ways. Patterns can be described, but nature is ceaselessly inventive. Reciprocity guarantees unending surprises.

Feelers

Who are the feelers? In Western cultural mythology, women are seen as more "feeling" than men. Countless couples such as Rachel and Barry belie that culturally engendered stereotype. In most of Western culture, women have more *permission* to be feeling; this does not make them more *naturally* feeling. As we see in our schools, males are socialized and praised for the aggressive, "unfeeling" position and females for "deferring" and being "sensitive." Feelers, male or female, relate primarily to their relatedness with the *other*. They are centrally concerned with *their* experience of the *other* when in relationship. They live in their inner world, where their basic values lie. This inner experience is the most important, the central part of the relationship to them. What happens inside each person is to them more important than what happens between the two in the "real" outside world.

According to her lover, Meryl is "floating through life." This means that at twenty-eight, she has gotten no more "real" than she was at eighteen or even eight. Of course, what is "real" is very different to the two of them. Meryl perceives herself as existing in a most real world; as a feeler, her hurts, joys, and flowing sense of life are exactly what "reality" is to her. She has difficulty understanding how anyone could not know this. There is some sense of playfulness in Meryl about her lover's "confusion," but there is also a distance and separation that she regrets. It is the latter that she talks about in therapy. As a fashion designer, she can put colors together as meaningful wholes, but in her relational life she feels separated.

Sherry is thirty-one. She comes to therapy basically because "My husband sent me. He thinks I'm crazy, or at least driving him crazy." She says this with a strange mixture of sadness and a slight smile. Her sadness is with the discordance between them because he does not understand. Her smile is her awareness of his complicity in his being driven crazy by her and his resultant connection to her because of that complicity. "He gets very upset when I say I want him to talk to me. He says he does want to talk to me, but he really doesn't. He got really upset with my asking him to leave work and meet me at the hospital when Kim cut her knee. It wasn't much of a cut, but I thought he ought to be there. It was the first time she had ever been to the hospital. He's usually not much fun. I don't want you to misunderstand, he is a good person and loves me and the kids."

Feelers, like Barry, Meryl, and Sherry live in very wide and disconnected personal spaces, so wide and disconnected that there are not many connections among external things in that "world out there." What happens inside feelers has little to do with what happens outside them. Were they having an affair, what they felt about their lover would have nothing to do with what they felt about their spouse. They disconnect the inner reality in which they live from the outside world of *others.* The feelers stay comfortable by refusing to see connections. They dissociate.

Danny is thirty-five and has been "brought to therapy" by his wife, Bev. She thinks that "thirty-five is time someone grew up." She says, "Danny roams and wanders through life. He'll just go out and buy a new car for me as a surprise, without even thinking about our budget. It's not even that we can't afford it; I mean he has a good job, but that's just not how adults act. He's so impulsive. He'll spend hours playing hide-and-seek with the kids, and the yard work never gets done." Danny nods his head in agreement. He has no defense, at least not yet. He does not really see these things as "a problem."

Perry has been in a primary relationship for seven years. In his absent-mindedness and impracticality, he might strike an outsider as comical or humorous, although that is not his intent, and surely not how his life partner sees him. His "forgetting" and putting the shampoo in the refrigerator rather than the bath cabinet eventually provokes anger, not laughter. Over time, his "not being able to find anything" becomes the source of irritation, not smiles. Perry will tell us, "I don't think I've done anything wrong, but somehow I end up feeling bad, as if I had. At work people don't think I'm a total spastic, but it feels that way at home."

Feelers are often dominated by shame, embarrassment, anxiety, and self-consciousness: the metafeelings that are intrapersonal, inside themselves. They deal with stress by displacement, or by sublimation. When these strategies fail, they move to anxieties, phobias, "acting out," and physical illness. They are often naïve about the world outside them, mostly because they have little real interest in it. Consequently, they can easily be startled and surprised by things from the outside. That the bank might actually close their account for being overdrawn upsets them—doesn't the bank know they are honest? They talk about and are upset over external things, but in fact are not really looking for an answer about real problems outside themselves. They are concerned with the answer from within: how the problem affects them, not how it affects others. Behavers label their attitude childishness, and see it manifested in the feeler's acting out (if you are angry at something, break a dish), making spur-of-the-moment and sometimes foolish decisions (buying a cute puppy that you have no place to keep), being impulsive about getting into and out of relationships, acting bizarre, and getting themselves into trouble, when, as the behavers put it, "They could or should have known better." Feelers often move into the world of *others* at extremes, in ways that suggest voyeurism or exhibitionism. They say, "Let's do it!" They deal in emoting, dramatizing, and "letting go." The inner world is most prominent. It is the pivot around which they organize their persons.

Behavers

Caroline and Walter have a twenty-six-year marriage. Walter stays uptight most of the time. He blames this on Caroline. He tells the therapist, "There we are in bed, it's eleven-thirty, I'm tired, just about to go to sleep, and she says, 'Well, maybe we ought to just get a divorce.' Hell, you can't just pretend you didn't hear, so I sit up and ask her what *that's* all about. She says, 'You didn't want to go for a walk this evening.' Now, Doc, does that make any sense? How can you get any sleep with that kind of thing? It was six hours earlier that she asked me to go for a walk, and I said I had to do the bills. That was it . . . then bam!"

Behavers, in contrast to feelers, are most concerned about the outer world. They live in the world of behavior, responsibility, and interaction. Their values reside therein. Walter does not see Caroline as "feeling." He sees her *behavior,* and judges it as irresponsible, irrational, and therefore impossible to understand; he translates this as "her being crazy." Behavers are concerned with closeness and stability. Experience in the relationship is secondary to these qualities. For behavers, everything is tied together; each item is in a neat compartment and all the compartments are contiguous. They perceive the outside world this way as well. Everything is related, everyone knows about everyone, everyone is watched and judged, all too often negatively. They feel this not in a paranoid individual sense, but as the way all of life really is. Their metafeelings are those connected to the outside: guilt and hostility.

Lamont dislikes coming to therapy. He thinks it is a waste of time. He thinks that if Merilee would grow up, there would be no problems between them. He resents her *forcing* him to come in to talk about feelings. He basically sees these feelings as her trying to get her way, to control him, or to get him to be or do what she wants. He sees her effort as doubly ridiculous since *he* "is the stable one." He is the one who does not complain, takes care of business, and hardly ever "gets upset." He thinks her parents spoiled her, that they did not make her grow up. Lamont is not much fun in therapy, for Merilee or the therapist. He is always picking at *others* and trying to catch them in mistakes. He has a need to correct the *other*. Sadly, none of this seems to bring Lamont any joy. He is an exaggerated behaver.

Behavers often project negative feelings onto others. Therefore, expecting the worst from the outside, they are seldom surprised, seldom childlike. What startles them is if they *are* accepted, *are* loved, if things *do* go well. Behavers try to deal with their stress by denial, withdrawal, or rationalization. When these fail, they tend to get depressed or develop physical illnesses; that is, they somatize. Others often experience them as inhibiting, controlling, or oppressive.

As you would expect from our earlier discussion about "already knowing," feelers and behavers speak very different languages. This language difference significantly reduces the likelihood of their being intimate. Behavers speak in blacks and whites. Feelers speak in grays. In our offices we listen to unending noncommunication between the two, as if a German and a Chinese were both conversing in their own languages, each insisting that the other either does, or at least should, understand what they are saying. The language of behavers is literal and certain. They mean what they say, and listen to others literally. What has been said previously is most important; the *other* is held to it. Nonverbal overtones are not validated. You cannot tease behavers: You meant what you said even if you thought you were teasing. There is no room for anything other than what was actually uttered.

In their language, feelers are not absolutely certain of anything, are metaphorical, and are hyperbolic. They seldom mean exactly what they say, and do not expect others to take them literally. Literal discussions confuse them. If they say, "I have never loved you," they are confused when you point out to them that they have often enjoyed your love and loved you back.

Bart is a behaver. If he says he hates you and never wants to see you again, he is apt to mean it in some serious way. He may well act on his statement, and expects you to hear it that way. His words have meaning as active intent, not just as a description of his internal state. Sue is a feeler. If she says, "I never want to see you again," she means that that is how she feels at the moment. There is no future intent, no sense of obligation to the words. Problems arise because when Sue hears Bart, she assumes he is speaking only for the moment, whether he knows it or not, just as she speaks. Conversely, when he hears her, he interprets her statement as intent and decision. He will do so no matter how many times she tells him that it was only what she felt at the moment. She is startled that he thought she meant it forever. They both listen to the other as if they were themselves speaking.

This kind of miscommunicating makes touching unlikely. Most often, the talking of such couples ranges from insidious negation of each other to overt conflict. You can see clearly here the underpinnings of the mutual accusing we described earlier. Unhealthy closeness, marked by judgmentalism, prejudgmentalism, and the lack of reciprocity, has captured the couple, and language is not translating their positions, but isolating them.

Having Bart and Sue in the office can be an instructive experience for therapists. The two can describe the same conversation, interaction, or happening, and their versions will have nothing in common. They disagree about the words each spoke, what was meant, why they meant it, what they should have meant, and so on, until the therapist must either question their sanity, question his or her own sanity, or realize that he or she is experiencing an experiential process between a dyad, and that that process is the *only* real truth present. The facts each defends are irrelevant.

Obviously, shouting across an experiential language barrier is not an efficient or functional way to communicate. All too often it is also very painful to both partners. Bart listens much better than he talks. He can hear many connections, but continues to believe he speaks monolithically. Sue talks better than she listens. She is poetic but careless. He is careful and prosaic. He is concerned with the sequence of things, the time, the place. She is concerned with none of these. Instead, the mood, the manner, the ambience, and the symbols make all the difference to her. Her memory is related to her current inner experience. His memory is related to the past, the sequence of events that brought things to their current state, and to the future, to where that sequence will lead. He remembers; she forgets. The words are important to him; the tone of the words are important to her. If he insists on living only in a behavioral world, and she only in a feeling world, their relationship will stay confused, like that of Georges and Albin in the film *La Cage aux Folles*. They will have to move deeper into closeness to maintain the relationship, to bring familiarity and security out of the confusion, to make familiar their differences, if nothing else. What they will lose in so doing, of course, is the very intimacy they have to experience in order to change, in order to learn a new and mutual language; the intimacy they need in order to learn even to accept each other, much less see each other as separate, different, but equally valid persons (as Georges and Albin fundamentally did).

The differences between behavers and feelers are not open to judgment. Neither is better or worse, right or wrong. Each is just a way of being. While in our culture more women tend to be feelers and more men behavers, gender does not determine personality and character. Biological gender is obviously *part* of our nature, but it neither confines nor defines. One of the highest prices of our current deficit of intimate experience is the loss of sharing between "masculinity" and "femininity," within ourselves and among us as persons, whether men with men, women with women, or men with women. This intimate sharing is the only life experience that breaks down such gender typing. In *The Hero with a Thousand Faces,* Joseph Campbell says, "To a man not led astray from himself by sentiments stemming from the surface of what he sees, but courageously responding to the dynamics of his own nature—to a man who is, as Nietzsche phrases it, 'a wheel rolling of itself'—difficulties melt and the unpredictable highway opens as he goes." We lose freedom in being defined by our "surfaces"—the freedom to be all that we might be.

Often, the dissimilarity between the feeler-behaver couple is most blatant in their sexual relationship. Therapists hear loud and strident complaints about their sexual differences. Usually the pair is actually complaining not of sexual differences, but of *differences in character.* Their descriptions of their own and their lover's or spouse's roles in the relationship are usually very accurate. Intuitively they have the insight really to see the *other* as they are. What they do *not* see is themselves, or the experiential nature of their relationship. Their simplistic solution to a given problem is for the *other* to change in order to be like them; they have no insight into what a relational catastrophe that would be.

Marvin is a feeler. He comes into the office and talks about his marriage. In speaking of his wife he says, "I don't understand her. I love to play. She never plays. It's always work. I always have to initiate our sex. She just responds. She is fine as long as I start things. I don't think it's fair that I should always have to. I want her very much to make the first move sometimes." Notice the "always," the hyperbole so typical of the feelers. Marvin goes on, "I think she would rather be doing her projects or cleaning the house. No, that's not fair, she enjoys sex. She just doesn't ever play with me, sexually or any other way." Marvin's wife is a behaver. She is tactile and a hugger, but less sexual, less romantic, and less pleasure-oriented. Such differences can be very painful and destructive of relationship; without intimacy, they can be devastating. Fed by intimate experiences, they can be the source of real growth.

The "sexual" differences that Marvin and his wife struggle with simply reflect a multitude of other consonant differences that in turn reflect the basic feeler-behaver pattern. Feelers play more, are more spontaneous, and are more initiating of new behaviors. Behavers show less spontaneity, work more, take fewer risks, and are more responsible in their relationships. They are more likely to resort to familiar behaviors, and are more managerial than creative. Feelers are oriented to the new, the unusual, and the unfamiliar. They are oriented to process and experience. Behavers are oriented to the old, the familiar, and the past or the future. They are oriented to goals and the relationship.

These are ways of being; they are stances and positions, not psychological definitions or personal judgments. They represent patterns in nature, and as Gregory Bateson says in *Mind and Nature,* "it is patterns which connect." What follows is an illustrative list of some of these differences, paired experientially. The traits are not descriptions of different personalities, but of relational experiences. Experiential pairing, in our usage, is always a relational experience, not the spatial proximity of two distinct personalities. A person who demonstrated characteristics of only one or the other would be so imbalanced as to constitute a personality or character disorder. Most of us, in our "normal" personalities, are off-center in one direction or the other but capable of manifesting ourselves within a certain range of the patterns.

Feelers	*Behavers*
Conceptual	Perceptual
See things in wholes	See things in additive parts
Overly concerned with own inner life	Overly concerned with other and external life
Experience and forget	Watch and record
Touch and participate	Look and listen
Process-oriented	Goal-oriented
Being somewhere	Going somewhere
Creative	Productive
Inventor	Implementor
Inventive	Pragmatic
Idealistic	Practical
Identify with parent of opposite sex	Identify with parent of same sex
Know what they want	Know what to do
Unorganized	Systemic
Space conscious	Time conscious
Heart sense	Head sense

There are further nuances of this particular experiential pairing that are almost impossible to summarize. Nonetheless, they are felt deeply in each such pair. For example, feelers know themselves to be lovable, but seem deeply to question their lovingness—whether their love (indeed, all their feeling) is authentic, lasting, deep, and real. Behavers know they are loving, that their love is lasting, deep, responsible, and real, but appear to painfully doubt their lovability. More specifically, they never seem to be sure that *others* really enjoy them as people.

Behavers are as good as their word. If they say they will, they will. They are compelled to do so, to move with the *other,* and to follow the rules. Feelers may or may not follow through on their stated intent. Being impulsive, they tend to respond to the admixture of their own and the *other's* feelings, rather than any *pro forma* response to expectations, either personal or social. The behaver sees anger as destructive, although he or she is generally angrier underneath than the feeler. To the feeler, anger is just another emotion.

These differences are fundamental in terms of how each *exists* in the world: the risking and creative feeler, the stabilizing and conservative behaver. Both are equally important and valuable, because creativity without stability is chaos, and stability without creativity is moribund.

This typology, or way of looking at patterns in relationship, is definitely an oversimplification. Trying to define persons by words is always an oversimplification, much as a map is an oversimplification of the land it represents. Again, Bateson in *Mind and Nature:* "For that which is not conscious, the language provides no means of expression." However, like a map, a typology can be very useful in understanding patterns and finding your way. In some respects, feelers sound like hysterics and behavers like compulsives, but they are not. There is a difference between a personality and a defense system. The pair do probably represent to some extent right-brain/left-brain predominances. Presumably feelers are predominantly right-brained, and behavers are predominantly left-brained. Although closer to reality, this categorization is still an oversimplification. The brain is just not that absolute. Humans are just not that simple. Feeler-behaver stances are not completely stable positions; each of us possesses all of these qualities and will manifest varying combinations of "feeling" and "behaving" at any given time.

Why do most pairings take this particular pattern? Why should pairing reveal any common pattern other than the obvious eternal classifications that we can see, like money, status, availability, beauty, or power? We believe that evolution is not random. It moves one thing toward something more complete, more whole. Life seeks to complete itself. The process is always one of becoming. The failures in evolution are not just nonsurvivors. The failures are the things that did not move on toward what they could more fully be. The fundamental point we are trying to make about experiential pairing is that couples combine in relationship in order to complete themselves. It is not a random process, or a process controlled by overt, outward qualities like those mentioned above—status, power, wealth. We select with astonishing precision that other person who can teach us what we need to know to be a more whole human being. We pair with the differences we need in order to complete ourselves. This pattern is the basis of experiential pairing. It is a paramount determinant of what happens in our primary relationships. It is the crucial reason why reestablishing a balance so that we may regularly experience the *intimate self* is so necessary.

The feeler-behaver pattern is the most common because it is the most direct representation of the brain's own internal pairing of left and right lobes; that is, it is a basic growth modality pairing whereby we each seek to become more of what a human being can be. It is a primitive-level pairing, like male-female, day-night, winter-summer, intimacy-closeness. The feeler-behaver pairing is common because most humans are by and large healthy, and thus participate in the mainstream of the evolutionary process. We can look at some of the other pairings, and see other patterns. These sometimes occur in basically healthy humans, but often they are the refuge of the more psychologically impaired.

Like-to-Like versus Shadow Pairing

We may pair with someone different from ourselves, but we almost always immediately feel close to those who are like us. We may even seek out alikes for relief from the arduous and often painful task of completing ourselves. With alikes we can be quiet and satisfied. Here we see two of the other occasional pairings: a feeler pairs with a feeler or a behaver pairs with a behaver. They chose quiet over growth. They have made a life decision, though unconsciously, that is the major determinant of how they will then exist. These couples are often seen by outsiders as being like a brother and sister, a business partnership, or two old friends.

Like-to-like couples are a small minority; most primary pairings are between a feeler and a behaver, who are searching for in each other what they do not find in themselves. Not that it is not there—they just cannot find it; it is lost to them. They "marry" their shadow and immediately start to complain about the very differences that made them choose them. In therapy we see many such couples, who have made their conflict about their differences the essence of the relationship itself.

Most of us, however, spend our relational lives struggling with our differences without making them the center of our daily living.

Pairing happens unconsciously. Like evolution, it is a powerful and enduring force. If pairing were simply a conscious, pragmatic decision, many people would simply not pair; if they did, their rational-social commitment would be too feeble to endure more than the honeymoon. People would pick friends to pair with, not shadows. But pairing is not a rational decision, and the commitment is more than social. We continue to seek the different, the unknown parts of ourselves. Nature protects itself from the death that comes with sameness. We are driven by a revitalizing need to seek the undeveloped part of our own being.

Orthodox thinking in psychiatry and psychology suggests that differences in relationship are basically characterological: a hysterical personality is attracted to a compulsive personality. People are attracted to their opposites, hence most marriages and relationships. We do not think pairing is that simple or empty of purpose.

For example, people do not usually have affairs with their opposites. Instead, they pick an alike, someone to provide affirmation and comfort, not challenge. It is as if they are having an affair with themselves. But they seldom form a permanent pairing with this person. It is a different experience and meets different needs. The involved person will tell you that the affair sustains and maintains his or her being. That may be, but it does not change it. Change depends on the confrontation of difference, which is not assured or automatic, but is *possible* in experiential pairs. Actually, more pairings fail in this way than succeed. That is, they stop growth instead of nurturing it. Our being captured by closeness has distorted the process. The lack of intimacy stifles and erodes growth. In intimacy, we grow with and into each other. We find in our experience with each other an awareness and consciousness of the parts of us we are out of touch with, parts we have never known or accepted. We can grow this way only in a balanced environment of intimacy and the healthy closeness needed to maintain the relationship.

It is only the recurrent intimate experience that can bring growth, change, energy, creativity, and stability to relationship. In accepting our shadows in the *other,* we accept *ourselves.* In accepting *ourselves,* we learn to love the *other.* This is the importance of our staying available to the experience of those differences. To shut down that experience, to get caught up with seeing differences not as experience, but as confrontive issues of right or wrong (as *I* involvements) or good or bad (*me* involvements), is to give up any opportunity of processing the deepest investment we each have in our primary relationships. As Confucius said, "By nature men are nearly alike; by practice, they get to be wide apart." When we are "wide apart" we cannot touch and intimacy is impossible.

Moreover, contrary to much of psychological theory, we feel that the part of experiential pairing that *is* characterological is not fixed. Character is to some degree relational, as we discussed earlier. Personality most certainly is relational. You interface with another as some particular you, with the *other* as some particular him or her, at some particular moment. This pairing determines much of what will be experienced in the relationship at that moment. What my personality will be at any random experiential moment is not a given. It depends on who I am with the other, how I am with the other, and who and how he or she is with me at that moment. Character is more stable, slower to change, and more deeply held than personality. It is more likely to show movement over longer periods of time. It *does,* however, change; humans are not captives of fate, be it genetic or historical.

I may be a feeler most of the time, but always with those who relate to me as behavers. In the presence of one who is even more of a feeler, I will become the behaver. My personality accommodates to the possibility of change and growth. This shift will be automatic and immediate if I am willing to risk growth, not willing to settle for quiet (or even painful) stability. It will not be conscious or willed. The pairing will seek a balance. I will automatically be part of that balancing. I will be what I need to be to keep the balance between the pairing of us, and between the *I* and *me* in myself, so that my *self* can be actualized. I will be different, as the pairing is different. That reciprocity is what makes pairing experiential. Character and personality will always be subordinate to the relational pairing. The state of being that allows us to be aware, to understand, to learn, to be in touch with this fact, is intimacy. Many people have difficulty accepting that character can be reciprocal. To us, that is a significant indication of how removed from the power of intimacy we have become.

The search for differences that we seek in the *other* explains many divorces and broken relationships. If, for example, one partner grows on her own, discovers more of herself, and finds new unknowns to seek, she will feel the need of different experiences in the *other*. This is why getting couples to grow together is so preferable in therapy to risking just one member growing. But if one has decided to grow, he or she will do so anyway, with or without the help of the therapist, and one can only hope the growth changes the *other* in ways that move them together. But change the *other* it will. Part of the work of growing is growing *into* relatedness instead of away from it.

Other Types of Pairing

We have used the "normal" pairing to explain the phenomenon of choosing our "shadows." We have looked at the pairings of alikes. These might be described as the two ground states. What are some of the other common experiential pairings in relationships? The possible variations are, of course, endless. The most growthful pairing is that of two very balanced persons. They each have a natural balance of intimacy and closeness; each has an intermingling of traits of both feeler and behaver. They process information and experiences in life equally well with both the left and right parts of their brains. They can easily exchange positions depending on what is happening. One can relate feelingly to the imaginative play of their three-year-old child, but take the main responsibility for auditing their finances. They are less bound by personal polarization than most of us. Such relationships are all too rare. They are what the healthy pairing of feeler-behaver can become if we continue intimately to share and experience our differences.

Another, usually less happy pairing that we see on occasion is that between a schizoid person (someone who is a "loner") and a very outward-directed, concrete person. The schizoid person lives essentially in his or her inner world and tends to relate symbolically to reality. The concrete person avoids his or her inner life and feelings and deals with the world almost exclusively pragmatically. He or she is above all a survivor. Not psychopathic, nor compulsive, but very practical and reality-oriented. Sometimes these pairings are growthful. More often, however, the two do not learn from each other. At best, they anchor each other in life. This is a useful function, but does not often bring either one to greater human wholeness.

The sadomasochistic pairing is another common experiential dynamic. We are referring not simply to the microcosm of sexual sadomasochism but the more general personal sadomasochistic experiential pairing. We suspect that here too the motivation is unconsciously the search for growth. The sadist and masochist are seeking to learn through experience about the other shadowy parts of themselves. They are like the alcoholic who drinks mistakenly thinking he is asserting his right to make his own choices, but does it in a way that is obviously *self*-defeating and *self*-destructive. However healthy their motivation in pairing, it assures nothing unless the implementation is equally real and healthy. And it is clear that you do not grow to feel better about yourself by beating on yourself or on someone else.

Another somewhat similar pairing is the rather odd tendency of some very bright people to pair off with a considerably less intelligent, comparatively "slow" person. In this context, "slow" is misperceived by the bright partner as synonymous with "realness" (much as in the retarded character played by Peter Sellers in the film *Being There*). The bright person, having a trait for which he or she has often received accolades, is seeking more "humanness," and pairs with a person who is not very bright, mistaking this trait for humanness. The one who is not so intelligent is looking for whatever he or she mistakenly thinks will bring acceptance and admiration. The search always fails. You cannot learn to be bright. You do not get human by being slow. Such pairs are correctly motivated to seek what they lack, but are looking in the wrong place.

Pairing to Avoid Growth

Different both from the genuinely growthful pairings and from those odd pairings that seem to be motivated by a desire to grow but are misdirected and almost always fail are those pairings that are motivated by a need to avoid any change. These are, of course, extremes. They include the pairing of the adored and the adorer. No real relationship is possible in such an experience. In fact, the impossibility seems to be exactly the commitment in such a couple. Narcissus and Echo are not real to themselves, so they cannot possibly be real with the *other*. He is totally *I* and she totally *me;* they can not be *selves,* so they cannot be intimate.

A variation on this theme is that of the cynical loner and the naive Pollyanna, where the fear of new experience is even clearer. The adored and the adorer may mimic relationship, but theirs is clearly a romanticized charade of real relationship. The loners-Pollyannas do not so much mimic as satirize real relationship. They exist in their own spaces and ways without even the external appearance of being connected. They are as caricatures acting out their separate roles, as if two actors with different scripts were performing at the same time on a single stage.

The dependent-dependent relationship is the pairing of two caretakers. Like two small children having to live in an adult world, they are protectors of each other against that harsh world. There can be no growth because the commitment is to avoid experience, to avoid risk, and this inevitably means avoiding intimacy.

The commitment to remain the same is seen frequently in the alcoholic/alcoholic-spouse pairing that we have described earlier. The intoxicated person cannot be a *self,* and by participating the partner is losing his or her *self* as well. Like the martyr-sinner pair, in which one partner is forever "bad" or wrong and the other forever "forgiving" or "giving," the alcoholic/alcoholic-spouse pair is common and effective in blocking not just intimacy, but also healthy closeness. As do all of these destructive pairings, it has a devastating effect on the children of the couple. The child's difficulty with intimacy may well be the most tragic legacy of such ungrowthful pairing.

The voyeur-exhibitionist pair can present itself either overtly or covertly. Whether it is overt, involving sexual acting out of other behaviors, or covert, and involves only one of the pair "living" life while the other watches, it stops intimacy and growth. You cannot live for someone else or have someone else do your living for you. Neither position is authentic; they are roles, and as roles allow no change. A variation on this pairing is the coach-star player couple (Professor Higgins and Eliza Doolittle), where the behaviors presented are more "wholesome" but the underlying pattern is the same. As we have discussed several times, the intimate person must be able to play: the coach does not get to play, and the "star" is no longer a real person.

The cynical loner-cynical loner pairing is less common but in its own way equally as destructive. Often these couples masquerade as two "independent" people. In reality, they are hiding from the world together and their "independence" is simply a disguise. They have little real relatedness to each other and usually know little about the other or themselves as people. The object of their pairing seems to be to accomplish just this end.

More extreme is the bitter, angry experiential pairing of two paranoid personalities—a union of defenses against what the two consider to be a hostile, threatening, and totally misunderstanding world. Growth, human or otherwise, does not occur under siege, with defenses bristling. Such pairs never join life; they battle life.

Perhaps the most destructive of all pairings is the relationship we can call addicted-addicted—the substance of the addiction or the resultant behavior makes no difference (it does not even have to be a chemical substance; it may simply be a behavior). These couples are overtly *self*-destructive and the union seems to be a mutual compact for just that. In this goal, they are eminently, and sadly, successful.

These are some of the more usual pairings. There are many others. Some are growthful, some promise growth but seldom bring it about, some are clearly motivated by a need to avoid change. In the first two cases, the pairing is either an extension or perversion of the feeler-behaver experiential pairing, which appears to be the prototype characteristic of most relationships, and to be the pairing that lends itself best to intimate experiential growth and change. Pairings in the latter case (designed to avoid change) are more severely distorted.

The feeler-behaver pair is the smallest system experience of the intimacy-closeness balance. It is the attempt, driven by nature, to balance a dyad, to prevent capture by one side or the other. Coming out of the unconscious, this drive represents the universal property of nature that strives for self-correction. In it we see our naturalness and our participation in that process. The drive toward our own evolution happens whether we are aware of it or not.

11

Personal Creation . . . Sexuality and Intimacy

Never does nature say one thing
and wisdom another.

—JUVENAL

When I *(Tom)* was still in training, which at that time was fairly traditionally psychoanalytic, I had occasion to see an uneducated, rural, elderly man. I asked him in the interview, as I had been trained to do, about his sexuality. He did not understand me, so I repeated my question. He still did not seem to comprehend what I was after. After several more attempts on my part, he finally asked me in a quiet voice if I was asking him about his nature. I had no real sense of what he meant by *nature,* but said, "Yes, is there anything wrong with your nature?" He replied with a quiet dignity and an accepting smile, "Doc, the worst I ever had was pretty good." I was certain by his manner that this statement was neither humorous nor a cliché to him. He was simply stating a truth as he knew life.

The old man had no confusion about closeness and relatedness. He was saying that his sexuality-intimacy was natural, and, as such, good for him in both senses of the word. *It was his nature.* He was not into *I* issues, taking care of the other; nor was he into *me* issues, having power or control. He *naturally* saw his nature as an integral part of his life. He experienced it as part of his being, not part of his doing. It was a component of his life that was as it naturally was. In being able to let his sexuality be that way, he was doing something that many of us have great trouble emulating.

To ask, "What is nature?" would, in an ironic way, move us further away from its essence. It is better to deal with what we *mean* by *nature* and *natural*. The words come from the Latin *nasci*, "to be born," *natus*, "born," and *natura*, "birth." They therefore describe an inborn characteristic; in other words, the way things are to begin with. It is not coincidental that *nasci* is also the etymological root of the words *naïve* and *native*. In true naïveness we are natural, childlike; and in being native, we recognize our connection to the rest of nature.

Denis Postle in *Fabric of the Universe* says: "Not only are we ignorant of the true nature of the universe, for which we might be excused; we are also ignorant of the true nature of ourselves." We would suggest that the two are the same and knowable to us only in the *intimate self*. Nature is related, always connected. It has all those qualities of "isness" that we discussed previously. It is easy, interconnected, nonintentional, nonconscious, without hidden agenda; it requires no thought to be recognized instantly. Nature is what undistorted humanness automatically sees as good, because it reflects the natural *self*. Nature has no metafeelings, only primary feelings. Although sexuality, felt as nature, connects us only one to another, its result is to open the door to connection to all else, for the direct experience of nature in any form is the ultimate integrating experience. It knows no better or worse, no judgment, only what is. Like that true "name" that wizards must know to perform magic, nature creates magic for us when we become part of it. That magic is the easy experience of *self*.

The enlightening session with the elderly man is vastly different from our experiences as therapists treating mostly middle-class people. Both of us have found that the majority of couples who present themselves in therapy with sexual problems instead generally have difficulties with their personal relationships. That is, they have problems with their closeness. A typical example: Dan is impotent, which leaves Ruby feeling rejected and frustrated. It becomes clear, after only a few interviews, that in fact Dan is furious about Ruby's need to control him. This is not a sexual problem but a personal problem, most easily, and, incidentally, most dishonestly, expressed in the sexual arena.

In contrast, what is so often initially presented by couples as a personal problem clearly emerges, after the same few interviews, as a sexual problem. Katie complains that Fred is never sensitive to her everyday feelings. He does not appear to know when she is tired, angry, hurt, lonely, or merely bored. Fred, on the other hand, feels that he is constantly being judged, prejudged, and accused: "She never gives me any feeling that I'm doing good, that I'm worthwhile." Actually, neither one is right about the other. Fred *is* sensitive to Katie's feelings; he knows immediately when she feels hurt. She, in turn, *is* constantly supporting and affirming him. His sensitivity and her supportiveness are both obvious to the therapist. So what are they doing? It soon becomes evident that Katie feels Fred is closed, unassertive, placative, tentative, unaware, and insensitive to her *erotic* feelings. Fred feels that she is sexually controlling, domineering, and totally incapable of being sexually satisfied, at least by him. What was presented to us as a problem in personal relationship and closeness turns out to be a problem in sexuality, an intimate impasse.

Seen this way, it is easier to understand why sexual problems are so difficult to deal with, often difficult simply to identify. Uncertainty about what sexuality is and is not, and our tendency to confuse sexual with personal issues, makes for problems in most of our lives. Think of your friends, your relatives, maybe even yourself.

Helen says: "Hal seems to be totally unaware of what I feel sexually. He doesn't know what to do or not do, what feels good to me or what hurts me. I know he's a nice person, and he isn't stupid, so why? Where is his head? I don't know for sure if he even thinks about it." Hal's kind of insensitivity, which we might call emotional rape, is in reality most often a personal problem. The feeling is usually anger. What Hal's anger is we cannot yet know, but Helen is angry not about sex per se but because she does not seem to exist to him in an *I-other* way. He is not close enough to her to accommodate to her. He cannot be in the shared space with her. As with many sexual complaints, the real issue is their lack of healthy closeness.

Kevin says: "I have a strong sex drive but she's not interested. She comes up and hugs me but then gets mad if I try to touch her or go any further." Kevin wants attention more than sex, and she cannot be "personally" honest enough to tell him she feels no room to be her *self*.

Denise says: "He never takes any sexual initiative. I really resent it. He never has, and I'm tired of it. It's not fair. I feel like I have to carry the whole burden." Denise wants to be wanted more than she wants. Her partner is dependent, and wants her to be responsible for whatever happens. Both are struggling with the closeness-relationship part of their lives. The problem is in their personal relationship, but is presented and consciously experienced by them as a sexual-intimacy problem.

Karen says: "He's premature. He won't wait for me. He's more interested in getting off himself. I've gotten to where I don't even bother to try." Again, the issue is really one of closeness, personal rather than sexual. He is hostile and evasive in their relationship. He cannot function in a healthy *I* way that would allow him to be in the shared space with Karen. Karen, on the other hand, has a neurotic *me*; she loses her own sexuality in her need for affirmation.

Randy says: "She's frigid. She can't climax with penetration." This ostensibly sexual problem is usually once more personal: She is so focused on the personal-closeness-relationship part of life that intimacy is seen as personally invasive. He is so insensitive as *I-other* that she experiences him as invasive.

Conversely, the presenting language can be personal, the problem sexual. The other side of this dilemma is just as common and confusing.

Lynn says: "He's always working. He never comes home. He works even on weekends. He might as well not even have a relationship. I wonder why he does. He doesn't enjoy being with me. He doesn't have fun with me or enjoy playing with me." Here Lynn is speaking of their sexuality, but presenting it as a personal problem having to do with their closeness relationship. She is not avoiding alluding to sex out of politeness or embarrassment; she is simply out of touch with her sexuality, her nature, as he must also be. She presents the problem as she feels it, as if it were a matter of personal living arrangements, the system of their living together.

Douglas says: "She spends all her time with the children. Our marriage hasn't been the same since our first child was born. It's gotten worse since then." Douglas believes that his wife feels safe only in being a mother, not in being sexual or intimate with him, not in wanting to play with him. To Douglas, she is not *natural* with him anymore. The issues are sexual, even though his enunciation of them is personal. He is out of touch with his sexuality, so he talks in personal terms.

Josh says: "She wants the house just her way. She spends all our money decorating, to make it exactly the way she wants it. You think she asks for my opinion? You think that you would recognize any of my influence if you came over to our house? No sir. I have to be careful where I sit in my own damn house. Can you believe that?" Josh's pain is real, but is it about decorating? No. He is saying that she does not accept him, or his sexuality, as he is: what he likes done or likes doing. Josh feels that he is not allowed to be himself, even in his own home. It is the nature of their intimate touching, not the closeness of furniture and wallpaper, that is hurting Josh.

Bernadette says: "He is so wishy-washy. If he buys something and it turns out to be broken, he has trouble taking it back. He's a patsy. He just won't stand up for himself. He is always being done in and taken advantage of. It really disgusts me." What is Bernadette actually saying? She obviously feels that he has no passion or conviction as a person. Translated into sexual terms, she is saying that he has no *self*-passion in his love and lovemaking. She talks of how they live, but the real problem is how they make, or, perhaps more accurately, do not make, love.

What is this strange and confusing connection between the personal-closeness and the sexual-intimacy ways of relating? Why the confusion of so many people speaking of one when in actuality the problem is in the other? We feel that this frequent distortion (that people speak sexually about personal issues and personally about sexual issues) reflects our imbalance into closeness. We are no longer clear about what we feel as *selves,* and use sexuality as a metaphor in our systems instead of experiencing it as a reality in *our* persons.

Why is it so difficult for us to put the two together? What are these powerful forces that can separate sex from relationship, make it so easy to compartmentalize them? What makes sex for some people so much easier and more exciting when it is illicit or strange? This view is reflected, for example, in Norman Mailer's remark that taking sin out of sex and making it normal and acceptable would reduce it to nothing but a feeble, occasional impulse. Studies like *The Hite Report* find that women have much more passionate responses in orgasm with cunnilingus and masturbation than with penetration. It has always been assumed that intercourse is the ultimate metaphor of connected relationship between men and women. Is it not? The *metaphor* certainly has tremendous meaning. Long ago Hippocrates said: "Male and female have the power to fuse into one solid, both because both are nourished in both and because soul is the same thing in all living creatures, although the body of each is different." Where is the *reality*?

Norma is married to a gentle and caring man, passive but "good," whom she "loves" deeply. She will tell you that she feels very close to him. However, Norma goes down the street every few months, always feeling bad about it, and beds down with a mechanic whom she does not even particularly like. One time they made love on the hood of the car he was fixing in his garage. Afterward, she asked him for a towel to wipe off some of the car's grease that he had smeared on her thighs during their encounter. Instead of providing a towel, he told her to go home and take care of herself. She walked home disheveled and humiliated; she is being used and she knows it. What makes her go back again?

Norma's husband is close but has problems with being intimate. He cannot be sexual with her. He has sex with her but cannot *be sexual* with her. These are different experiences. Although he goes through the physical motions, he is not having a sexual experience. He is caring and solicitous, he is a lot of good things, but none of these attributes are intimate, and therefore they are not sexual. He does not share his nature with her; he is not with her naturally. She experiences his accommodating *I,* not his natural *self.* The mechanic is anything but solicitous. He certainly does not care, and is not even polite about it. Why does she go to him? He is all *me*: what he wants, how he wants it, and what he enjoys. What pulls her toward him is that she can feel him enjoying her. She is looking for the *self* experience, the truly sexual. Like so many of us, unfortunately, she thinks, "Real sex must be the opposite of what I have with my partner, since what I have there is not the experience I want." When she finds out, after some time, that the mechanic's *me* is not what she is seeking either, she finally comes into therapy.

Norma is looking for a way to touch and be touched while being herself, close to another, openly and easily. She wants to be sexual, not in the security of her private fantasies, but in a real relationship. She needs to experience closeness and sexuality together. Norma is desperately searching for intimacy, the experience of being in her own space while she has the safety and comfort of a shared space. To be intimate. To be really sexual.

Gary sees his sexuality with his lover almost as a job. Not quite a chore, but very much a service. He knows he feels little joy in himself in their "sexuality." He accepts this loss of desire, somewhat sadly, as an inevitable part of a long-term "relationship." He has become less himself in a very real way, though consciously he does not really understand what has happened. The slow erosion of the relationship, as both his hurt and resentment mount, will mean that eventually he will have neither the relationship nor his sexuality. Gary overtly sacrifices intimacy for closeness. He will say, "It's worth it to me to have someone." But he does not "have someone"; he has a "sense of security" that is neither real nor sustaining of his personhood. To be sexual goes beyond having sex.

Todd comes in because his marriage is not going well. His wife is not happy with him or the marriage. He feels lost. There is no animation apparent in him until he begins talking about sex. But it is not his wife he is talking about; it is his secretary. He describes what "good head" she gives, how much fun she is, how she loves their lovemaking. When asked what kind of "head" his wife gives, he answers indignantly, "My wife doesn't do things like that. What kind of woman do you think she is?"

The sadness is that when his wife comes in to see us with him, it is apparent that she is more than willing and able to be as sexual as he appears to so passionately desire. He is simply not ready and able to accept and enjoy her sexuality. He is so afraid of mixing closeness (the personal) with intimacy (the sexual) that he lives in a sexual limbo. He cannot be both sexual and close at the same time. Perhaps his wife cannot put it into words, but she does know what is going on. Her marriage does not allow her to be herself. Will she nag, be angry, pout, have an affair herself, give up on sex, or "make him pay"? Such behavior happens more often than not. Everyone is real, whether their spouse or lover knows it or not. She *is* a person and will react to the loss of *self*. Whether she does it healthily or not is the *choice* she has.

George is an absent husband, often traveling on business, having a life of his own. Meanwhile, he "drops his wife off" at our office, in order that the therapist can "help her to become more sexual," and despite him, after some years of therapy, she does become sexual. She finds her nature, wants to experience it often, and moans in ecstasy when she does. Does this make George happy? No. Now he comes in to see us himself, depressed, anxious, and somewhat emaciated. He wants to know what is going on with his wife. He says he is less sexually potent than he used to be, that he is concerned that his wife may be seeking out other men, and he is considering hiring a detective to check up on her. George got what he wanted, or what he thought he wanted, sexually. However, personally as well as sexually, he is clearly less happy and satisfied. He should have realized that we all must be careful what we ask for; we may get it.

Pairing is experiential. We live together in an exquisitely precise balance. We rely on the other to remain pretty much the same. It is our neurotic contract. If the other changes dramatically, we had better be prepared for some significant readjustments within ourselves. It *is* a myth that it takes two to change things. George could feel sexual (out of town) while his wife was home mired in her need to stay close and personal. When she became sexual with him, he was experientially shifted into the personal. He was not prepared for what he had always thought he wanted. He could not be intimate with her when she was ready for it.

The difficulty of experiencing personal and sexual feelings together is very apparent in George's reaction. He is not unique. The problem he has is probably the most common problem in paired relationships. It most likely accounts for the singles' bars, singles' nights at the church, and similar institutions. What are people actually looking for in such places? Sex or personal relationship? Do they know the difference? It is likely that even in singles bars people are painfully looking for both sexuality and relationship, but have not the vaguest idea of how to put the two together. Their encounters never seem to work out, because of our pervasive difficulty in experiencing both closeness and intimacy at the same time.

Is then the solution to learn how to have "personal" sex? No. Whatever personal sex is, it apparently is not what couples are searching for. When two people who really care about each other are making love, and in the midst of their passion she says, "I really love you . . . Go ahead, don't wait for me . . . Am I doing it okay? . . . Take your time," what happens? All of these are affectionate personal expressions, but he loses his erection. Or he says, "Are you all right, honey? . . . If I'm hurting you, just say so . . . You're the finest woman I know . . . Are you making it?" Again, quite personal, but she dries up. Why is this?

A new couple comes in for therapy. Over the past year or so, they have felt closer and more loving than ever before in their years of relationship. Unfortunately, she has simultaneously lost almost all sexual interest in him. How can we understand this? A middle-aged man comes in who has not been sexual with his wife in over a year. When he finally gets around to talking about it, he says that he does still feel sexual. We then inquire why he cannot be sexual with his wife, to which he has no answer. He does not know. If we listen to him, he shares his pain but cannot explain it. He is not unusual; many people feel this way.

The paradox is that so often we are turned on when we are not really close to the other and are turned off when the other reminds us that we are close to them. It almost seems that sexuality and personal closeness are not compatible. Couples usually deal with this problem by simply separating the two feelings. In radical form, that was Norma's solution: She walked down the street to have sex with someone with whom she had no personal relationship. Likewise with Todd: He enjoyed his secretary while defending his wife's so-called virtue. Both Norma and Todd separated sexuality and closeness completely and acted out the separation. Gary simply sacrificed one for the other, assuming that a long-term relationship meant a loss of sexuality, erroneously believing he could make the sacrifice forever. Most couples do not actually act it out, but they do divide the feelings in relating to each other. The result is that they are not sexual, or do not enjoy being sexual, or try in a multitude of ways behaviorally to separate their sexuality from their personal relationship. Lon buys his wife costumes and wigs. Miriam fantasizes that her lover is the yardman. Gloria plays roles, a slave girl one night and a princess the next. Kerwin pretends his lover is someone different every night. Many of us prefer sex in the dark so we can have fantasies, even if we do not consciously recognize them as such. Almost all of us have better sexual experiences with our spouses or lovers in motels, hotels, or anywhere away from our homes, away from what we associate with closeness and the personal. To play, to be free, and to be our sexual, abandoned, careless selves, we will risk almost anything. Either that risk or, sadly, we try nothing at all.

There is a wonderful short story that I *(Tom)* heard years ago about a man who spent his time making love to most of the women he met. When the lovemaking was over, he would always turn his back to them and go to sleep. He finally met a different kind of woman. He made love to her and then as usual rolled over to go to sleep. She cuddled him. He was shocked to feel her reach around his hip and cup his now limp penis in her hand. His first thought was, "Another one of those women you just can't satisfy." Soon, however, he heard her breathing slowly. She was asleep. She slept, her hand cupping his small limp organ, while he anxiously stayed awake all night. He did not remove her hand. When he left in the morning, he had no intention of ever seeing her again but found that he could not forget her. He sought her out again, and the same experience occurred. Finally, he began to understand that this was indeed different. One time after making love, instead of turning his back to her, he remained face to face, cuddling her. For the first time in his life, he could sleep in a woman's arms. He had discovered the secret, the secret of moving easily in and out of closeness and intimacy. Being close in the foreplay, being intimate in the sexual passion, and moving easily back into the closeness. Separation does not work, nor does merely being close. Only the beautiful dance from one to the other feels natural.

Separation does not work, despite many sex therapists' claim that "Sex is sex and has to be seen as such, not as something that has much to do with relationship." If it has nothing to do with relationship it may be fun, it may be good exercise, and you may have an orgasm. However, sex as sex is just a "screw," with all the mechanical implications of that word. It is not making love.

Unfortunately, many people miss the connecting idea that in the sexual act we are literally *making love.* In this meaning is a profound sexual truth. Something is there after *making love,* which simply is not there after a "screw." Both may be fun, but "screwing" does nothing to enhance or energize relationship; *making love* does. It creates something. Since both are fun, how can you tell the difference? You know by how it feels afterward. After "screwing," you turn your back and forget it. After *making love,* you see the other a little differently, with a gentle gladness, even some gratitude, that the other has let you be close, shared with you, and let you know him or her so intimately. *It makes love.* That is, it creates more love than was there before, even if only for the moment. Its creative essence makes it intimate. It energizes and enhances the closeness of the relationship.

We have spoken of the importance of both closeness-relationship and intimacy-relatedness, and the need for a balance between the two to form the matrix of love. Sexuality is one of the pivots. In it, the *me* and the *I* are merged, experienced simultaneously as *self.* Real sexuality is the prototype of the intimacy-relatedness experience: being yourself fully while accepting the *other* as he or she is fully.

We believe there are two major reasons for the difficulty we have in experiencing personal (closeness) and sexual (intimate) feelings at the same time. There have been several well-thought-out theories proposed in answer to this question. One of the most impressive is the work of Geza Roheim, the earliest psychoanalytical anthropologist, and a colleague of Freud's. Roheim suggested that when man moved from being a hunter-gatherer to being a farmer, he needed some methods of inducing fear, guilt, and anxiety, to control other men by, in order to assure the inheritance of property, which is the basis of all law and order in a permanent society. Sex surfaced as the most readily available behavior-feeling to be anxious, fearful, and guilty about. (Hence, women became sexual property, and their chastity the insurance of legitimate inheritance.) In this way, sexuality became "captured by the system." The antisystem postures—prostitution, pornography, etc.—then became distortedly "sexual." The *nature* of sex has been distorted for a long time.

This distortion is a manifestation of civilization, of system. On a simpler level, we can also point to two phenomenological reasons. The first is that we have unnaturally genitalized sex. When we, the culture (system), co-opt sex, we make man into "a prick" and woman into "a pussy." Genital encounter is a wonderful experience, but if your sexual experience does not penetrate the *self,* as well as *I* or *me,* your person, your body, your mind, your spirit, all of you—from your toes to your taste in art and books—you remain separated from your nature. You are not more human than you were before the experience. You are not energized, enhanced, and re-created. You have not *made love.* You remain the same *me.*

The second reason is the reverse of the first: the total removal of the *me* experience (genitality) from the sexual relationship. People become so involved in the *I* experience that they cannot let go of accommodating to the other person long enough to be genital at all with them. If you cannot exist as a *self* naturally, in your nature, you cannot be truly sexual.

However important genitality is, however gratifying it is, it is but a part of sexuality. Sex has other dimensions, which are not more important but are just as important as genitality. Even more pointedly, these various dimensions form a wholeness that is greater than and different from the sum of its parts, and in which our true nature is emergent. Sexuality is our relatedness to the total physical world we live in. It is how we *be* in the world we live in. The world of trees and smog, the world of Joe and Emma, the world of fish and stars. It is not what and how we *do* in the world. That is closeness. Sexuality is "living in the world in good faith," and most particularly has to do with the pleasure we feel with the world we so live in. It has to do with joy in, satisfaction from, and connection with that world. In other words, it is feeling intimate with whatever the *other* is, whether a woman, a man, a rose, or the brisk air.

Sexuality encompasses much more than trophic genital impulse and gratification. If it were merely a matter of copulation, we would not have evolved beyond spiders or rodents, or wherever in the evolutionary line we predate any notion of individual "identity." Evolution involves the emerging complexity of all aspects of our being to assure our survival. The sexuality of humans is much more complex than that of other mammals. Not simply because our sexuality is conditioned by and coexists with other personal and social feelings like guilt and shame but also because human sexuality is in general multifaceted. It is productive of as well as being the product of these facets. It has been so shaped by the process of evolution to increase the chances for our survival, and thus further evolutionary progress.

Paleoanthropologists Donald Johnson and Maitland Edey speak to these issues in *Lucy, The Beginnings of Humankind*:

> . . . if one is going to have fewer offspring one had *better* have a larger brain to take care of them. . . . In the case of primate evolution, the feedback is not just a simple A-B stimulus forward and backward between two poles. It is multi-poled and circular, with many features to it instead of only two—all of them mutually reinforcing. For example, if an infant is to have a large brain, it must be given time to learn to use that brain before it has to face the world on its own. That means a long childhood. The best way to learn during childhood is to play. That means playmates, which, in turn, means a group social system that provides them. But if one is to function in such a group, one must learn acceptable social behavior. One can learn that behavior only if one is intelligent. . . .

The complex feedback loop is apparent and would have to involve the complexity of our sexuality, since it is the very instrument of the process. Unless we understand and appreciate these multiple facets, we will fail to understand human sexual difficulties. Full humanness disappears into the convoluted preoccupation with sexual gymnastics, orifices, and positions that supports the whole how-to industry of sexual advice and apparatus. Our obsession with sex as genitality, as sexual technique, is a lowering of humanness to a level far below its common denominator. The common denominator is our nature, the unending creative energizing that is intimacy.

Spiritual Sexuality

Alice comes in because she wants to talk about her lover. She says this up front. She wants to know why he has little or no sexual interest in her. She is not worried about his being unfaithful; she is fairly clear that he is just not sexual. As she talks, we get the picture of a man who is not interested in much of anything. We hear no passion about any aspect in his life. Of course, we realize we cannot know him through her. She only shares her experiences. However, we can feel a sad emptiness in what is going on in their relationship. Alice is searching for an answer; unlike many, she has come into therapy before getting so angry or resentful that she cannot deal with her lover at all. She still cares. They have a chance.

Sexuality in humans is basically spiritual. By spiritual, we mean that in humans sexuality is more psychological than it is simply instinctual. We use the word *spiritual* in its oldest meaning, "breath." This moving of air in and out is the most fundamental experience we have in our connection to the world we live in. As such, the need to be spiritual is a pragmatic truth, a basic biological and evolutionary aspect of our sexuality. As the old rural man said, it is our nature, our being a part of nature. Our sexuality includes an unconscious need, which at its best eventually becomes conscious, to be unendingly aware of our interdependence with everything and everyone in our environment. In some very meaningful ways, what we as a culture have done, are doing, and will do in our own living space highlights the real difficulties we are in with our sexuality. We are everywhere ecologically out of balance. The sexual impulse and act, if fully human and thus intimate, is the most primitive and natural experience we have of our connectivity and interdependence. Your nature *is* your nature; your genitals are not. If you are not spiritually connected to your nature outside yourself, you cannot be connected to your nature and passion inside yourself. As the English critic Cyril Connolly said, "The man who is master of his passion is reason's slave." And normally also a slave to systems.

It is not merely poetic when people say of sexual climax, "I go out of my mind . . . I come right out of my body . . . I feel whole." This sense of being connected to the all is an important experiential facet of sexuality. The same sensation underlies the words men and women will cry out during orgasm—"Oh, God," or "Ooooh" (like a mantra chant); they are often spiritual, connecting, and transcending. To live you must breathe; to be alive you must have *spiritus*.

These are not theoretical speculations about the adjunctive, spiritual components of human sexuality, but realities that we as therapists deal with all the time: sexual problems between couples are mainly experiential, not physical. We have to be concerned with those experiences. We need to facilitate the intimate-closeness experiences in families, so that the sexual healthiness of both parents and children in those families will be enhanced. X-rated videotapes, the sexualization of advertising, the T&A movies for teens, and the swinging singles scene are not going to do this. If we become clear that increasing a child's experience of his or her connection and sense of belonging to nature will significantly increase the likelihood that he or she will mature sexually in a healthy way, then we will have also become clear about how we can help this growth. If, in all family experience, we facilitate the experience of connection, of interdependence, of the ecology of the family as a *natural* entity, then we have increased the probability of all family members being more fully and healthily sexual.

Juanita and her husband arrive at our office. He does not want to come in because he knows why she does. He is embarrassed. Juanita wants to know if her sexuality is normal, since she is partial to making love in the living room, during the day, or in other playful and different ways. He says that he has enough trouble just dealing with her in bed, and that she is "like this" about everything. She is confused, afraid that something is wrong with her. Most people have gotten so far away from their *spiritus* that those who are sexually alive (in all its meanings) question their normalcy.

Curiosity and Playfulness

Apart from what we have called the spiritual quality, what are some of the other facets of sexuality that, while nongenital, are part and parcel of the sexual experience? For one, sexuality seems to be inseparable from curiosity. Sexual humans are curious humans, and curious humans are sexual. Curiosity is not simply being interested in or concerned about: It is actually a delight in knowing, a beautiful lack of fear of the new and unknown. It is a connected position in which you are a part of nature and explore it with relish. Curious children delight in learning and, because of this pleasure, learn well. Learning for them is not work but play. Every new discovery is in a small way like an orgasm. Children who are free sexually are curious children. They want to know. The same is true as they become adults. Free sexuality does not mean promiscuity, which again is a confusion between genitality and sexuality. On the contrary, people who are free sexually do not tend to be promiscuous. They have no need to act out. The most common statement we hear regarding people's sex lives is that they are dull, uninteresting, and never innovative. Such boredom occurs only when neither person is curious, or when neither will *be* curious. Intimate humans are available to the new; as Nietzsche phrased it (in *Eternal Recurrence*), "Even a thought, even a possibility, can shatter and transform us." Such transformation is part of sexuality.

The next facet, one related to curiosity, is play. Play is nonintentional being. It is the congruence between being and doing in humans. *Homo ludens* is the playing, exploring, and learning human. It is the willingness to risk being in the world as we are, without intent or goal, just for the sake of being. This playfulness allows us to avoid capture by the familiar in our culture, and the familiar in our relationships. Play is the only way to deal with the system without being captured by it. In naming sexual stages "foreplay" and "afterplay," we acknowledge our confusion about our sexuality. All sex is play if it is natural. Sexuality is, as Freud suggested, the natural tranquilizer, the counterpoint to the anxiety imposed by adaptation and civilization; that is, closeness, relationship, familiarity, and system. Sexuality, in being nonintentional, physical, connective, risking, exploratory, is the essence of intimacy. It is a playing in which we adults can learn anew, as we learned as children. Not only the new of the *other,* but, more important, the new of *ourselves.*

Body Image

Clayton has come in to see us four times now. He still has not really said why. If we can patiently accept his timetable, eventually he will let us know. Two years ago he had an auto accident in which his leg was badly hurt. He has healed physically, but that leg is now a little shorter than the other one. It has lost some of its musculature and is scarred. Clayton has not healed in other ways. He has lost his sexual drive, without consciously knowing why. For some time he assumed that he was still recovering from the trauma of the accident. Now he knows that it is more than that.

Body image and body awareness are also facets of sexuality. They reflect how comfortable one is with one's sexuality. The importance of body image to sexuality is part of what is so destructive about the body-beautiful cult—not the body healthy, but the body beautiful. To borrow an old cliché, your sexuality is not just skin deep. As part of nature, all healthiness is beautiful. In the real sense of body image, how likely one is to deal with stress on a cellular level (somatizing), on a personal level (emotionally with oneself), or on an interpersonal level (emotionally with others) depends a great deal on whether one is sexually active. Active not genitally, but totally: psychologically, spiritually, curiously, environmentally, and playfully. Our complete sexual image seems to shape our body image. Those of us to whom sexuality is an intimate manifestation of our connection to life perceive our bodies as healthy (and care for them as such) irrespective of the current systemic fad in "what looks good." Whether we do this in turn determines our predisposition to somatize, internalize, or externalize stresses. Conversely, the way we feel about our bodies, other bodies, gender in general, humanness, the environment our body is in, the ecology, and the world will reflect in one-to-one correspondence how we are sexually. Being part of nature, you cannot escape your nature.

Creative Sexuality

The creative facet of sexuality is evident. Obviously, sexuality creates new life. It does this literally and, just as important, does it metaphorically. Other kinds of new life are given birth: paintings, sculptures, symphonies, poems, novels, bridges, designs, ideas, cultural origins, and personal impulses in our relationships. Sexuality pushes us not just to clone but to create, to evolve, to move, to grow, and to change. Nature is pragmatic. Our nature has reason and intent. Sexuality energizes our challenge to the familiar and secure, and has all those qualities of the intimate experience that we have described: to be fully sexual you must, for example, feel accepted and unjudged. Sexuality is also our greatest insurance against the seductiveness of death. We struggle unendingly in life. Death means we can finally fully retire and just be still, quiet, unasked of, without demands or tomorrows, allowed to sleep. The absolute, final tranquilizer. How could that not be seductive? Poets have long known this. From *The Faerie Queene* by Spenser:

> Sleep after toil, port after stormy seas,
> Ease after war, death after life does greatly
> please.

Familiarity, closeness, security, being part of the system, all experiences we each have in life, have the same seductiveness. To escape being lulled into the living dead is not easy. The only assured antidote is intimacy. Of the varied intimate experiences, sexuality is the most directly re-creative and committed to the ascendancy of life over death. It is nature.

Creativity and chaos are close cousins. Chaos is the inevitable outcome of creative risking if there is nothing *but* creative risking, with no closeness and familiarity, no system. Again, it is the balance we must seek: the familiar, the new; the secure, the risky; the close, the intimate; the system, the dyad. Can we find a balance? Sexuality, in this sense, is the natural (pragmatic) cure for cultural inertia. It balances our being civilized with a creative risking that ensures that the culture changes, evolves, and remains organic; that is, remains a part of nature.

We find in our sexuality the most important of all experiences for a human to know: the experience of survival. Sexuality is fundamentally committed to survival, biologically and psychologically, for individuals and for a species. It teaches us that we are more alike than we are different. Perhaps here, more than in any other way, we see how disconnected from our real sexuality so many of us are. In the *making of love,* even though we are different people with different anatomies, a beautiful truth of nature appears. Immediately after the orgasmic experience, on a very deep and primitive level, we softly know that we are more alike than different. We are so much alike that anatomies, colors, orifices, genitals, or preferences in desires make little difference. Without this knowledge, we would end up separate, discrete, and competitive. With it, we know, feel, and sense our organic natural relatedness. That we see such extreme competitiveness (sexual and otherwise) in our culture is simply one more indication of our imbalance. The close-familiar-relationship side leaves us seeing *us* as different from *them*—men from women, Americans from Russians, blacks from whites, even Lakers from Celtics. *I* sees *me* as different from you; only in my *self* can I see your *self* as more like me than different. You and *I-me* as a natural relation. It is enough that the full human has to deal with the natural existential aloneness of life. To remain islands, isolated as different, is more than we can stand.

As islands of difference we pollute our waters. We do not see our survival in its wholeness; we are interested only in our own security. When this happens, the system has captured us, whether it is national policy, local economy, or our primary relationship.

Sexuality teaches us, more than any other human experience, about death and ending. A Renaissance expression for orgasm *was* "a little death." It is the only experience we know that has an ending with no sense of loss, rejection, or separation in it. On the contrary, after orgasm, we feel more together, more alive, and more connected, even though we have ended. That is the importance of *making love* rather than "screwing." We feel closer. The knowledge that ending is okay if it is shared, is a part of living, and is a part of nature, comes from *making love*. It teaches us that death too is a part of living and cannot be separated from the rest of life. Through sex, we experience the journey of life in intimacy. We get free of the system. In closeness and familiarity, life is a discrete series of steps, places, jobs, tasks, and other activities. In intimacy, we learn that life is one continuous being.

The two ways of experiencing life, closeness and intimacy, are very different. As my *(Tom)* mother once said, "If a sad and tearful person tells you *why* he's crying, then he's not as sad as he was when he couldn't tell you why." In intimacy, I do not explain, but share my tears with you; I am myself with you. In myself, I feel what I am with you. When I move to my *I,* I mostly feel for you; I react and accommodate; I am dealing with relationship, not being. If I were off crying alone, I would feel *me,* only what I am internally. We humans have difficulty allowing ourselves just to be, to allow ourselves just to cry in the presence of the other, just to laugh in the presence of the other, just to be naturally as we are. In other words, we do not feel free to be our *selves.* This reluctance is most evident in our sexuality.

If you ask people why they cannot talk about their sexuality, usually their excuse is that it is "too personal." This response paradoxically indicates that they do not experience their sexuality as a dimension of *self,* but as a relationship to the *other,* between two people. The interpersonal source of their feelings is further seen if we ask whether they talk to each other about their sexuality. The answer tends to be no, because what they say might leave them vulnerable to being hurt or retaliated against. We all feel threatened about our sexuality because we have, sadly, come to believe that it is relational, in the sense that it is defined by *others,* even available for debate and argument in the *close* relationship, rather than relational in the connected-intimate sense.

But this is not sexuality; there is no passion in such a life position. Observe a couple at a party. She looks across the room at a man and finds him sexually attractive. Her partner is watching and feels threatened and angry. Then she starts feeling guilty, then he is ashamed of himself, and so it goes, on and on. This pattern is how they display their own "sexual" struggle. In genuine sexuality, she is enlivened in her looking, he is enlivened by her enlivenedness, and they make love that night, further energizing and re-creating each other. Even if my lover leaves me for another, am I neutered? Yet that is how we tend to deal with what we call sexuality. In truth, my sexuality (as an aspect of my reality, a part of my nature) is not rejectable or disposable. It is not *defined* by *others.* It is instead *experienced* with *others.* We have spoken of some of the nongenital facets of the genuinely whole sexual experience. One's sense of connectivity or spiritual ecology, one's curiosity, one's body language and connection to environment, one's playfulness, the risking and challenging of familiarity, the creativity and response to new experience, the behaviors challenging the inertia of culture. We have spoken of what we can learn: that we are more persons than men or women or even humans, that we can die, can end and be reborn, that we are a part of nature.

There are other things that sexuality clearly is not. Sex is not the motivation in rape. Something personal is, usually the rapist's anger, fear, and need for control. Someone who is truly sexual cannot commit rape. Nor is there much doubt that sadomasochism has little to do with sexuality, despite the amount of money that people spend on its cultural manifestations. Sadomasochism really has to do with a personal perversion manifested in sexual behavior. The personal perversion is the issue; the sexual behavior is merely the vehicle. By personal perversion, we mean the deep neurotic need to either control or be controlled. The fact that the experience occurs to the context of sexual contact is an example of the narrowing of sexuality to genitality. Sadomasochism is not in touch with the other 98 percent of what makes up natural sexuality. If seen as a sexual problem, it cannot be helped or changed. The issue is one of both masochists and sadists needing to be grossly dependent; the sadists are just waiting their turn.

Is the exhibitionist seeking sexual genital permission and affirmation, or is he asking the more personal question of whether, if he is acting in what he himself perceives as an unacceptable way, he will still be accepted and loved? One day a male exhibitionist walked into our clinic, garbed in only the traditional raincoat. He knocked on each office door, and "flashed" when the doors were opened. By the time he had finished his rounds, the police had been notified and arrived. They arrested him. When someone asked him why he had come to a psychiatric clinic to flash, he said sadly, "I've never done this before, but I've always wanted to. I thought I would be safer in a psychiatric clinic, I thought you would understand. I was wrong." Then he began crying. He was wrong, not in the sense that he would not be understood, because his *personal* problem was understood, but because his pseudo-sexual behavior was not acceptable. As we have seen before, here is a case of personal doubt presenting itself as a sexual problem.

What about the voyeur? What is he or she looking for? Is it sex, the primal scene? We suggest that perhaps instead they are seeking relationship and closeness: One draws close to see the *other*. Is a foot fetish sexual? Could not a shoe be the fetishist's symbol of a nonsexual person as well as a vagina? Adult sexual abusers of their own or any other child—are they sexual? We most seriously doubt it. Their behavior is more likely to be based on primitively and psychotically personal issues. In all these "sexual" problems, there is no intimacy, no connection, no relatedness, no spirituality, no creating, and no being naturally who you are and letting the other be who they are. Without these feelings present, the fundamental issue is not sexual; it is personal. They are problems of the *I* and the *me,* not of the *self. Self* cannot behave in these imbalanced ways.

Sadly, most "sexual" behavior is also not sexual. It is of *I* and *me,* not *self.* When *me* predominates, sex is overgenitalized. When *I* predominates, closeness precludes intimacy, as partners placatively accommodate to the *other*. Again, the issues become personal, not sexual. The relationship, the closeness, familiarity, and security, become the focus of the struggle. The new, the creative, the playful, the curious, the spiritual, and the ecological are not experienced. Yet this pathology has not only its destructive dimensions, but also some seeds of growth. Like the shy child trying to attract attention, people who are only being personal in their sex will feel the need to move, to search for what is missing. Their dissatisfaction almost always ensures this movement. As painful as growth makes the relationships, it does at least give them the opportunity to change. Nature is life. It always moves in one way or another.

I *(Pat)* once attended a meeting where a group of men were standing together commenting on the women who came in and out of the room.

The men's conversation was ribald and full of sexual innuendoes whenever a woman in a short skirt or tight sweater appeared. Then in walked a woman who radiated real sexuality. Not only were there no comments, but the male group rather uneasily broke up. True sexuality intimidates most of us, because we are so removed from our own real sexuality. We cannot tolerate being faced with our alienation from our passion, and our personal realities. We cannot just be what we are. It bothers us when we see someone who can.

If we are to teach healthy sexuality in families, we need to find ways to evoke, elaborate, and applaud in our children, our spouses, and our *selves* the risking of being in the family in new ways. New ways of being that we and they have not been willing to risk before: First, a willingness to acknowledge that we are all dependent on one another because of our natural connections, rather than our needs. Second, an excitement with spontaneous playing and creativity. Third, a curiosity about the unfamiliar. Fourth, a spiritual, empathic awareness of our common humanity. These experiences are far more important to our becoming fully sexual human beings than untold hours of instruction in genital acrobatics. For, whatever else sexuality is, it is foremost an intimate experience. It is the prototypical intimate experience. Genitality makes up no more than a minuscule percentage of our sexual being. A person who can be fully intimate in all the other ways we have been talking about can easily become capable as well of the mature and gratifying genital experience of sex. Our ordinary humanness is what teaches, not the how-to manual.

12

Personal Practice . . . Marriage and Intimacy

Freedom is nothing else but a
chance to be better.

—ALBERT CAMUS

We have talked about experiential pairing as a natural force; we assume that it was happening early in humankind's development, long before someone created difficulties by tagging a word like *marriage* onto it. However, words do contain truths, and one of the significant aspects of the word *marriage* is its confused etymology. The Latin *maritus* and Sanskrit *mas* (or *maryas*) designated a male. The Greek *meirax* designates female, as do the Welsh *merch* and the Lithuanian *merga.* So from the beginning there has been confusion about the institution of this "merger." The struggle between male and female over how much input, power, and presence each should have in pairing—what their roles in a "marriage" should be—has gone on since history began and has transcended the *relational* qualities of pairing itself. Humanity has created difficulties by systematizing a natural experience. In acculturating pairing to a social contract involving property rights and inheritance, a religious institution lost from its original spiritual roots, and a political institution sustaining cultural systems, we create the very confusions we see in *marriage's* etymology.

These issues of sexual politics, gender roles, and cultural-religious-economic systems are recurring, and will doubtless continue to resurface in the further evolution of marriage. We are presently in the midst of a dramatic and powerful struggle of male and female to provide a better relational basis in marriage, one that makes it a more viable and creative institutional underpinning for families than the purely "systemic" marriage that has begun collapsing in the past century.

If we understand that "marriage" in cultural use is an institution, as opposed to "pairing," which in nature is a natural experience, then we must ask where, as an "institution," marriage is going. But first, what do we mean when we call marriage an institution? An institution is to society and culture what an element like iron or hydrogen is to the physical world. It is a basic building block. Moreover, it may be changed by its relationship to other basic elements, as iron is by oxygen when, over time, it rusts. So marriage, a cultural element, is altered when exposed to the current family element, or even the shifting sense of what a person is, or what a woman is, or what a man is, or, more interesting, what a soul is. Cultural elements mutate cultural roles and institutions, just as would be true of natural mutations. That is, a mutation that changed "pairing" as a prototype of nature would, of course, change what we see on the cultural level as "marriage."

Marriage as an institution will undoubtedly survive, despite changing times and cultural uncertainties, simply because it is at least grounded in a reality of nature; that is, experiential pairing. We need to look at the most enduring cultural changes in order to see marriage evolving. Some apparent changes in its forms are not actually changes in its reality at all.

For example, in recent times people have been more openly examining and challenging orthodox (state- and/or church-sanctioned) marriage. There is greater acceptance of (and sometimes encouragement of) living together as an alternative. This cultural transition, too often one that tries playing with the concept of commitment by playing with words, can cause meaningful problems in paired relationships. The political, economic, and social issues strongly affect relational feelings. Cultural roles and positions are pressured by natural pairing (in ways that are usually unconscious), but they also, in very real ways, pressure how we live and feel with each other. This convergence of the two (the natural and the cultural) is the very balance between intimacy and closeness that we are discussing. In *The Human Animal,* the anthropologist Weston La Barre says, "If our present analysis of human nature is at all correct, neither Culture nor man is omnipotent." As we discussed, we are a product of the balance and *exist* in it.

In terms of their capacity to relate healthily, on the pairing level, people who live together are as married or unmarried to each other as a corresponding group of "married" people would be. Our question is, "What is this couple's relationship to each other, what is the commitment?" Marriage, in this sense, is not a legal or social construct but a state of primary relatedness, an evolved natural state that exists as the basis of family. As we shall discuss later, family does not necessarily mean having children, but is instead a life position (a way of existing in the world that is).

A highly significant evolution, less self-evident than changes in contractual form, *is* taking place in marriages: There is a—we think salutary—movement away from marriage as the ultimate basis for systemic security toward its value as a possible source of joy and growth. To note this movement may sound simplistic, but in fact the concept of marriage as a source of *self*-development and creativity as well as a source of security is a major cultural shift, although not a total reversal of emphasis. Security remains an important concern in marriage. As noted by the American social historian Lawrence Stone (affective individualism) and others, the shift has been in the balance, to a more even position between security and creativity, one that is attempting to facilitate what we have described as the intimate relationship. This is healthy movement, away from the capture by system that unhealthy closeness represents. This systemic capture and its effects, particularly on women (but also on the personhoods of all of us), have been written about by sociologist Nancy Chodorow. In *The Reproduction of Mothering* she speaks to the effects this has on parenting practices, and therefore perpetuation of the systems. If changed, "Children could be dependent from the outset on people of both genders and establish an individuated sense of self in relation to both. In this way, masculinity would not become tied to a denial of dependence. . . . Feminine personality would be less preoccupied with individuation. . . ." The imbalance between security and creativity in relationship is a reflection of our mistaken concepts of male-female, closeness-intimacy, system-dyad.

From Security to Creativity

On a particular Sunday morning, I *(Pat)* arose in an angry mood. I did not know why. Actually, at the time I was not taking enough responsibility for myself to even wonder why. I went down the stairs and into the kitchen, where my wife was quietly and contentedly reading the Sunday paper. I proceeded, for the next ten minutes, to bang and clang, complain about the coffee, the lack of cereal, and whatever else I could find to be bothered by. I managed to get in several irritable jabs at her, the newspaper headlines, and the day itself. I was not particularly aware of my tone then; I was just "waking up." After a while, she looked up at me and softly suggested that I go back to bed. I asked why, full of irresponsible innocence. She replied, "When we got married, I didn't agree to let you ruin my life." She was right. We are all slowly waking up as persons to this truth. If people's entire day-to-day experience of marriage (and the pairing underlying it) were open to this knowledge, they would change. They would find their *intimate selves*.

An insistence on the right to *selfhood* for both partners is not just a passing cultural fancy. As can be seen by our country's 50 percent divorce rate, it is a major reevaluation of the whole notion of what a marriage is supposed to be. With the work force now 50 percent female and women slowly moving into leadership positions, the concept of both woman *and* man is changing in very real ways. The traditional marriage that is the cornerstone of property rights, established religions, political hierarchies, the male-dominated economic arenas, and an educational system that trains consumers, competitors, and confused communicators is, of course, still with us. Those facets that prove useful to healthy social maintenance and human relationship will stay, but they are no longer sufficient in themselves. And the *self*-destructive components are changing, because they must be changed if we are to survive.

Teresa has been married for twenty-two years to a very successful man. They have a big house, big cars, and three children, who are doing well in the best schools. Teresa belongs to a big church, is a good wife-mother-hostess, can comfortably afford to buy what her family needs and wants. She will tell you that Russell is a good man. Yet she comes into therapy. Why? Because she has had very little happiness, joy, or pleasure for many years. She wants something more. Not because she is selfish or needy. The security of marriage is simply not enough. She is missing the experience of *self*, and so missing the intimacy that would change her marriage into a generative and growthful experience. She wants to be a person. In all likelihood, so does Russell, even if he is not conscious of this desire.

As we said earlier, the pairing of two individuals creates family, and as family is a primary life position, changes in family engender changes in the rest of the culture. One way to see the roots of this cultural shift is to observe changing concepts of the individual, for these will influence and give direction to pair behavior, although not significantly to the pairing process. The pattern of evolving concepts of the individual can be traced through our religious, philosophical, and psychological systems. By changing our perceptions of our identities, religious leaders like Jesus, Buddha, Mohammed, and Luther moved the culture. Philosophers like Locke, Nietzsche, Hegel, and Marx had impact as cultural originators of another kind. Psychological theorists like Freud, Pavlov, Jung, and Rogers have contributed more recently to the change in our cultural values by redefining our views of human nature. Most recently women writers and theorists have contributed new viewpoints on our natures as females, males, and persons. Icons of our popular culture, our movies, our music, our technologies, etc., have perhaps a more immediately pervasive effect on our sense of ourselves (the Beatles, for example). All these shifting concepts of the individual then manifest themselves in our concepts of relationship, whether it be marriage or its emotional equivalent, and so affect its cultural evolution.

In talking about closeness in relationship, we have discussed the idea of sacrifice of *self* (the subordination of person) to institution or system. Confinement to these sacrificial, constructed roles can turn a paired love relationship into a heavy, serious, and unjoyful grind. We create an imbalance that leaves us in a boring, erosive, ungratifying, and uncreative personal prison. We lose the excitement of courtship, along with the expanding and sustaining creativity of our original love. We neither take that walk on the beach together nor bring that feeling home with us. How have our current concepts of the individual led to this imbalance? Consider the mistaken notion of *self* that has emerged most strongly in recent decades, and trace what it has done to the notion of marriage. These are the decades of "do your own thing," variously called "the *me* generation," "the cult of narcissism," "creative selfishness," etc. This distorted notion began slowly, but has greatly accelerated since World War II. The idea that identity was either an *I* issue, distorted into a manipulating-controlling part of us, or a *me* issue, distorted into a totally internally determined presence in the world meeting only its own needs, began to stress traditional marriages in an outwardly noticeable way.

Donald claims that Rose has forced him into coming to therapy with her. He says that he is okay and just wants to be left alone to "do my own thing." Apparently, this is what Rose was also doing, until she decided that there was something missing in her life. Rose began to notice that she did not feel like a person with Donald or with herself.

A marriage of two dissimilar people separately trying to "do their own thing" is almost a contradiction in terms. It certainly presages an unending, confrontive struggle. How do you "do your own thing" in a relationship when "doing your own thing" implies a withdrawal from relationship? We end up with two unacceptable alternatives: either a "traditional" marriage, wherein the *self* is submerged and sacrificed to a prescribed and constrictive set of rules, or a separate but equal independence, which suggests the antithesis of marriage by any definition. How can both partners be married and at the same time achieve personal fulfillment? That is the real issue and the real question we must address.

Flight to "Freedom"

Let us look for a moment at how the dilemma has progressed in the past few decades. At first, as the importance of personal freedom was increasingly insisted upon, our response was not to enlarge the marriage space, but to search for more personal experience outside the marriage. Many women, thinking that men were achieving *selfhood* through work (which is, in fact, *not* the case), sought *selfhood* outside of their primary relationship. They turned to relationships with other men and women, both friends and colleagues, to increase intimate (not genital) relationship—relationship in which they were allowed to be themselves. This reaching out to *others* was all to the good *except* as it was used as a way of avoiding the issue of what was missing in the primary relationship (and thus was much the same as what men were doing at work and in other activities). Like the stereotypical husband's watching football or stopping on the way home to have a drink with the "boys," a life of longer hours at a new job or new involvements with *others* can become merely a relief from the boring unfulfillment of the primary relationship. The original romance, the creative tension of the differences experienced in the intimate relationship, is gone. We flee in confusion from our inability to relate personally, sexually, intimately, and enduringly. This is a far cry from "they got married and lived happily ever after."

Carla is forty-one and has been in a committed relationship for nine years now. She is an executive whose career is more "intimate" to her than her lover. She not only works long hours, but, perhaps more meaningful, she continually makes choices indicating that her work is her first priority. Instead of leaving the office early and making a joy of their anniversary, she is late at work, late getting home, late to the theater, and then "late" in understanding why her partner is upset. She has, like many of us, successfully found a way to avoid intimacy in her relationship. She may indeed be intimately involved at work, but we must look carefully at this. People who are open to intimacy, who experience being a *self* in one way, usually do it in all ways; it is their nature. This is not always so, of course. There are people who can deal with *impersonal* intimacy, in art, music, or writing, but are unable to deal intimately with personal relationships. Such people are caught in a different place in their growth than most of us. They have found a window to intimacy, but have ceased looking for the doorway. In Carla's case, however, we suspect that she is struggling with *I* and *me* issues: She is not finding *self* at work or at home.

Dennis and Barbara are in their mid-forties. They have been married for more than twenty-three years and have two children in college.

Dennis is a physician, working from 6:00 A.M. to 6:00 P.M., going from his office to work out in the gym, then to a lounge to drink with friends. On weekends he plays golf and goes to various social and civic meetings. In her leisure time, Barbara plays tennis on three different teams and belongs to so many useful organizations that she cannot remember where she is supposed to be on what day. The two pass like the proverbial ships in the night. Their sex life is practically nonexistent, and both would be totally shocked to feel intimate with the other, because their whole marriage is designed around their staying away from each other.

Of course, the push for *selfhood* is not new—indeed, it is pushed by the nature of experiential pairing. The shift we are seeing is that it is more out in the open, causing real behavioral and cultural changes—among them the frequency of divorce. Attempts to avoid confronting conflicting demands for personal freedom have brought us trial marriages and "separate lives." Neither of these work, in the sense of solving the problem. Too many relationships end up as two lonely parallel lines that are always even but are never meeting or touching. Affairs, "swinging," promiscuity, pornography, etc., avoid intimacy by separating sex from personal relationship. Divorce avoids the question of how to be oneself in marriage, by giving people the false hope of reexperiencing romance and excitement in another "marriage." But the impasse rises again, usually more quickly with each successive "marriage." More and more, partners become obsessed with personal fulfillment, searching for themselves in *others,* and allowing the demands of "identity" to overshadow acceptance and a capacity for dealing with differences in relationship.

In *Hamlet,* Shakespeare wrote:

> This above all: to thine own self be true,
> And it must follow, as the night the day,
> Thou canst not then be false to any man.

It is to our *self* that we must be true, and in so being we will then "be what we are" (not be false) to our *other.* You cannot find your *self* in *others,* and "identity" is not difference.

Marge is only thirty-five but is already winding down her sixth relationship. She comes in for therapy because her parents want her to, but she seems to be in no distress personally. She talks in a rather straightforward manner about the excitement of meeting a new man, the courting, the sex, and the romance. She is mystified by why the passion goes away, other than to conjecture, "I think getting serious ruins it." This statement is one we frequently hear in our offices: "Commitment destroys romance." It is the same idea as the sign outside a church announcing, "Love—The Ultimate Self-Sacrifice." If these are in reality what love and commitment do, who needs them?

It is clear that the most striking deficit of marriage or committed relationship as an institution (in terms of its meeting these shifting concepts of the individual) is its failure to fulfill the deepest personal, sexual, and spiritual needs of the two partners. As psychotherapists, we hear this lament from couples over and over. The form of the lament is usually fairly predictable, because the traditional system has given us culturally enforced gender-specific roles. Typically the husband says, "She's cold, unresponsive, not turned on, not interested in sex, unexciting, uncreative, drab, flat, gloomy, and too involved with the kids." In other words, she is depressed sexually and not growing. He does not understand her depression but is simply enraged by it. Typically the wife says, "He won't relate to me as a person. He won't talk, listen, touch, or hug. He works all the time. He doesn't know his kids or me. If I told him a dream I'd had, he'd ask what the hell difference it made." In other words, he is cut off from his personhood, his sensitivity, his feelings, and his creativity. She does not understand his withdrawal, and is likewise enraged. Although this is the "typical" (stereotyped) example, its real significance is in its demonstration that the lack of intimacy is what is distorting both. The distorting would be just as true if the roles were reversed.

Is there hope for such a couple? Yes, but a solution to such distortion is not simple. Currently, there is much instability in marriage as an institution, and great increases in the personal mobility of those married. Moreover, the culture has opened the secrecy and privacy of marriage to continual scrutiny. A torrent of information flows out in books, magazines, television, films, and radio talk shows. Some are good, some bad, some relevant, and some ridiculous. But all are examining, exploring, and revealing the games we play with each other. We emphasize the carnival aspects of easy divorce, affairs, uncommitted relationships, and "sexual freedom," the boredom, hurt, and loneliness. It is not just that bad news makes good entertainment; there is an aspect of reality to the changes. Look at the divorce, suicide, and alcoholism rates. These are real. Both traditional marriage and its alternatives are under attack, and often rightfully so.

Some see the disquieting drive for *self*-fulfillment as another surfacing of hedonism in a world that has lost its moral purpose. For those chasing the cult of "me" or the ego gratification of "I," this assumption may be true. But there have always been hedonists and narcissists; their view of "self" and so of relationship simply presents old problems taking new shapes in another culture. There is certainly no question that we currently have our full share of such people in this culture. However, the real shift, for most of us, is a culturally expanding and naturally based desire for the return to a more spiritual and experiential position, a cultural questioning of patriarchal marriage. This shift is seen in the very real changes in our attitudes regarding the individual rights of all humans, ethnic and gender roles aside; in our crying need for a balance in which personal fulfillment can become a way of experiencing *self,* a way of experiencing intimacy. This position is naturally moral—as all nature being itself is moral. The desire and even demand for this intimate experience is spiritual desire, a longing of the human spirit, and that is why we spoke previously about the relevance of concepts of the individual in religion, philosophy, and psychology to our concepts of healthy relationship. By tracking the evolution of the human spirit, we can learn how two people can join without losing the spirituality that humanizes and personalizes them, the natural human spirit.

From *The Soul of the Indian* by Ohiyesa: "Nearness to nature . . . keeps the spirit sensitive to impressions not commonly felt, and in touch with the unseen powers."

Because many husbands despair of the marriage relationship's offering any opportunity for a real increase in their joyousness, and because, on the contrary, they indicate by their behaviors that pleasure, joy, and freedom are to be found only outside the marriage relationship; because many wives also despair of the marriage relationship's offering any opportunity for increased personal experience and growth, and indicate by their behaviors that identity and personal fulfillment are to be found only outside marriage, the marriage relationship has become distressingly unstable. Both husbands and wives are suddenly propelled into highly mobile, unstructured, and morally malleable life positions, which bring them close to the alienation of chaotic loneliness and fragmented identities. Who is the husband who can talk easily with a woman at work or in a bar, but spends his hours at home in silent communion with the television set? Who is he? Who is the wife who chats so vivaciously and personally with the neighbor, who is so expressively persuasive in her own work, and yet just circles around the house engaging in seemingly mindless activities while her spouse stares equally as mindlessly at the TV? Who is she? Is she his wife? Is he her husband? Why, when they are so effortlessly animated in their respective worlds outside the home, can they not be so with each other? (This exact dilemma may be present in any paired relationship; we use "husband" and "wife" to name life positions.)

Private Marriage in the Public Eye

Our paradigm is not an unrealistic parody of marriage, nor is it new. It is, to some degree, true of the majority of marriages. Sometimes the roles are reversed, but the story remains the same. What is new is that this common failure is now out in the open, on television and in books, no longer a secret. The opening up of the secrecy and privacy of marriage has led to a new honesty concerning sexism, sexuality, and sociopolitical structures, which in turn affect ecology, religion, and global conflict. We have unfolded the protective silence about marriage that, even a century ago, was mandated as the foundation for the likewise mandated silence concerning other established cultural institutions. For as we stated at the beginning, the human-pairing relationship is the basis for all our other forms of relating. As the smallest system, it is the prototype for all other systems.

The breakdown of secrecy is seen even more directly between individual husbands and wives. They talk to family members and to others with whom they are intimate, about themselves, their relationship, and in some cases their sex life. In many ways, their openness is what is making clear to them that something is missing in the marriage. It is not simply "talking" about our marriages. People have "talked" about their marriages throughout history. What has changed is that we no longer talk in the context of secrecy—in the context of the traditionally established institution.

Paradoxically, we are more free to talk to others, but less free to talk to our spouses. We can quarrel in front of others, but cannot resolve the quarrels between just the two of us. We have been liberated to talk about relationship but not relatedness, about closeness but not intimacy. People discuss their marital state socially. But what they talk about, usually in "jest," is its nonmarriageness, how it is not a real marriage and not meeting their needs. An unfortunate side effect of this negative "show-and-tell" is that we usually get support and agreement from our friends, family, and confidants. Seldom do they confront us with *our* marital sins or shortcomings, *our* ways of stopping the intimacy that we say we want. Their support often reinforces the problem, for it encourages us to continue to see our dissatisfactions as being caused by our spouses.

Naomi is eighteen years into a marriage with which she is not happy. At thirty-eight, she still is not doing anything about her dissatisfaction. For the past ten years, she has increasingly seen her husband, Willis, as the problem. She believes him to be unloving, uncaring, dull, immobile, and incommunicative. But instead of attempting to talk to him, she seeks condolence from her sister Madeline, who feels unfulfilled in *her* marriage. Naomi complains, "I wish Willis would grow up. He still needs a mother." Madeline cannot afford to think about parallels in her own marriage, so she deflects: "Oh, I know. They're all that way." Naomi persists: "I don't think we've been out in six months. All I do is take care of him, the house, and the kids. And damn it, I work too." Madeline, still threatened, replies, "He just doesn't think about how hard it is on you." The conversation continues in this vein. What Madeline does not say to Naomi is "What are you doing to change all this? How are you with him? What are you doing about you?" Madeline is supportive but not helpful. It is the same as the man complaining about all of his wife's shortcomings, whose friend noncommittally answers, "Well, you know how women are." This kind of support does not help. It does not make one deal with oneself. It gets the distress out in the open, breaks through the secrecy, but it leads to no emotionally connecting or correcting experience.

Trying to "Fix" Marriage

Our dissatisfaction with marriage is now out in the open. The institution is no longer a sacred monolith. It is discussed everywhere, from television to church bulletins, as we search for whys and ways to make it better. The trouble is that most of the proposed solutions deal only with the relationship, the closeness, and the role side of marriage—for example, books on improving your "sex life," articles on ways of juggling two careers, or discussions of ways to "divide the responsibilities." Therefore, even if the proposed change seems correct and healthy, nothing else changes, and the attempts may create more of a problem, instead of being a part of the solution.

One supposed remedy to this marital struggle was *exchanging* roles. He and she switch their gender-typed traditional responsibilities. However, there is no finding of *self* in this exchange, just as there was no finding of *self* in the original traditional roles, because these are all *doing* behaviors and have little to do with our being. As such, whatever the assignment of roles, they are often resented, and detrimental to the creative, growing process of *self*. He simply becomes indignant and wishes he were doing something else instead of "spending time with her." She fumes as she perceives his lack of enjoyment and wishes she were almost anywhere else. They may be "closer," but they are no more intimate. The organized, imposed solution is making the problem more acute. He does not get to know that he *wants* to be with her. She does not get to know that she *wants* to be with him. We do not get free of the system by constructing new systems.

Another supposed remedy is *personal freedom* in roles, where the function of what a husband or wife is "supposed to be" is left undefined, and "being a person" comes before being either a husband or a wife. Again, we see how this liberation from roles (in itself healthy) can become part of the problem (become a role in itself). Couples in pain want to know why "being free" leaves them less free. They have become more tied to the relationship-closeness part of their marriage because they must negotiate and accommodate to avoid roles, and in doing so, of course, must become "closer." These couples tend to be less secretive, openly admitting that something is wrong. He can say directly that he is not getting what he wants. He does not want to "have to come home immediately after work" or "go on a family vacation." She does not want to "visit his family on the holidays" or "invite him to my company's functions." Both feel that being a person is necessary and important, but do not know how to be *married* as persons. Their openness often leads to "living" outside the relationship, such as having totally different lifestyles, totally different friends, and pretending that this does not affect the marriage. If such a couple has children, it also leads to a sense of disconnection between marriage and family. What these parents do is seen as less important or meaningful to their children, since the children are expected to understand automatically that their parents are persons. Both want to be what they want to be, not what they are expected to be. They are confused in believing that personhood can be found in avoiding roles any more than it can in living them. Having to "not be something" is as much a role as "having to be something." There is no freedom in either.

What is happening today is that family is becoming less related to marriage, behavior less related to feeling, and personhood not related to relationship. Something powerful is shifting and moving in our views of marriage, yet in the transition coming out in very confused ways. We see the confusion continuing even after divorce, as couples stay in contact and retain some semblance of a relationship, or remarry and form unusual network families of various combinations. Terminating the marriage does not terminate the confusion.

Marriage and Intimacy

Family and marriage are inextricably tied, because pairing creates family. Therefore, family, in any meaningful sense, is a natural state. It is not defined by having children, but is instead a state of potential. *Marriage* is the word we use to signify the pairing that creates this natural state. Only by understanding that in its naturalness marriage is a spiritual state will we be able to answer the question of how we can be married and at the same time be our *selves,* personally fulfilled. The other spiritual state of existence is the individual, and the only relatedness that allows the two spiritualities to exist together as such is intimacy. Intimacy is necessary for true marriage to exist.

Personhood and relationship are equally important: they are the two sides of the balance. Personhood is not "doing your own thing" or "being free to be you." *It is being able to be your self.* Intimacy is the two partners being *themselves,* and accepting each other as such. Our culture's current grab-bag of experimental forms of sequential marriage, sexual behavior, and "me-first" lifestyles, along with the weakening of family forms and traditions, all reflect how far the pendulum has swung away from intimacy, and the resulting pain that this imbalance has produced. The problem has been present, especially in Western civilization, for a long time; only the overtness and pervasiveness are new. Having broken apart, traditional forms cannot be (and should not be) forced back together by religious zealotry, governmental propaganda, or cultural fads. But their collapse represents an evolving change that has caused pain and dissatisfaction, and so must be addressed.

To reiterate, it is clear that marriage serves obvious social values that have long been successfully managed by the traditional aspects of the institution. These are maintenance-closeness functions: the preservation of property and legal rights, child rearing, political and territorial control. Stability and maintenance are real needs, but our overinvolvement with them has diminished the ability of both men and women to be *themselves.* It also leads us to be overinvolved in our suprasystems. We spoil the ecology outside us because we are living in a spoiled ecology inside. Nonetheless, although a reversion back to some of the traditional values may be painful, we are wrong to throw out the whole tradition because we have woefully misused it. There are traditional values that represent good, functional aspects of relationship-closeness—as we have said repeatedly, it is the balance we need. The traditional values found in courtesy, respect, commitment, sharing, and the like are necessary parts of healthy closeness. Ridding ourselves of the unhealthy capture by the system is imperative, but we must remember that healthy closeness is equally as important as intimacy.

Marriage can successfully serve the personal and sexual needs of the individuals married. It would not survive as an institution if it did not allow and potentially promote growth; it would not continue to be a part of evolving nature. It is the failure of marriage in this individual area, by a lack of intimacy, that lies at the core of the disturbances we are experiencing. On an individual basis, marriage cannot exist as a mere social institution; it must be the most meaningful thing in your personal life, the pivot around which the continuing growth and evolution of your personhood occurs.

Primary pairing has customarily provided adults with the basic needs of childhood that were provided by their original families, such as security, dependency, familiarity, a group-social identity or base of operations, and a matrix for socialization and continued learning about living with *others.* This function is tremendously important; it sustains human closeness and relationship. But it is not sufficient to sustain our health as persons. The intimate aspects of play, *self*-expression, individual growth of *selfhood,* as well as exploration of sexual feelings and actions, are equally necessary. Just as our original families did, our pairings must offer us intimacy as well as closeness. It is naïve to believe that closeness issues, like security and group identity, are any more or less meaningful in our childhood than our *self*-identity, expression, play, and growth functions are. Unfortunately, it is likely that a deficient intimate experience in our adult relationship will be a continuation of the imbalance of our previous family experience. In experiential pairing, in choosing our primary relationship, we are in some respects looking for a way to complete our growth as a child and become a whole person. Herein lie the discontents and unmet deep needs that make marriage based solely on security untenable. The search for security simply perpetuates our childhood conflicts by stopping our growth.

We have seen a profound change in our society. The woman who once married for economic and/or territorial security is being replaced by the woman who wants to be economically and territorially self-sufficient, and is looking for someone to "allow her to be herself." The man who previously sought the security of a base camp, a caretaker at home to let him wander and compete "out there," is replaced by the man looking for someone who can "release the fun, play, and sexuality in him." Both, however, are still missing the point. The relationship-closeness side of marriage, security in any of its forms, cannot alone provide what each partner is actually searching for. The same mistake can be seen in those who choose a partner to meet dependency needs or to process their identities. You cannot find your *self* in the *other* person. You cannot get permission to be you from the other person. You cannot get the other person to parent you into your *self.* You cannot be you by not needing the other person. You cannot make a man-woman marriage out of a child-parent, parent-parent, child-child, child-adult, parent-adult, or any other fixed and secure combination. These common distortions are for maintenance and are usually used in the service of unhealthy familiarity and closeness; not for creating, finding, growing, or becoming.

So a marriage must find a way to be both a place of role and ritual and a place of *self* and spirit. In *Contributions to Analytical Psychol-*

ogy, Jung said: "Seldom, or perhaps never, does a marriage develop into an individual relationship smoothly and without crises; there is no coming to consciouness without pain." This pain is the work of experiential pairing. Ideally, "marriage" should provide a nourishing medium within which each person can grow into his or her own personal fulfillment. It should promote maturation, expand each person's awareness of who he or she is, what he or she feels and wants, and how those desires and feelings can best be lived out. Far from being antithetical to your ability to find a *self,* a healthy marriage never jeopardizes your sense of identity as to who you really are. It enhances, enlivens, energizes, and renews, until truly being oneself and being in relation are indistinguishable. The modern struggle we have been looking at (the assumption that commitment and relationship are curtailing personal freedom) is a sad misunderstanding of what *self* is. Responsibility in relationship is not a diminution of *self;* it is a direct outgrowth of *self.* People's inability to discover the intimate experience in their marriages is the basis of the increasing pain and lack of personal fulfillment that therapists see in their offices every day.

The only true freedom is the freedom to be what you are as a *self.* Complete *self*-responsibility is the only road to complete freedom. As you learn this, there is less and less choice about *what* to be. When you can freely be your *self,* you are what you are. Your continuing freedom is only to grow and expand, not to be something else. An oak tree cannot choose to be a holly bush. That is not freedom, it is not nature; it is license. Exchanging relationships will not lead to your *self.* Being your *self* is not *defined* by relationship, it is instead *found* in your relatedness. Most couples do not understand this; even less do most families. The faith in sequential relationships as a path to *self*-fulfillment is perhaps attributable to the mobility of our society and the loss of stable but altering extended family systems. In previous times, experiences for changing as well as for learning socialization were available *within* the family. Now they are more likely to be sought outside the family sphere. It may also be that couples today do not view the family as being at all pertinent to experiential issues. This hypothesis gives us insight into what has been called the "generation gap," where a lack of sustained in-family values and life patterns has led to an expanding movement away from the intimate experience. For too many of us, there has been a centrifugal flinging outward, away from family and relationship, to "find ourselves," instead of a centripetal movement inward, toward intimacy with those closest to us. The latter is the only way to find anything, and especially the *self.* We find our nature only by participation in nature, in the nature of being a *self,* in the nature of the primary relationship, and in the nature of family.

13

Personal Training . . . Family and Intimacy

By law of nature all men are equal.

—DOMITIUS ULPIAN

As is true of our potential for closeness and socialization, our *availability* to the intimate experience is taught and learned in our early experience in our original family. The molding of our inborn nature happens in our most simple true system, the family. In this sense, there is no nature-nurture dichotomy. The entire progression, from genetic makeup to a parent hugging a child who has grown into adulthood, is all a part of nature. This chapter does not pretend fully to explore the psychodynamics of family life. Instead, we want to describe the ways in which the original family experience determines, shapes, or at least affects our availability for both natural intimacy and natural closeness.

Are there close families? Most of us would respond yes. We recognize or remember families that we thought of as close. Often, what we recall is a feeling we had when around them: They were families we felt we might have liked to be part of. The members all seemed to accommodate well to each other, to "get along well." Are there intimate families? These are much more difficult to recognize. We all know, or have memories of, families that seemed spontaneous, very open with each other and astonishingly devoid of roles. They might be loud and confrontive, but were also impressively honest and tactile in sharing their positive feelings with each other. They were passionate families, but rather chaotic, and certainly not the accepted cultural model. Yet frequently their house was where the children in the neighborhood tended to congregate. Are there families that are both intimate and naturally close? There certainly must be, but they are so rare that few of us would probably even recognize them.

We have described the relationship between intimacy and closeness, the experiences that bring about an optimal natural balance between the two, and the failures of experience that create imbalances. Our context so far has been in the one-to-one relationship, the dyad. Such relationships offer the potential for depth, passion, and growth in personal experience, *if* we can successfully manage to blend closeness and intimacy. To be able creatively to fuse the two—natural closeness and energizing intimacy—brings us to the experience of *self*. The likelihood of intimacy decreases with the degree of interpersonal closeness, but when we can bring it about, our personal growth and gratification can be profound and expanding. What then happens in the family? Families are intricate, often indescribable meshes of close relationships and intimate experiences, real or possible. At first glance, because of both organic and cultural pressures toward closeness, it would appear that intimate experiences in the family are even more unlikely, more difficult than in one-to-one pairing. The pressures toward closeness are organic because the very biological nature of child rearing requires bonding and caretaking. Bonding is a powerful drive. Child rearing, even with the cultural distortions we have imposed on it, is a powerful biological instinct. Yet despite these compelling commitments to closeness, the natural intimate tendencies and drives of children provide a saving counterbalance. In the words of Longfellow in "My Lost Youth":

> A boy's will is the wind's will,
> and the thoughts of youth are long, long
> thoughts.

Such long, long thoughts help prevent total capture by the system, at least until the children are "civilized," which often means until they enter society by going to school, or day care, or into some other social system. While home, unless the parents are already significantly neuroticized, the balance between natural intimacy and closeness remains healthy. There is not yet sufficient demand from the system or the parent to change it.

Our educational institutions basically teach system; that is, they teach closeness. The word *education* comes from the Latin *e ducare,* to lead out. However, instead of leading out to fuller expression of *self,* our schools become instruments to lead us into a greater sameness, a greater capture. Instead of teaching us creative thinking, they teach us how to give the answer the "system" wants, the "right" answer. Students who give creative responses are often dissuaded, whether overtly or not, from risking being different. We are not speaking here about whether the "answers" on the multiplication tables are optional; of course they are not. What we are speaking about is that same capture by the system that prevents people from learning out of their own experience. This is *self*-destructive, both literally and metaphorically, to the species. We teach coordination, living for the system, instead of cooperation, living as *selves* within the system. Nowhere is the fear of risk and creativity that has captured our culture so evident as it is in our "education."

In *A Sense of the Cosmos,* Jacob Needleman says: "But what is admirable in the child is his integrity—the almost total unity of his innocent mind with his body. *That something of this organic unity should continue to exist as his mind is informed about life on this planet seems to me to be the basic aim and problem of education.*" And, we would add, of life. Learning to learn as a wholeness and learning to learn from our *self* experience would be a better goal. The *self* teaches *and* learns naturally. Schools as a community of *selves* would be both more effective and more human. They would be more in tune with our nature.

The obvious fact that human beings basically learn about intimacy in the family makes the experience of the balance between closeness and intimacy that occurs within that family the central determinant of our availability to intimacy in close relationships. This fact remains true of "family" even though our cultural concept of what family is has changed over the years. We now think of family as "nuclear family," but previously it was "extended family" and prior to that "tribal family." The cultural form affects how such teaching and learning takes place but does not alter the operational fact that "family" is *where* it takes place. Perhaps it would be more accurate to say that the natural capacity for intimacy is either reinforced or obdurated in the family. The capacity for intimacy is natural.

It is sad if children miss the creative joy of having intimate experiences within the family. More unfortunate and painful, however, are the long-term effects this deficiency has on them as humans. It is in our families that we learn to be or, too often, learn how not to be persons. We learn how to *behave* in family life, as well we should, but we also learn, or should learn, how to *be* persons. The paradox is that if we genuinely learn to *be* in families, we will have little or no difficulty learning how to behave. If we instead learn how to behave, we may or may not learn how to be. Obedience does not assure humanness. *Self*-discipline does; it is based on a genuine love of your person. *Self*-discipline literally means to be a disciple, one who follows out of love, of your *self*. You realize *self*-discipline in learning how to be yourself with others. Learning to be your *self* with *others* openly and healthily is the primary experience one has living in a natural family, as child, sibling, or parent.

All of us come from families. As such, family is a prototype of nature, certainly of human nature. Family is an internalized symbol for us all. Your "family" may be in your thoughts, it may be in your memory, or it may be in your fantasy. But the symbol is always there, in you and in me, in the orphan, and even in the alienated. It preoccupies the psychotic. It is an overriding symbol that basically determines the course of life in the neurotic. A human being without family is inconceivable, even if that family is a vague and confused introject (an internalized active image). The only likely exceptions would be the sociopath and psychopath, but they too have their own families. We might not recognize them, but they are there. The battered and abused child has *some* concept of family, even if most humans would not accept that concept as "valid." Humanness cannot exist without family, for the nature of humanness is relational.

Family begins biologically in pairing. Experiential pairing creates families. Experiential pairing, based on the powerful need in all of us to complete ourselves, provides the natural basis for creating others, and so families. Looked at this way, transient sequential pairing reflects an unwillingness to commit, not to "marriage" or "relationship," but to the work, pain, and hardships of the task of experiential pairing. The task of joining with another person (different enough from ourselves to assure us the opportunity of finding the parts of our persons we have still to grow into) is difficult psychic work. The Jungian shadow becomes our potential spouse. Those who avoid this powerful prototype pair with either someone they can only be close with or, alternatively, someone they can only be intimate with. In either case, the possibilities of a growthful, natural balance of closeness and intimacy are diminished. Both avoid the natural possibilities of experiential pairing. Those who can only be close dependently rely on the *other* to do, be, feel, and think what they cannot do, be, feel, or think themselves. Therefore, they never know their wholeness. Those who can only be intimate independently rely on the fact that the *other* is just another version of them. The relationship is like living with yourself. You never grow because you are never confronted with any humanity different from what you have already experienced. You are imprisoned in your own likeness. Out of these two ways of avoiding experiential pairing come abusiveness, escalating unhappiness, and our high divorce rate. The only real basis for an emergent relatedness, and thus emergent family, is experiential pairing.

You learn how to deal with experiential pairing in your original family, your operational family. This simply means that you learn there how to relate to someone who is, in some significant ways, different from yourself. Your father is clearly different from your mother. Your father is different with your sister than he is with you. Your mother is different with your brother than she is with either you or your sister. Your brother and sister are both different, and each is different with you. You are different with your first cousin and very different with your best friend. Perhaps even more important, all these relationships differ at different times. How does the young child, initially committed by nature to being himself or herself, deal with the moving chaos of these ever changing differences? How children deal with that chaos will then determine how they subsequently deal with experiential pairing. What they learn will determine how well or poorly they will manage to combine natural closeness and intimacy in their future relationships; most significantly, how well they will manage them in their own families.

The Risk of Intimacy in Families

Kenny is six years old. He is the youngest of three children. His father is a reasonable but controlling, compulsive person, who regiments his family. Kenny's mother is a rather passive person who has been depressed for years. Her depression finally brings her, with her family, to see us; they have been in family therapy for three months. The mother has just started to again see herself as a person. Today Kenny sits on the sofa looking intently at the therapist. There is silence. The therapist asks Kenny, "Is there something you want to say to me?" The child turns and looks around at his family. His father says, "If you have something to say to the doctor, say it." Kenny looks puzzled, turns to the therapist and blurts out, "What do my mom and dad do in bed when they're not asleep?" There is now a loud silence. His older brother snickers self-consciously. Finally the father states, "There are some things we don't talk about, Kenny. When you grow up then maybe you'll understand." Unsure about his response, turning to the therapist, the father continues, "Perhaps you could answer his question in a way he could understand." The therapist responds, "I think he would prefer for you and his mother to answer." The mother speaks for the first time, with a great deal of feeling: "If he didn't need to know, then he wouldn't ask. I think this family is just too secret. Why don't you answer him? He has rights too."

Kenny risked being different from his family's usual ways of relating. He succeeded. As we often see in young children, the innate willingness to risk breaks through. His risk allowed the others to be different. His capacity for experiential pairing in a healthy way grew. If the growth continues, he will most likely take this capacity on to the family he will later help create.

Carson is fourteen. He is a creative, assertive, confrontive, but loving teenager. Susan, his mother, comes out of the same mold. The father, Roger, has a moderating influence on their relationship. He is not passive, just gentler in his way of relating. The younger sister, Robin, frequently observes passionate exchanges between Carson and their mother over issues ranging from schoolwork to chores. One evening, not too different from many others, Susan and Carson are arguing vehemently over his desire to try driving the car before he gets his learner's permit. The discussion gets very loud, but is soon over. Carson relents and goes to his room, his loud logic not convincing the parents any more than his impassioned pleas; he accepts their decision. Susan then turns to Roger and says, "You know, I really admire that boy. He has a lot of spunk." Carson did not hear her say this, but he knows she feels it. Roger laughs, enjoying both of them as people. Robin is present and hears all of this and grows from it. Roger and Susan are engendering in their children a healthy foundation for experiential pairing. Carson will probably have an easier time than most in balancing intimacy with natural closeness. We can guess that the same will be true for his sister.

These two examples are somewhat different. Kenny is an exciting beginning. Carson is an exciting accomplishment. Both are unusual, at least in a decided minority. Two other general outcomes to these situations are far more common: Kenny could have kept quiet about his curiosity and conformed. Carson could have gone on fighting, become a rebel, and perhaps ultimately wrecked both the car and himself. In other words, Kenny could have given up his differences, avoided intimacy, and subjugated himself to the security of becoming one of them and staying familiar, sinking into the security, however precarious, of maintaining closeness and giving up his own being. Carson could have given up his closeness, his relationships, and gone through life rebelliously, destructively asserting his pseudo-independent differences, his false intimacy. Both would have taken these mislearned experiential pairings into their future family. Carson might never even risk having a family. But were he to have one, he would almost certainly raise rigidly conforming children. Kenny, in contrast, would have reared rebellious, self-destructive Carsons. The frightening phenomenon of "skipped" (alternating) generations of neurotic behavior (the rebel and then the conformer, the successful and then the failure, the mover and then the stayer) is something therapists see all the time. The behavioral pattern swings back and forth for generations. It is ample testimony to the power of mislearning. It is why the balance of intimacy and closeness, and the corrective experience in pairing that such balance engenders, is so crucial.

Closeness in Families

Families, by their nature, make intimacy difficult. *Family* as a word is, after all, the source of the word *familiar*. Closeness, for a variety of easily understandable reasons, is the highest priority in family life. Relationship in family life is far more important than experience. Closeness is therefore more important than intimacy. Family is a system. Family life has to be maintained, bed and board provided, meals cooked. People have to get up, fix breakfast, go to work, go to school. The infant has to be fed, even if it is two o'clock in the morning. These essential maintenance responsibilities have to be attended to for the family to survive. Stability and predictability are crucially important. Mother and father each need to know the other will get up, go to work, get the children off to school, take care of the home, watch over their health, earn a wage to pay the bills. Each has to be certain that the other will continue to perform these duties, both for their survival and for the children's. Stability and constancy are primary values; they are the underpinnings of maintenance and predictability. They become primary values because they are realistically necessary to the family's functioning effectively. Effective functioning means the survival of the family as a system. All of these values, of course, promote closeness.

This closeness in families is real. Babies really do have to be fed in the middle of the night. Diapers do have to be changed. Bills have to be paid. Someone has to earn an income. The toilet has to be cleaned occasionally. Meals have to be prepared and dishes washed. Someone has to scrub the pots. All of these tasks are real: the grass cut, the laundry done, repairs made, clothes mended, sickness attended to, and financial preparations made for the children's education and the parents' old age. The needs of one child at any given moment have to be negotiated with the needs of another. The needs of either parent, immediate or in relationship to each other, have to be tangibly managed. Without closeness, families cannot survive.

Because closeness is both real and functional in families, continuous relationship is emphasized over experience in relatedness. This is almost unavoidable, since closeness assures maintenance, stability, and constancy in a primary group. Six people living together in a house makes for literal closeness. Family members *will* be familiar with each other. Taking care of infants and children requires being close; watching a toddler near the edge of the steps or walking down the driveway means staying physically close. This proximity is in addition to the unending peripheral attention and constant mental monitoring of children required of all parents. Under such circumstances, opportunities for enhancing experience (promoting intimacy) become something of a risk and a luxury.

This perception is where capture by the system occurs. Intimacy *seems* a luxury, yet without it closeness becomes merely roles and postures. The family fails in its primary function of producing mature, feeling, relating human beings. The risk in emphasizing experience comes from the creativeness of intimacy, which is neither predictable nor constant. Families are understandably fearful of risk, change, and strangeness. Maintenance is a powerful force in the family. The family system becomes more important than the individuals that make up that system. The flaw, of course, is believing that one has to be sustained at the expense of the other. It does not; nor do we have to choose between intimacy and closeness, just as we do not have to choose between breathing in and breathing out. When closeness excludes intimacy, we have been captured. We have lost choice.

Accepting Difference

The five-year-old boy is playing by himself in the corner of the living room. The father turns to him and asks, "What are you doing?" He replies, "I am talking to you." That is a direct, experiential, and intimate response, the kind small children are prone to have naturally. The father responds with some irritation, "That isn't what I asked you. What are you doing?" He now says, "Nothing." The father is teaching him relationship (closeness) rather than reinforcing his experience (intimacy). He is being taught not to share the immediate experience, but to stop and figure out what it is his father is really asking, and then to answer his question. He is learning to be a member of the family and of society. Unfortunately, he is also beginning to lose his capacity for immediate intimate experience, the capacity to be just who and how he is at that moment with another human being.

Ellen is nine. She is the eldest child. As is so often true, her mother was a much better parent by the time she had her youngest child, Brad, who is now four. He is a delight to his parents. He is loving, outgoing, happy, enterprising, and wonderfully playful. Ellen, in moods that seem on the surface unprovoked, is frequently angry with her younger brother. She pushes, shoves, hits, and often breaks his toys. Her behavior (not that unusual between siblings) is an issue of closeness. The mother, however, does not deal with it on that level. She does not talk to Ellen about her behavior, as she clearly should do, for they are obviously behaviors that seriously disrupt family relationships, the group's ability to live together. Instead, she talks to Ellen about her anger with her brother. She insists that Ellen should not feel angry; she addresses the issues of experience and intimacy. Ellen *is* angry. That is what she feels.

She has a right to feel what she feels, even if she does not have the right to hit Brad or destroy his toys. Her capacity and ability to experience, to be intimate, are eroded by her mother's response. If this pattern persists, Ellen will grow either into a rebelliously acting out, angry adult, or, just as sadly, into an overly controlled, inhibited, guilty, "nice" person. The intimate experience, in which she would be accepted as she feels, allows change. "Controlling feeling" does not.

Patrick is fourteen years old. He is playing in the side yard with some friends. One of them is seventeen. Something happens, and Patrick and the seventeen-year-old get into a fight. The father is standing on the screened side porch. He watches the beginning of the fight. Seventeen is quite a bit bigger than fourteen. At the start, the fight does not go so well for Patrick. The father remains uncertain about whether to intervene. He decides not to. Patrick finally begins just to hold his own, and soon the fight breaks up. The seventeen-year-old leaves. Patrick, who was aware that his father was watching from the porch, walks into the house. As he walks by, not looking up, he says to his father, "You darn near misjudged that one." There is a *real* risk to intimacy, in parenting, in living.

All three of these examples involve some decision on the part of the parent as to whether relationship or experience, closeness or intimacy, should be attended to. The decision is seldom rational or conscious, it is usually emotional and preconscious. Do we like our child so much that we overprotect, or do we love them enough to tolerate risk? Do we need the constant stability that requires everyone to feel the same way, or are we able to accept a larger wholeness that includes difference?

Liking and loving are intermingled feelings in relationship, and are sometimes subjectively indistinguishable. This is especially true in families. Certainly, each is part and parcel of both closeness and intimacy. Nonetheless, liking is somewhat more important in closeness, and loving somewhat more prominent in intimacy. Our language reflects this emphasis. To like and to be alike have essentially the same meaning. Originally the word *like* meant "common body," later "corpse," and still later it came to mean "to please." Presently, it means "to be similar to" or "to be pleased with," and to be liked is to please the *other*. These are primary motivations in family life. Most members of a family mistakenly struggle with the need to be alike; to be part of the "common body." Much of the impulse comes from the general discomfort in parents with their own differences. They give the impression that to have a relationship, two people have to agree, have to be alike. But as Schopenhauer phrased it, "We forfeit three-fourths of ourselves in order to be like other people." The child follows the same misbelief, as he or she struggles and strives to be alike, and so liked. The child comes to suppose that to be different, which often means to be yourself, means not to be loved. Since, to a child, being loved means to be, to exist, the confusion and distortion can be profound. Children may grow up believing that they exist only when they are "loved." That is obviously untrue. To believe it is also very, very painful.

You exist as yourself. Relationship is not definition. To believe otherwise is to commit yourself to a lifetime of dependently seeking meaning in other people's feelings for or about you. You can grow up believing that the only way you can be loved is to become like the other person. You can end up equating closeness, security, and stability with love and intimacy. You can end up a robot, a psychological corpse. You can grow up committed to security at the price of not growing, not being your own person. The result is not really security at all, but neurosis, a living death.

People are in fact much more alike than they are different. We do not have to strive to be alike. Why endeavor to be like your parents or your siblings, when enormous species, genetic, and familial similarities already exist? However, similarity is not sameness. Nature makes billions of snowflakes, all similar but no two the same. The same is true of persons. There are no two people who are the same, not even identical twins. Each of us, as children, has the right to grow up with our singularity, since we can be unconcerned about the overwhelming ways we are similar. Our major task as parents in a family is to create a space within which each child can grow into his or her accepted uniqueness.

Teaching Metafeelings as Feelings

What is required is the space, the opportunity, the freedom to be. Feelings do not need to be taught in families, only behaviors. You feel naturally. You feel before you are aware of feeling. Your feelings are part of your nature. You feel first and only then think of what you are feeling. Feelings arise out of your natural *self*. We learn on the *self* level only in the intimate experience; that is, we can really change only ourselves; no one else can do it. *Self*-learning is the only learning possible at that level of being. If *others* could teach us feelings, they could change our nature.

When we suggest that you cannot teach feelings in families, that you can only provide the space and opportunity for the intimate experience within which they occur, we are speaking of our primary feelings: feelings we are born with, such as joy, sadness, anger, fear, and sexuality. Families can and do teach a multitude of other secondary and more complex feelings. These we have discussed as metafeelings. They are usually feelings about having feelings. The family can teach children to feel guilty about being angry, ashamed of showing tears, embarrassed at feeling sexual, modest about their natural bodies, self-conscious about showing primary feelings, and shy about human relationship. Families can convert anger, a natural and healthy feeling, into hostility, an unnatural and neurotic feeling. They can convert sexuality into a violent expression of power over another human, and out of this distortion construct the whole sadomasochistic nightmare. They can convert empathic sadness into the hypocrisy of maudlin condescension, change an assertive sense of *self* into self-righteousness, or turn fear into obsequiousness or tyranny. They can do these things just as well as teach respect, kindness, consideration, and politeness. Families can and do teach all these metafeelings. But in the service of ensuring closeness, stability, alikeness, continuity, and obedience, and generally civilizing and socializing the child to fit the family and social mold, the "controlling" metafeelings are proliferated. They are the stuff of which neurotic and psychotic worlds are made. Not all metafeelings are bad (for example, politeness and consideration are enablers of relationship): the problem, once again, is the imbalance. Healthy closeness gives way to capture by the system; useful socialization becomes destruction of the ability to experience.

We make a distinction between counseling and psychotherapy that is germane to this description of the differences in families. The differences are between *emphasis* on closeness or intimacy, teaching feelings or nurturing their development, and being responsible for changing *others* as opposed to providing a relationship within which the *other* assumes responsibility for him or herself. Counseling deals with closeness; it reteaches metafeelings so as to be less destructive; the counselor assumes responsibility for changing the client. Psychotherapy deals with intimacy rather than restructuring closeness. It is concerned with providing a nourishing relationship within which primary feelings develop and mature into naturally being themselves. Experiential psychotherapy concerns itself with the client's developing a sense of his or her own responsibility for living. The same difference in focus is quite apparent in the two major forms of family therapy. The strategic family therapies are very effective forms of counseling. In experiential family therapy, the emphasis is instead on nurturing and reinforcing the capacity of each member of the family to be intimate within the close confines of the group. Experiential therapy attempts to prevent capture.

Families, like counseling, generally do well constructing closeness, teaching metafeelings, and staying responsible for the growth and change in children. Families have a more difficult time promoting intimacy, nourishing primary feelings in relationship, and fostering a sense of *self*-responsibility for happiness or unhappiness in family members. It is generally much easier in a family to either overtly agree, or at least covertly go along with, the decision to avoid dealing with meaningful issues that would cause members to reveal themselves. Seldom do parents or children volunteer to be different, to explore differences in a risking manner. The differences we "live out," like being rebellious, are not risking—they are just another form of capture. It tends to be much easier for parent or child to discuss the fact that someone in the family is being selfish or unfair (metafeelings) than it is for them to comfortably talk with the rest of the family about their anger or sexuality (primary feelings). It is vastly more probable that blame will be the subject of a family discussion than that one member of the family, parent or child, openly will discuss his or her own responsibility for their own pain and unhappiness.

Fear of Not Getting to Be a Self

Why is there so much difficulty in being intimate in the family, in just being who you are and sharing what you feel? The difficulty is not rare or occasional, but characteristic of how we live together in families. Its universality is seen in the overwhelming, often-stated wish of so many people to be something other than what they are. Not to be *someone* else, but more as if they are saying, "I would like to be whatever I am not." The parent wants to play more, be less responsible, be like the child. Children want to be independent, as they mistakenly perceive their parents to be. They would rather go to work than to school. The girl wants to do what the boy does, the boy what the girl does. The father would rather make furniture than work at the office, would rather be a writer than an accountant. The mother would rather be a doctor or an actress than a realtor, a lawyer, or housewife. Always something we are not. Why? Would we be different if we lived in Denver rather than in a suburb of Atlanta? If we were richer, thinner, married to someone else? Whole industries have been built around these discontents and fantasies.

The fact that we feel these constant, vague, and uneasy dissatisfactions about what and how we are does not mean that we really want to be somebody else, somewhere else, or with someone else. But it sounds that way, and some do actually act out their fantasies. In reality, however, these stirrings most likely reflect our uncertainty over whether we have ever *been ourselves*. Instead of wanting to be someone else, we simply want to be sure that we have come to be *ourselves*. We are further plagued by the mistaken belief that everyone else but us is getting to be themselves. The proverbial search for identity begins early in the family. An intellectual, conscious awareness of who you are does not satisfy that need. It is satisfied only by the repeated intimate experience of being just who you are, comfortably and in relationship, particularly within your family. True identity has to do with *self.* The *I* or *me* experience does not provide us with that certainty. The child can be quite effective and real in getting what he wants from parent or sibling. He can be fully him, alone, sitting on the bed in his room. But neither experience tells him of him*self.* He can know himself only when he is being fully himself, not alone but with another member of his family, and feels fully accepted in so being. Humanness is relational. Identity comes out of *self,* and *self* is always related.

From Juan Chi (in Wu-Chi Liu and Irving Yuchung Lo, *Sunflower Splendor*), about A.D. 250:

> He could be heard, but not seen,
> sighing sorrows and full emotion
> self-tortured he had no companion
> grief and heartbreak piled upon him
> "Study the familiar to penetrate the sublime"
> But time is short and what's to be done?

Given the realities of family life, the pragmatic requirements of maintenance, constancy, stability, predictability, and the predominant push for closeness, can families afford to foster intimacy? Can they even tolerate everyone in the family getting to be himself or herself? Obviously, families as we have described them would be reluctant and at best confused about promoting intimate *selfhood* among its members. It is as if they believe that chaos would be the only possible result. The husband might or might not come home after work. He might independently spend the income on buying a new BMW instead of paying the rent or the mortgage or the children's college tuition fees. The wife might become so involved in her own career or interest that she would forget that the children are at school, or spend the income on a sailboat and leave for the Caribbean. The son might decide to quit school in the eighth grade, or make sexual advances to his sister. The daughter might decide to wear only bags for clothing and never take a bath again. Why do families project such beliefs (why does civilization in the form of governments and religions perpetrate them)? In truth, given a family's avoidance of intimacy, their commitment to frequently neurotic closeness, these irresponsible events might come to pass. They sometimes do. People can live out what is not their nature if they have no connection to *self,* no experience of intimacy.

In *Janus,* Arthur Koestler speaks to this issue of the "dangerousness" of people existing as intimate selves: "Throughout human history, the ravages caused by excesses of individual self-assertion are quantitatively negligible compared to the number slain *ad majorem gloriam* out of a self-transcending devotion to a flag, a leader, a religious faith or political conviction. Man has always been prepared not only to kill, but also to die for good, bad, or completely hare-brained causes. What can be a more valid proof for the reality of the urge toward self-transcendence?" It is capture by the system, not *selfhood,* that is so "dangerous."

But given the beautiful support and acceptance of being yourself in a family, it is inconceivable that such chaos would ensue. Quite the contrary, we suggest that such a family would be naturally closer, more stable, more supportive. How could it be otherwise? Because of their ongoing intimate sharing, each member would be exquisitely sensitive to the *others'* wants, needs, joys, and hurts. They would exist quietly confident of a reciprocal sensitivity. Anyone who does not believe this is bound to have a profound distrust of nature, or a cynical ignorance of how nature works when it is left free to do its work. Families are natural. They should be left to function naturally. In nature, system is not opposed to individuation. Centrifugal movement is not excluding of centripetal; they work harmoniously and naturally. The end result would be a sensitive balance between natural intimacy and natural closeness in a natural family. The only dangers are either imbalance or unnaturalness, both of which we sadly already experience in the majority of our current families.

Intimate Parenting

Ideally, what kind of family could bring such a natural balance about? What kind of family would graduate children into an adulthood as capable of being intimate as they are of being close? Such a family would, of course, begin with two parents, who were capable of being both intimate and close. Both parents would have considerable awareness of their commonalities, *and* their individual histories. They would know how much they were alike, but at the same time have a sense of the *other*'s uniqueness. They would feel no need to be *more* alike. They would enjoy their differences. More feelingly than factually or consciously, each parent would have an awareness of the ways in which he or she was different from the other. Each would be willing openly to express and share those differences with the other. Each would have a constant sensitivity to the differences of the other. Perhaps most important, each would have a willingness to learn from the differences experienced in the other, and to grow in both personhood and daily life through their experience of those differences. We are describing ideal parents. We are also describing an ideal relationship, a relationship of ideal experiential pairing, within which experience each person grows in humanness. They learn from their sensitivity to the differences in each other. They not only accept those differences, but experience them in a growthful way. They expand themselves. These are the ideal parents, ideal founders of families. Are there such creatures? Probably not, but some people come closer than others. How can we recognize them?

Intimacy in Parenting

Anna and Rob have been married for six years. Sometimes she dresses in a rather Bohemian fashion: purples and oranges, silks and burlaps, or tailored blouses with ballooned Oriental pants. She is an experimenter. Sometimes her experiments fail. She dresses in such a disaster one evening. Rob greets her as she comes out of their bedroom, and begins to laugh uproariously. She is plainly taken aback. He continues to laugh, tears rolling, raucous in his mirth, comfortably unaffected by her dismay. Within a few moments she too begins to laugh, grinning at first, but then just as unrestrained as he is. Soon, both are laughing joyfully and wildly, much as young teenagers will laugh together for no apparent reason. In this moment, Anna and Rob come close to our ideal. Can you imagine them telling a child who is angry to go to his room and stop being angry? It is unlikely. They might, as responsible parents, send him to his room for acting out his anger, being hostile, or being destructive, but not because he was simply feeling anger, a very human primary feeling.

Such parents are equally intimate and close to their child. Anna and Rob are making love in their bedroom on a Sunday afternoon. The door is shut but not locked. Their four-year-old girl, who has been taking a nap, comes in and stands beside the bed, watching. They stop and turn to her, without shame or self-consciousness. The child asks, "Are you mad at each other?" Anna softly replies, "No, why do you think that?" The child says, "Oh, you looked like you were fighting." Anna responds, "No, we weren't fighting. We were loving each other." The child looks confused: "Oh." Anna asks, "Would you like to get in bed with us and love?" The child nods and climbs up into bed with her parents. Soon she is sitting on her father's back saying repeatedly, "Gid-up, gid-up." Rob and Anna are laughing. They are loving as children love. It is as active and noisy as was the lovemaking the child watched and did not understand. They were being intimate with their child. They taught her no metafeelings. The child left, laughing delightedly. They made love. When they came out to the den she was happily playing with her toys. She looked up at her father and said, "Gid-up."

Tom had six children. The youngest girl was seventeen and special to him, probably because they were very much alike, with the added attraction of her having some of her mother's traits, the ones he most liked. In many ways she embodied the relationship between him and his wife. The girl began coming home later than the time set for weekend nights. It would be twelve or twelve-thirty, when the established curfew was eleven o'clock. Tom repeatedly admonished her for being late. She would always remind him that she never had agreed to the curfew. What could he say? He simply pulled rank: "Well, that's when you are to be home." After one of these exchanges she said, "Dad, what are you concerned about? I am responsible and take care of myself. I don't get into trouble. I don't get drunk or stoned. I'm not cruising around in fast cars. You pretty much know where I am and whom I'm with all the time, so what are you worried about? If it's sex, then what's the big deal? I could have sex at nine-thirty. I don't have to wait until after eleven. So what are you talking about?"

Tom felt a vague discomfort that, in some ways, she was right. He said, "Let me think about it." He walked away, and she went on her date. Tom was pensive for a few days. He thought repeatedly about what his daughter had said. He finally talked to her again: "You were right in what you said to me. I do feel you are responsible and take care of yourself. But I still want you to come home at eleven. Not for your sake, but for mine. I start listening for your car. When you don't get home, I lie awake and worry about whether you're okay. I don't like doing that. Maybe I worry too much, but I do worry, and I don't want that. So why don't you get home somewhere near on time so I can sleep. Do it for my sake, not because I'm trying to keep you a virgin." She smiled and said, "Fine, at least that makes sense. Why didn't you say that in the first place?" She faithfully arrived home around eleven every time she went out, at least until she left for college.

Glen is forty-four years old. He is playing tennis on Sunday afternoon with Neil, his neighbor and best friend. They play frequently, and as Glen is a more talented player, he usually wins. But not today. Today he is losing. Between sets they take a break and sit down on the bench for a few minutes. Neil says, "You feeling okay?" Glen grins and replies, "I didn't get much sleep last night. Scott called me at one-thirty. Said he'd had too much to drink and wanted me to come get him, all the way across town." Neil shakes his head sympathetically: "I'll bet that really pissed you off." Glen smiles again and says, "No, actually it was kind of strange. It made me feel good. I've been telling those kids for years that their being alive and all right is more important to me than sleep. I told them to call if they had been drinking, and damn if

Scott didn't listen. Lisa and I agreed that we are going to sit down and talk to him tonight. Hopefully he's learned something about alcohol. But other than that, I'm sure pleased with what he's learned about caring about himself."

These parents we have exemplified were intimate and close to each other. They were equally capable of being intimate with their children, allowing them to be just who and how they were as persons, *with them.* Rob and Anna's four-year-old really learned something about what a physically loving human is. Tom's seventeen-year-old was listened to; the roles of father and daughter did not capture them; she was responded to, not by a programmed relationship, but by a father who really shared himself. Glen and Lisa's eighteen-year-old was not only accepted but celebrated in his choice of being himself healthily. Even if the acceptance is simply in his parents' smile, he will know it. And he will grow from it.

Intimate experiential pairing, like Anna and Rob's, immediately extends itself to the child. Alone and together, this couple was capable of being who and what they were with their four-year-old. Clearly, the child was learning to be herself with her parents. It would be more accurate to say that she was not learning *not* to be herself. We have little doubt that when another child is born into Anna and Rob's family, the same will be true. Even further, we have little doubt that the relationship between the children will be equally close and intimate. Everyone in the family will learn and grow because of the unique differences of each member. Like snowflakes, they will be close but not alike. As Elizabeth Cady Stanton said: "Nature never repeats itself, and the possibilities of one human soul will never be found in another."

Most families are not this way. What usually filters down to the children is a fear of intimacy and an unhealthy addiction to security, closeness, stability, and order. Individuals, as persons, must be cultivated as *selves.* Couples must be cultivated as a fertile union of *selves.* Families must be cultivated as a garden of *selves.* Was that not the original message of the genesis of families? The garden symbol is found in most genesis stories, of which the biblical version is probably most familiar to Western civilization. God provided his first human family with the closeness of Eden. Everything was assured and guaranteed. No greater closeness, security, predictability, or stability could be asked for. Why were our "original parents" dissatisfied? They wanted the freedom to be themselves, to choose to be right or wrong, to grow, and to risk in the hope of expanding. They wanted freely to choose, freely to risk truly existing in the image of God. God, in infinite wisdom and love, gave that gift. It makes no difference if you see God as nature, the unconscious, Judaic, Christian, Islamic, Buddhistic, or any other way. The gift is the same. With it came a true Garden of

Eden. A family within which every member was free to choose, to be himself or herself, to be both close and intimate, and to manifest his or her own unique nature as part of the wholeness of nature.

Cultivating Selfhood

When we discussed acceptance, we said it was a position that took effort, took a commitment and the labor to make it manifest. It takes exertion to be a person who can accept. The same is true of being a healthy family. It takes commitment and effort. It must be an active process. It is difficult for us in our agonistic Western culture to understand this, because familial acceptance is a way of being more than one of doing. Nonetheless, such acceptance is an active process. It is a commitment to living, to growth. It is having the same investment in our children's emotional health and growth as we do in their physical, mental, academic, and athletic well-being. To make this effort, parents must have the same commitment to themselves and with each other. In *Patterns of Culture,* Ruth Benedict said: "Our children are not individuals whose rights and tastes are casually respected from infancy as they are in some primitive societies. . . . They are fundamentally extensions of our own egos and give a special opportunity for the display of authority." Displays of authority are not acceptance; *healthy* closeness does not destroy *self.*

We earlier spoke of "cultivating" people, couples, and families. The metaphor expresses what should be real. A good farmer *tends* nature. He or she allows what nature offers to happen in the most growthful way possible. Reaping the best people possible is much the same process. A commitment to tend nature in families is in reality a commitment to living on all levels. To experience life, not just watch it go by. To experience our children, not simply observe them growing older. To experience our spouses instead of merely watching them from up close. To experience *ourselves,* not to linger about waiting for someone else to free us. Instead, too often, as Emerson said, "We are always getting ready to live, but never living."

Such awareness requires this active process because most of us will get little support from our culture, society, or peers. Two weeks of vacation per year to devote to play, to rest, to being yourself, and being with your family, is a very small priority to place on things of such devastating importance. Two weeks of a year to re-create *ourselves.* The choice is a statement of where we currently are as a culture and a society. I *(Pat)* had the opportunity a few years ago of spending several hours with an Italian gentleman. He was a mid-level executive, the father of four, married for nineteen years, who worked for an automobile company. One thing he could absolutely not understand about this country was our institution of two weeks vacation a year. He himself had four times as much formal vacation each year, two months entirely given to being with his family, being himself, playing, and enjoying life. I had no reply. Much of what we all see in families that we do not like, what we worry about in our own families, derives from our overinvolvement in closeness, in "security." Play, risk, creativity, animation, and intimacy are all too often missing from family life, and all too vital to be compartmentalized in "vacations" from our "real lives."

14

Personal Expansion . . . Evolution, Ecology, Creativity, and the Unconscious

It may be that our role on this planet is not
to worship God—but to create him.

—Arthur C. Clarke

Why did Archimedes jump out of the bath and shout, "Eureka!"? Was his response not his *intimate self* shouting in relief? Did he not feel the immediate, wondrous connection of *self* with nature? Not simply the excitement of intellectual discovery, but the joy of being momentarily intimate and, as is always true with intimacy, the joy of learning something new. Was he not learning something new and different about himself and his nature, an awareness that his human nature is part of all nature, finding an even more exciting awareness—the knowledge that what he is as a human being allows him to more surely know all of nature. Intimate self-knowledge becomes an exciting, eternal, widening sense of connection with what there really is in nature. Human beings, seeing nature as a fabric within which they are woven, can then experience the connections that make knowledge possible. This is a way of knowing that comes from being connected, in contrast to knowledge that comes from being convinced of what things should be. It is knowing from what *is,* not what is supposed to be. It is experiential, not judgmental. You can know only you, you can know intimately only what you are connected to through your *self.* And only in that experience can you change personally. Only in that experience do you feel your basic humanness, your commonality, your being so beautifully a part of nature.

We individually have the same difficulty as those who "study man." In *Reinventing Anthropology,* Stanley Diamond wrote: "The anthropologist who treats the indigene [native] as an object may define himself as relatively free and integrated, a subject, a person, but that is an illusion. In order to objectify the other, one is, at the same time, compelled to objectify the self." This dilemma, the more formal statement of what we earlier described as the difference between the knowledge of connection and the knowledge of assimilation, is an academic way of discussing the pairing of closeness and intimacy. The knowledge of assimilation, closeness, system is just as important as that of connection, process, intimacy, but we are *self*-defeatingly overbalanced in its direction. As Diamond goes on to say, "If self-knowledge is irrelevant, so is self-criticism." We can know *ourselves* only in *process,* in our experience of our participation in nature. That reciprocal relationship is our commonality.

The *I-other* dyad (the *I-me/other* connection of intimacy, and what we have described as the intimate experience) becomes the prototype for our understanding of everything in nature. We can understand things only out of a clear acceptance of our being integrally connected to those things. It is the *experience* within which we know, because only in it do we experience nature with its intimate connections. The dyad is our metaphor in an existence defined by metaphors. It is probable that all of our metaphorical systems are symmetrical, for they appear to mirror a common truth of nature. Psychology, biology, chemistry, physics, sociology, and all the other metaphors of nature that we term "sciences" will probably converge, as they develop in understanding, in a consensual, communal, unitary system. The same holistic "system" will be the basis of music, of the arts, and of mathematics. The underlying natural fabric will be seen in its symmetry, in all of our knowledge. Natural truth is process, not stasis. This principle is one that the *intimate self* immediately recognizes. All of nature, including human beings, participate in this process, and can therefore experience it and know it.

If this is indeed true, then everything from God to atoms "knows" the same process. That universality is the most profound implication of intimacy. All of us, God, trees, fish, atoms, you and I, know the same truths. Nature always knows what it needs to know. Not being *intimate selves,* we become unnatural, and have no way of knowing what we need to know, no way to take in the knowledge so immediately available in the intimate experience. The *intimate self* knows another person, or a flower, much more fully than the *I* that looks at the other as someone or something "out there," or the *me* that sees only its own reflection.

Nature knows what it needs to know, but only in the moment. God or nature, who or whatever one calls the wholeness, would have no growth, no motion, and certainly no joy in preknowing everything. All the dimensions of life are marked by motion and growth. There is an expanding perimeter of new knowing radiating out from nature, from us. This is what we mean by creativity. We create new space and knowing with each new way of being, experiencing, seeing, hearing, or existing. Paradoxically, if you already knew everything about your spouse there would be no further reason to be married; if you already knew everything about life, there would be no point in living. Fortunately, this is not possible, for, like you, your spouse is constantly changing, and life is too.

For most of this century, the human unconscious has been viewed in a negative way, seen as a cesspool of conflict, neurotic drives and impulses, an uncontrolled danger. This evaluation is a profoundly distorted and perverse concept of the unconscious. The unconscious is the natural part of us, the part of us most congruent with nature. The unconscious perpetuates in humans the wisdom of animals and plants: a wisdom that so perfectly manages breathing, heartbeat, and the intricate chemistry of our human bodies as exquisitely as animal and plant ecologies manage to keep their balance—when not interfered with by us. In this ecology, the unconscious is an essential part of the *intimate self*. Listened to and believed in, the unconscious allows more knowing, and creates more relationship. The unconscious takes us back to the natural by putting us back in touch with our nature.

Evolution is the growing unconscious. The anthropologist Claude Lévi-Strauss said that every conscious point has its unconscious counterpoint. The obverse of this is not, we believe, true. The expanding perimeter of not only our evolution as a species, but more particularly of our growth and movement in personal relationship, depends on our trust in the unconscious, our acceptance of its constantly "creating" nature (in other words, it creates new points that are not represented in consciousness). There is no certain, predetermined conscious set in relationship. The risk in life is a true risk, the risk of being intimate. We learn something new and are changed. Our perimeter enlarges; we are in touch with more than we were before the intimate moment. We move out into the unknown and make new connections. These vitalizing new connections are primarily unconscious. We feel the energy, the animation, and the connection, even if we are unaware of it. Since the unconscious is our deepest bond with nature, through it we know a little more of all of nature, including human nature.

As part of the same reciprocal, natural universe, we are responsible for our *selves*. Blaming *others* is both pointless and futile. Blaming your spouse, your lover, your parent, your child, your God, or any external *other* is not only futile, it is unnatural and arrogant. Have you ever seen a wild animal blame another? Can you imagine the grass dying under the fallen pine needles spending its energy blaming the pine trees, rather than doing its best to break through to the sunlight again? A tuft of green grass pushing its way up in the midst of a macadam driveway is an impressive sight. It is also intimate. To abrogate your responsibility for your *self* is to separate your *self* from nature, to become captured by your own system or, even worse, someone else's system. Wild animals do not, of course, paint Sistine Chapels, nor does grass create mathematics; we are conscious as well as unconscious. But the "art" is a reflection and experience of nature, and the mathematics is inherent in "what is." Remaining balanced is still our natural need, and in us becomes a *self*-responsibility.

In *Personal Knowledge,* the physical chemist and philosopher Michael Polanyi says: "If we ask whether Euclid's theorems existed before they were discovered, the answer is obviously No, in the same sense as we would say that Shakespeare's sonnets did not exist before he wrote them. But we cannot therefore say that the truth of geometry or the beauty of poetry came into existence at any particular place and time, for these constitute the universal pole of our appreciation, which cannot be observed noncommittally like objects in space and time." Truth, beauty, and love are dimensions of reality, not aspects of culture.

Intimacy as Ecology

I *(Tom)* once had a dream in which I had a "conversation" with God. I kept calling Him, and when He finally answered I told Him I was very concerned with what was going on down here. To my surprise, He wondered why. I told Him that there was a lot of pain and suffering down here, people were hurting and starving, and violence was getting out of hand. He said gently, "I didn't know that." Enraged, I asked Him why He did not know that. He said, "When I put you all down there, everything was fine." I asked, "Well, where have you been?" He said, "I've been tending my rose garden." I was even more infuriated. He listened patiently to my tirade, then replied, "Tom, aren't you having any fun? You sound distraught." I railed at him again. Finally He said in a compassionate tone, "I hope you find more joy in your life. I have to go back to my rose garden. You know, Tom, you might consider farming trees."

We are not only *responsible for* continuing to experience and learn more, we are also *responsible to* what we do know. It is senseless continually to complain about the foulness of our water while we continue to pollute it, even though we know what causes pollution. We are irresponsible, but we are not ignorant. We can know as nature knows, or we can choose not to. Apart from human beings, and perhaps domesticated animals, nature chooses to live by what it knows. We think it hardly arguable that it lives more sensibly and perhaps even more compassionately. But man's arogance goes beyond his refusal to learn from nature, including his own nature. He presumes to teach nature what nature already knows. Some of our interventions are enormously helpful to us; some, however, are disastrous to all of nature, including our own. The polio virus probably does just as well in nature, despite man's developing a vaccine to protect himself from it. In such cases, we are not attempting to reteach nature. We are simply being an inventive part of it. Bacteria do not appear to have been daunted by the advent of antibiotics. Humans, at least for the time being, just get along with bacteria a little better. This is different from our attempting to reteach the human body what nutrients it needs in order to stay healthy, simply because these new forms of nutrients suit the mechanics of the food industry and increase their profits. Nature knows what nutrients the human body needs, and in what form they are best ingested.

Such unwarranted intervention is on the same level as our trying to reteach primary feelings. You cannot teach humans how to feel angry, sad, or sexual. You can teach them metafeelings, frequently unhealthy ones, such as how to be guilty, ashamed and embarrassed; sometimes helpful ones, such as caretaking, consideration, and politeness. We cannot teach intimacy, but we can teach man to be fearful of it. We can make him afraid to know, and unwilling to be responsible for himself. When we do, we pay a heavy price.

Healthy ecology is best visualized as a dance. Our human nature dances with all *others* in the natural community. Any fear we develop of experiencing our nature makes us an awkward and stilted dance partner. If we are petrified by dogs, they are much more likely to attack us. Those afraid of the water end up being the ones who drown. By and large, human beings have become wallflowers at the dance of nature. In most instances, we feel exactly the same wistful longings but fearful inability to be ourselves, do what we want to do, be what we can be, that most wallflowers feel at dances. Most of us are watchers, not dancers. We are not living, but fearfully maintaining our secure but deadened existence. We watch life on television or, just as unsatisfyingly, we watch life among *others* instead of living it *ourselves.* We watch life literally, not just metaphorically. It has become our politics, our sexuality, our morality, our spirituality. We watch and vicariously pretend to be. To understand this is to comprehend the insanity of the person who continues to smoke while at the same time obsessing over whether he should stop eating eggs because of the cholesterol in them. Or the insanity of the person who claims that killing everyone in a small rural village is a way of making it peaceful. Or the absurd conviction that imposing your doctrinal beliefs about religion or morality on someone else will increase the spirituality of mankind. Our basic insanity is our unnatural conviction that what we believe and want in our private, self-constructed, and unreal worlds can be imposed on the rest of nature, including human nature. It *is* insanity. It is righteousness, judgmentalism, and irresponsible blaming. The *intimate self* knows better.

We spoke earlier of islands of loneliness. The image is the poet John Donne's (from *Devotions upon Emergent Occasions*): "No man is an island, entire of itself; every man is a piece of the continent, a part of the main. . . . any man's death diminishes me, because I am involved in mankind; and therefore never send to know for whom the bell tolls; it tolls for thee." We know of no more relevant way of addressing the major issues facing humanity today than to deal with the lack of intimacy, to understand the conditions that are conducive to it, and the conditions that make it unlikely. We are convinced that crucial problems like the threat of nuclear destruction, world hunger, terrorism, and nationalistic megalomania will not be dealt with simply politically. They must be dealt with personally. They will be dealt with when we are neither willing to destroy our *selves* nor need to destroy the *other*. In intimacy, we are clearly aware that the destruction of either partner in a dyad amounts to the destruction of both.

Primary pairings are societal phenomena as well as individual experiences. Intimacy is paramount in both; the lack of it is disastrous in both. But we have to begin in the simple, one-to-one, human relationship. You and me. We are far more alike than we are different. Can we reclaim some natural balance? Be more concerned with creating, energizing, enhancing, knowing, and growing? Otherwise, our erroneous conviction that security lies in maintenance and closeness will undoubtedly come full circle, and confront us with our foolishness by destroying us. Evolution is an ongoing process. Nature provides opportunities, not answers. There is no lasting security. When we refuse to risk and therefore avoid intimacy, we are trying to stop the evolutionary process. We do not succeed. Nature, relationship, moves on. We simply become further out of touch, and therefore less likely to survive—either in relationship or in nature.

With the growth in population, with urbanization, industrialization, with the increase in the speed and ease of transportation and information dissemination, human beings have become closer and closer. In consequence, we have become more and more involved with, and addicted to, the closeness aspects of relationship—maintenance, familiarity, and security. We let our systems identify us. Our uniqueness is hidden, even from ourselves. The consequences are what one would expect. There are few human beings now who know where the animals or even the flowers are, know in what direction home lies, know when it is safe to be where, whom it is safe to be near, know how to be easily and naturally themselves in their environment. There are few humans who in the intimate experience of their environment are part of that environment and participate joyfully in that knowledge: grow from it. Most of us have lost our balance in the intimacy-closeness matrix, lost our balance in personal pairing, in primary relationship, in our sexuality, in our family life. It is in these areas that we fundamentally learn the balance, or imbalance, of intimacy and closeness. For better or worse, such learning then affects all levels of our being: work, community, government, nation, and world. The cradle of learning for this powerful and essential balance between intimacy and closeness is the one-to-one relationship and the family experience. Here is where we become addicted to closeness and fearful of intimacy. The difficulties humans have establishing a gratifying intimate relatedness to the world around them simply reflect the more microcosmic, individual experiences they have had in relationships and in their families.

Our lack of intimacy (in our *selves,* our pairings, and our families) manifests itself in divorce, spouse abuse, child abuse, alcohol and drug abuse, neurosis, and even psychosis. On a broader social level, lack of intimacy brings us terrorism, war, starvation, acid rain, and potential nuclear destruction.

The pain and tragedy brought about in individuals and families by a failure of intimacy is lamentable. The perversion of nature on the global level brought about by the same failure of intimacy is species suicide. The means to correct this failure depends on our ability to become more easily intimate in our close relationships, pairings, and family. Politics will not suffice: nor dogmas, nor laws, nor any *system.* We cannot drop out of the evolutionary process. We cannot commit ourselves permanently and irrevocably to maintenance and familiarity. Most significantly, we cannot give up our intimate evolutionary thrusts in our personal relationships and families. We cannot, so long as we are alive, exist entirely in the stasis of security and closeness. Given a personal experience in intimacy, human beings will remain a part of the natural process, capable of evolving, free to change course and position in the time and space of the rest of the world. Given intimacy, we will survive and even flourish. Nature is not perverse. If we live comfortably within nature, we will not perversely destroy ourselves. That is the ultimate importance of intimacy. If balanced with closeness, it assures survival and growth. Security assures neither.

We can more clearly recognize the patterns of nature by observing on the macrocosmic level that which we more easily experience in the microcosm of interpersonal experience. In *The People of the Lake,* Richard Leakey says:

An alternative explanation for this heretical un-Western behavior [primitive man not amassing food and possessions] is that they [primitives] have a firm security about their way of life. As Rodney Needham has said, their behavior suggests that gatherer-hunters have "a confidence in the capacity of the environment to support them, and in their own ability to extract their livelihood from it." Life for most gatherer-hunters is a steady rhythm of work, leisure, and socializing. They move with an easy nonchalance from camp to camp, not with a fatalistic resignation, but with a confident assurance that stems from a true intimacy with nature.

Let us suppose that thousands of years ago human beings lived in a balance of closeness (maintenance, familiarity) and intimacy (renewing, energizing creativity). The balance was not simply primitive society's philosophical approach to life, but was their existential reality. Existence depended on both intimacy and closeness in a very pragmatic way. You maintained your familial group closeness and your tribal closeness for safety, good hunting, and the various other life activities that required maintenance, predictability, and real accommodation. The closeness was not neurotically compelled but naturally and healthfully chosen. The familiarity of your cave, your valley, and your clan meant security.

Balancing this closeness was a healthy intimacy, a connection to nature that allowed learning and creating. Intimate risking, which led to increased connection, more animation, and further *self*-knowledge, was certainly as important for survival as the natural closeness that it engendered. Without closeness and attention to maintenance there would have been unending risk, perilous change, and growth without direction. The clan would not have survived. Without intimacy, without the *intimate self* experience, there would have been stagnation, mislearning, and an inevitable alienation from nature. Again, the clan would not have survived. We are not proposing a pastoral, "happy" prehistoric man. We are speaking to the reality of both closeness and intimacy as core biological and evolutionary life dimensions. Civilization has *profound* impact on the changing course of humanity. We *are* suggesting that, unfortunately, one of its major impacts is the systemization of man.

Compare this construct of the clan member of thousands of years ago to the increasingly urbanized, industrialized, informationized, systematized person of today. Compare him with us, not romantically, but in the practical sense of how we live in the world today. The modern man usually has no immediate contact with his own territory, his food supply, his clan, much less his neighboring clans, his animals, or his plants. He is a man detached from nature. He is probably intimate only in his dreams, and he laughingly comments on how strange his dreams are. He touches very little, and when he does, he feels awkward, so he touches less and less. He is out of contact with his own physical healthiness. The likelihood of any experiential growth, change, creativity, or personal animation in him is minimal. He is unlikely to be living in the world as it really is. He is even less likely to be living in the world as he really is.

This hypothetical man is one of the many people who come to therapy. In them, the intimate experience has diminished to a degree no longer compatible with personhood. The *intimate self* is actively participatory and concerned with growth, not detached, uninvolved, or mainly concerned with maintenance and stability. It is committed to evolving rather than revolving. The *intimate self* is unafraid of change. It not only seeks change but allows it to occur, in contrast to the fearfulness of change so characteristic of modern man. The *intimate self* has the assurance and comfort of knowing it is always a part of a community of *others* that change with it. It never feels the awful loneliness of modern man, but changes in connection with an ever-changing world. The *intimate self* is also unashamedly adaptive. It has no pride. It has no need to protect its system. It can change with the change in the *other*. It moves with life as it evolves, with no apparent need to stay the same because of an investment in maintaining itself as is, or a fear of being different. Natural as the unconscious, it moves as we as humans move in our dreams. It is always relational because of its ever-present awareness of connection with the *other:* it has no need to be special; is content to be part of nature. Consequently, it has no need to be right; it is content just to be. Therefore, it never feels alone.

Intimacy as Creativity

When we refer to the *intimate self* as "it," we of course are not describing an entity separate from the person, but an integral part of all human beings, probably the most vital part. It is the part of us that ensures first our survival (through continuing evolution) and second our creativity. What does creativity mean when we are describing human relationship? How is one creative in relationship? Obviously, by participating *in the relationship* in a new and different way. The result, of course, is a new and different relationship, even though the created difference may be slight. Years of continuing slight differences keep the relationship viable and a creative joy. There are few experiences in life as energizing as someone who is very familiar acting differently. It is much more exciting than a stranger being strange.

There are many "different" experiences that occur between two people that are not creative and do not energize relationship. To be creative, change must be experienced *in the relationship,* not simply affect the relationship. In fact, these latter experiences usually harm the relationship, either directly or by keeping it from changing. A person who has difficulty with his anger with his lover may begin to play golf on the weekends in order to avoid confronting his anger. His avoidance will change the relationship, but probably for the worse. The person who has been spending all of his nonworking time dependently near his lover because he has difficulty establishing his own personal space may enthusiastically decide to join a Saturday-morning bike club. His active choice probably will make a creative difference in their relationship, for the change is done *in relationship,* and without anger. The choice is *self*-responsible. The behaviors of the two people are the same; the experiences are different. The creative differences are commonly such rearrangements in personal spaces. They almost always involve a new and different feeling shared with the other, a different way of being behaviorally, a significant shift in the attitude of acceptance, or a new sense of connection with each other. They make experience different.

What causes change on a larger scale (culturally, on the system level) is a much-debated subject. Cultural anthropology has moved from the cultural evolutionism of Spencer and Marx to the diffusionism of Frazer to the cultural relativism of Franz Boas. In more recent years we have fused functionalism and structuralism into the current structural-functionalism. As a colleague who is both biologist and anthropologist says, "Anthropology seems a science in search of a paradigm." On the one hand we hear, in *The Imperial Animal,* Robin Fox and Lionel Tiger say:

> The insights gained from the evolutionary, species-wide perspective . . . leave us less helpless in the long run. Without this perspective, we are not tackling reality but only our own cultural versions of reality—and often just our conceit about what reality should be. Most of our problems . . . have to do with the constraints and distortions of behavior that we create, or, to be kind, that are created by the almost impossibly difficult context into which we are trying to fit our evolved human behavior. . . . If there is any hope or confidence in the future of man, it resides in the lie this perspective gives to the dismal theories of culturalists of whatever school. If man were indeed a blank slate for his culture to write on at will whatever perverse message it chose, we would be in even greater peril than we appear to be. . . . Men do not need to learn or to be taught that slavery and exploitation are inhuman. They know they are. And they know this because they are human themselves. . . .

On the other hand is the classical cultural anthropological position that cultural evolution has replaced biological evolution in man and, as anthropologist Marvin Harris says in *Culture, People, Nature,* "All cultural differences and similarities have been produced by divergent, convergent, or parallel evolution"—all types of *cultural* evolution.

The role of particular creative individuals in changing larger systems is especially debated. We would think that since culture is a system, changes in culture are most often systemic. That is, they have their roots in closeness (economics, wars, etc.) instead of intimacy. The intimate acts of individuals are most often either consumed or co-opted by the system. But we feel that cultural forms have their prototypes in the intimate unconscious, and that individual creative differences are probably a major force in *provoking* the system to change itself. Art, the creative act (intimacy), in whatever form, is the primal initiator of change in humans as individuals. This changing is always relational, coming out of *self,* and therefore contains elements of both individual and society, closeness and intimacy, system and dyad. These changes usually take place in "quantumlike" jumps, and then disseminate to manifest themselves in longer-term effects in other areas of the system. Innovators from Plato, Copernicus, Joan of Arc, Shakespeare, and Jefferson to Marx, Margaret Mead, Picasso, and John Lennon have greatly influenced the flow of history: They changed how people saw themselves, as well as how they saw each other and the world around them. With few exceptions, such creative people always seem to bring us closer to the realization that all of nature is one. In being creative, one literally creates a new place to be. If one then connects with another, this newly created space allows the other a new way of being. These newly created spaces become a new part of the ecosystem, a new expression of the unconscious, a new movement in the expanding perimeter of our true environment.

Early man had to be creative in order to survive day-to-day, had to create new solutions to life and death problems, and find new answers for newly discovered questions. The need for new words to formulate and communicate those answers, or words to create new internal maps of territory, relationships, and being, was a reality of living. As societies have become increasingly complex and diversified (and therefore closeness-oriented and maintenance-addicted), creativity has become the province of only "special people," "artists." These "special people" are expected and allowed to be countercultural. They constantly challenge the current culture, and question the answers of the cultural guardians, the experts, the cultural maintenance men. The "special people" can still be creative because they have not been captured by the culture's systems. Our cultural images of the artist, the scientist, the revolutionary, and the naturalist as misfits or eccentrics sadly convey how fearful of change we have become in our society. Our images of creativity are either satirical and negating, or worshipful and romanticized. Our fear of the creative *intimate self* is very real and operational. Creativity has become a countercultural risk, rather than the natural ally of cultural health and growth.

Currently, even the counterculture is declining. Rebellious creativity is as highly specialized, localized, and suspect as it has been at other times in the past when the "culture" overwhelmed the individual. Well-publicized pseudo-creativity, mass-manufactured creativity, and mass-marketed creativity crowd out the natural realities. "Creativity" in the service of cultural maintenance, consumer economics, and shaping public opinion is not creativity. We have co-opted even the bizarre for systemic consumption. If slasher movies, nuclear toys, child pornography, and government terrorism are part of the system, part of security, a way to make money, and a way to control people, then there is little left in our institutional repertoire to express genuine creativity.

In *The Counterfeiters,* Hugh Kenner speaks to this loss: "And to see art in this way progressively losing its skin and bowels, progressively firming and flexing its epistemological skeleton, is to see mimed the retreat of all experience whatever from full apprehensibility (hence the shrill rage of [D. H.] Lawrence). It is always so, in the realm of the counterfeiters. Imagination, grown specialized, is not fed on visions but is curious about applications." This "art" in the service of system is, of course, not art at all.

Our institutional emphases serve our concern with closeness and stability at all costs. The constant complaints that we as therapists hear in our offices, that you hear at work, at parties, or in your neighborhood, reflect this oppression of intimacy and creativity in favor of maintaining the close, and closed, system. "I wish they would just give me some responsibility." "I would just like a chance to be a little creative, to have some input that makes a difference." "Nobody listens to a damn thing I have to say." "I wonder what it would be like to be a carpenter, this office work sure gets me down." "Is this all there is?" "I would like to contribute something." "I would like to help but I don't know what to do."

There are, of course, always exceptions. A patient of ours who was a very successful businessman running a large corporation had hired a young M.B.A. to fill a responsible position in his company. After three months on the job, the young new executive shared with his employer his impression that, after having looked closely at the operation for three months, there was not a thing he would change. The young man was let go. Security is not an end point; it is often an end. Might a person who seeks the "perfect" partner be looking in the wrong direction? Might not a wife stating that she is perfectly satisfied with her relationship to her husband suggest to us that everything is not well in the marriage? As therapists, we have sat with scores of depressed couples who said that things were "perfect." Then why did they come to us?

Nicholas is one year short of his thirtieth birthday. He has been to college, has an M.A., and is finishing his Ph.D. Emily, his wife, is concerned because Nicholas constantly talks about doing something else, living somewhere else, and generally being someone else, and she experiences this as a rejection of her. It is not. Nicholas is searching desperately for some way to be himself. He intuitively fears being captured by the system. That intuition is rather common. In most it will remain a fear, an abiding discontent, or, perhaps worse, be acted out in some uncreative, unproductive rebellion against the system. With such rebellion, you remain a captive of the very system you are trying to avoid. Nicholas wants to find something outside himself that will give him a sense of being free. He will not find it outside himself. Emily's concern is appropriate if she is fearful that he will dissipate his personal energies in abortive discontent. But more likely, and even sadder, she is concerned about security. If that is true, she participates in keeping Nicholas as he is. Only if one of them, or both, can risk the *intimate self* experience (being themselves with each other in their world as it presently is) do they have a chance to find what they both so desperately want: he, his real freedom, and she, real safety because of a newfound sense of freedom to be herself. People searching, like Nicholas, are usually looking for intimacy, in themselves, in their relationships, in their marriages, in their careers, in their lives. The clearest manifestation of such intimacy is the creativeness of a new experience and the vibrant animation that accompanies it.

Creativity must be reclaimed as the province of all of us, both in our relationships and in our culture. It does not suffice for only the "special people" to have it. The only way to ordinarily and commonly be creative is to ongoingly and ordinarily be intimate. Only in this way can we constantly re-create ourselves. Our more usual, secondhand recreations (going to the movies or watching television) cannot substitute. Creativity has to be experienced in relationship. Only in that related re-creating can we expand our connection with each other and with our world. That is "living in the world in good faith." Intimacy and closeness are again balanced. We have better maintenance, easier familiarity, fonder remembering, less confining predictability, more appropriate consciousness, natural roles, and better time and space orientation. We have more healthy generosity, more energy and creativity, heightened animation, contact with our unconscious, increased freedom, re-created spirituality, openness and risking, and a sense of timeless and spaceless being.

Beauty, love, and good faith flourish in such a balanced matrix, one that mirrors the patterns of nature. Like musical harmonies, the balanced matrix has overtones, undertones, and resonances that make each new experience slightly different from earlier ones. Living this way, our relationships, our family, our work experience, our being within ourselves, is never the same. It is always renewing, and we continually learn. The basic and essential quality of the intimate experience can be stated simply: "I am going to be me regardless of the other, but I am going to be me in unremitting relation to that other while I am being me. I will be what I really am, while creating space within which the other can be whatever he, she, or it is." That is the essential function of the *intimate self.*

Dreams are this way, nonverbal communication is this way, real creativity is this way, the unconscious is this way, evolution is this way. All of life and living in the world in good faith are this way. Art is clearly this way. Artists are the painters of dreams, poets of evolution both personal and physical, playwrights of the unconscious, and choreographers of nature's dance. Artists know that all but intimacy is a compromise; a realistic, important, pragmatic, and necessary compromise to assure the closeness and accommodations essential to stability. But a compromise nonetheless. Compromising takes us momentarily out of the flow of natural time and space. Momentarily we forgo the creative risk, the evolving, energizing changes, and the natural dance. But without healthy closeness, maintenance, and stability, intimate creativity could not occur. Newness can occur only in order. Even artists are involved in the stability and concern with closeness. "There is no personal freedom," says Charles Hampden-Turner in *Maps of the Mind,* "in seeking to conquer ecological connectedness." Healthy closeness is the order of ecology, just as intimacy is participation in it.

Dreaming and Intimacy

In another dream of mine *(Tom),* God talked to me, again only as a voice. God said, "Do you know you are a member of the Boy Scouts?" I replied, "No, I didn't." God went on, "Do you know you are a member of the NAACP?" Once again I said no. "Do you know you are a member of the Ku Klux Klan?" No again. "Do you know you are a member of the Society to Preserve the Whales?" No again. "Do you know you are a member of the Nazi party?" No again. "Do you know you are a member of the Sandy Springs Garden Club?" No again. This went on. Finally I asked, "What do I do in these organizations?" He said, "You are president." I asked, "What do the others do?" He replied, "They are the president, too. Everybody is the president." I asked, "Who does the work?" He replied, "I do." Without expanding on either the personal or philosophical implications of the dream, it describes for me what we have been saying throughout this book. We are all part of all of nature. There are really no separate camps. We are part of what we affirm, *and* what we abhor. Only by knowing our participation in the things we abhor can we change them and return in faith to the natural evolutionary process. God, whatever God is to you, really does the work. But that makes us more, not less, responsible.

If you accept that dreaming is an unconscious, natural, and creative activity, then the connectivity we experience in dreams, the metaphors that emerge from our internal symbology, can teach us much about intimacy. Dreaming directly reflects the unconscious, and the unconscious is both natural and communal. Dreaming also has obvious conscious components that reflect our daily experiences, worries, and frustrations. However, we are unconscious when we dream. Even in daydreaming we are in an altered state of consciousness. Deeper than sorting out the day's experience, dreaming obviously has natural and biological functions. Dreaming is closer to nature than it is to civilized social experience.

I *(Pat)* have for years used dreams as one of the ways to deal with troublesome personal issues: I ask myself to dream about a problem. I am looking for a new way of seeing and dealing with a personal dilemma and often find that my dreams respond to the request. Sometimes the response is clear, and directly useful. More often, the response is symbolic or metaphorical. The latter, of course, leaves me with an inherent ambiguity. Like those who listened to the Delphic oracle, I may learn some essential, illuminating truth about myself, or I may conveniently misunderstand the dream in a self-serving way. I can never know for sure what the symbols "meant." Generally, however, my dreams reteach me the importance of being myself in relationships. They remind me to suspect the systems that can so easily and unsuspectingly capture me, and to commit myself to a constant return to my nature. I have learned to listen to my dreams. When I do not, I inevitably end up unhappy, ungentle, uncaring, and unnatural. Neurotic behavior never gains the end it supposedly is designed for. It does not make us safer. I have come to suspect any preoccupation I develop with security.

Dreaming has many of the characteristics of intimacy. It is creative, intense, animating, and energizing, and can be growthful, depending on how seriously we attend to it. Dreams are a direct connection to our unconscious, our communal nature, our *intimate selves*. In dreams, our experiences are heightened as they are in the intimate experience. The normal rules of space and time are abandoned. The world of dreams does not operate by cause and effect: Our dreams have a natural connectivity, in both metaphor and symbology, that is remarkably intuitive of personal truth. The connections exist not only within a single dream, but run from dream to dream over the course of our existence.

Dreaming is a universal human experience; quite probably, it is at least metaphorically characteristic of our relationship to all living things. Recent research is continually suggesting new functions of dreaming, both psychological and physiological. Since as experiential therapists we view physiology and psychology as interchangeable and unitary, we would like to add a suggestion for a natural and fundamental function of dreaming. Dreaming may be the brain's way of being intimate with itself. We have said many times that the intimate experience is the one dimension in which change on a *self* level occurs. Without this change and growth, there is only dying. It would be astonishing if nature did not build in some mechanism to foster and protect life. A process to assure a slow but constant reenergization, reanimation, and re-creation of the psychic self. The renewal would have to be a constant, experiential reconnection to the unconscious, the deepest natural component of living beings. Through the unconscious we remember our environment, our ecology, the intimate wholeness of nature, including human nature. Dreaming allows us the basic experience of the *intimate self* unendingly and quite effectively.

The Intimate Unconscious

> To him who in the love of Nature holds
> Communion with her visible forms, she speaks
> A various language.
>
> —William Cullen Bryant
> "Thanatopsis"

Earlier, we said that the unconscious is not simply a chaotic, seething mass of primitive drives, conflicts, and primary-process thinking. Rather, it reflects the reassuring fact that we as human beings are profoundly rooted in a universal natural reality or matrix.

Consciously we are only peripherally aware of this, except in passionate moments. Intimacy reminds us. We are part of a larger whole, each individual part of which contains its total, natural, beautiful wholeness. The unconscious is the most powerful and significant expression of the *intimate self*. To stifle intimacy is to curtail the unconscious flow. We become deprived of our connections to our natural world, and exist only in our constructed worlds. We become creatively and relationally impotent. If we cannot occasionally but repeatedly live in our conscious lives as we live in our dreams, we slowly atrophy. Both our *selves* and our relationships slowly expire. In the words of Henry David Thoreau, "Dreams are the touchstones of our characters." In them we are reconnected to our unconscious. To trust consciousness more than unconsciousness is to forgo intimacy. It is to move to an addictive, apprehensive concern with closeness and with our personally constructed worlds. We must surely begin to see that the "dream" is more real and rational than our own constructed reality. Is mutually assured nuclear destruction rational? Is acid rain rational? The "dream" is part of real time and space. It dramatizes the process of life as it really exists in nature. This is why art, in all of its various expressions, gives the only permanence to culture, history, and the evolution of life. Only that which exists in the multidimensional, ever-changing world of time, space, and being can survive. All that exists in constructed worlds, idiosyncratic worlds of need and security, disappears with the death of the maker, whether individual or societal—both Caesar's power and the Roman Empire.

"Unconscious" is not really a useful or descriptive word. It simply means "that which is not conscious," which really tells us nothing about what it *is*. The negative name belies the power of the concept. Perhaps "unconscious" should be renamed the "intimator," the natural connector, the natural spirit, the nexus, or, perhaps, in Paul Tillich's phrase, the "ground substance." Whatever it is, it is a universal natural constant, not an absence of something else. We do not call God the "inhuman." We do not know what God is, or nature is, or life is, but we give them names that signify what they seem to be, not what they are not. The unconscious is actively powerful and universal. Not to trust it is not to trust life itself. Life is risking. Without risk there is no intimacy, and without intimacy there is no life. Consciousness is proper and cautious. For all of its importance, consciousness paradoxically is more affiliated with death and dying. In its awareness of death, and its fear of it, consciousness expends most of its time and energy trying to prevent death, rather than promoting life. In contrast, the unconscious has a natural concern with life. To the unconscious, death is simply part of the cycle of life. Consciousness is concerned with "knowing." Not knowing leaves us insecure. "Knowing" is placed in the service of keeping us from dying. It thereby forgoes its natural function: intimately knowing the *other* and actively promoting life. Consciousness defends against its own demise. Thus it moves us into a frightful paradox, because the only real security there is, is death itself.

What we do not know consciously is much more important to our living than what we do know. The willingness to *be* when we do not "know" is far more creative of intimacy than what we *do* when we do "know." What we do not know is the substrate and nourishment out of which life emerges, with which it grows, re-creates and renews itself. Not knowing guarantees evolution, both personal and physical. It makes life happen. To define God, as most humans do, as one who preknows and prejudges everything not only makes the deity dreary and boring, it also makes God simply another construct of ours, another prejudgment, another nonreciprocal source of blame and judgment.

The capacity each of us has for life in the natural world, life in relationship to *others* simply as we are, depends primarily on how many of our unconscious skills and processes can be transferred into an alive consciousness. The only vehicle of this transfer is the intimate experience, whether we are experiencing trees, stars, flowers, music, books, lovers, children, parents, spouses, strangers, friends, or enemies; only intimacy allows change.

We cannot be intimate consciously, only unconsciously. Closeness, healthy or unhealthy, happens only in consciousness. Intimacy is the movement into the unconscious with another while you are awake and not dreaming, neither day nor night dreaming. We are not fantasizing; we are really there with *others* when they are really there with us. Intimacy is always relational. In the intimate experience, you know exactly what I know, what Anna Pavlova or Picasso knew, what Buddha or Saint Theresa knew, and, perhaps most important, what your mother knew when she was being honest. You know what God knows; you know your true ecology. The only path to this knowledge is the *intimate self.*

Epilogue

Life is not a problem to be solved but a reality to be experienced.

—SØREN KIERKEGAARD

In *The Art of Intimacy* we have shared the personal struggles of many of the people we see in therapy. In large part, their struggles are their search for intimacy. What then of Sarah, the woman first met in the Prologue, who came in depressed and unconnected to her husband? Will she find what she seeks, learn to be joyfully Sarah, connected intimately to her world? What of William; will he learn to relate—as him*self*—to another? What of the multitude of other Sarahs and Williams who do not see psychotherapists at all? What can they do to realize themselves? Or you and I, walking the beach in Acadia or Point Reyes or along the Outer Banks of North Carolina—can we become connected to our past and future, know our nature? Can we learn there, in the words of e. e. cummings (from *95 poems by e. e. cummings*):

> For whatever we lose (like a you or a me)
> it's always ourselves we find in the sea.

Our experience as therapists sadly suggests that what most of us will do is to continue to think "we need 'solutions,'" continue to ask for "answers." "What do I need to do?" "Tell me how to solve the problem." "Show me the way." I *(Tom)* had a client once who complained after five or six sessions that despite what he was paying me, I had given him no advice. I explained to him that the reason he was paying me was that it is very difficult to find someone who would *not* give him advice. And I suggested that if he did not believe me, he should simply stop the next five people he met, tell them his problems, and listen to all the free advice they would be glad to give him. You cannot be advised into *selfhood.* You cannot be "told" who you are. There is no list of things you can *do* to *make* yourself *be* more naturally who you are.

Clearly, issues of intimacy are not *doing* issues but *being* issues. But just as clearly, "What can I do?" is the typical, expected response of most people in Western cultures. We are a "doing" people. If we have a problem we *do* something about it. This attitude is also true of most therapists; being members of the same culture, they feel compelled to *do* something for their clients. At some level they assume that they should be able to figure out, then tell the client what "to do" to solve the problem. As experiential therapists, we believe on the contrary that if the problem is one of intimacy, of *being* a *self,* the fix-it approach is not only unsuccessful, but detrimental. We are tempted, of course, to advise, but the truth is that we (that all therapists) can only know what *we* would *do* (in being *ourselves*) in a given situation. Like all therapists, we often succumb to the illusion that we can transfer our *self*-knowledge to our clients, but such intervention simply makes the client an agent of our personhood, instead of a person in his or her own right. Until people learn to change themselves out of their *own* experience, they cannot grow.

Were the therapists in the same interpersonal or intrapersonal situation, and *they* were to *do* what they had suggested, it would probably work for them. The *doing* would be consistent with the *being.* For the client following these instructions (implementing external advice), the results will bring about no internal change and may even be catastrophic, precisely because the doing is not congruent with the *client's* being. "Doing" has no inherent rightness or appropriateness; it is totally dependent for its effectiveness on its naturalness—its congruence with the nature (being) of the doer. In other words, its *selfness.* I *(Pat)* was once seeing a depressed man who passively was allowing himself to be abused by his employer. In an impatient moment, I succumbed to the illusion that I could and should tell him what to do. I told him he needed to share his anger with his boss. On his next visit to see me, the man wryly said that he wanted to share with me the news that my suggestion had not turned out too well: "Like you told me, I decided to tell my boss how mad I was. So I did. He got real upset, and then said some things that got me pretty upset. He kept talking that way, so I finally slugged him. He fired me." Even though the client in his wry tone signified that he understood I had not told him to "hit his boss," we both knew my "advice" had not helped him change in his being, as him*self,* and from his own experience. He may have been less depressed, less passive—but as an agent of me, not as himself.

What *others* respond to in us is our *motivation.* This sensitivity to the implications of our behavior is most easily seen with children. If you accidentally hit a child, even painfully, while playing with and enjoying him or her, he or she seldom acts hurt, and seldom complains. In contrast, when you barely touch a child in anger, he or she screams as if beaten. Why the difference? It does not have to do with what was *done.* The response of children to similar behaviors appears to depend on their unconscious awareness of the motivations of that behavior: the *being* of the actor, not the act. Moreover, the response does not seem dependent on the child's perception of the *feelings* accompanying the behavior, but specifically on his or her perception of the motivations. You can be upset (as, for example, when a child runs out in the street after a ball) and thus strike the child. But if your motivation is not to hurt or punish (pass judgment) but to reach him or her, the child is seldom distressed by your upsetness or frightened by your actions. Conscious motivation, of course, is often very different from real motivation. The child listens to real motivation. We can punish a child for "misbehaving" when the behavior is fairly normal and it is we who have had the "bad" day. Of course, if the adult's behavior is excessive (a parent is so distraught that he or she breaks the child's arm), motivation is irrelevant, but such excess is not natural, and the child responds to that unnaturalness.

Real motivation is an expression of congruence between being and doing. My *(Pat)* client's boss could not be aware of my therapeutic motivation, only of my client's belligerent goading. The two were not the same. Congruence of doing and being, then, is necessary in order for us to *do* something about becoming intimate.

In *The Art of Intimacy* we have described the three *functional* components of personal relationship: *I* (personality), *me* (character), and *self* (connection). Because of the emphasis on goal-oriented doing and behaving that characterizes our society, and our therapists' training primarily in ego analysis and *I* therapies, our psychologies are primarily ego psychologies. This emphasis accounts as well for the abundance of self-help, instructional psychology books. They tell us what to *do,* and we assume those lessons are teaching us how to *be.* It is a sense of this imbalance that led novelist and physician Walker Percy to subtitle his book *Lost in the Cosmos: The Last Self-Help Book.* For what he laments in that book is our lack of intimacy with each other and with all of nature.

Doing and behaving are teachable. We can instruct people in how to be close. We can counsel them. We teach what is not known, and can be enormously effective in developing new behaviors that enable people to relate more effectively to each other; that is, we can teach healthier closeness. But we cannot teach intimacy. To say so is not to imply that psychological teaching and instructing are not tremendously valuable. It simply means they are not relevant to developing intimacy, the essential complement of closeness.

Feeling is not teachable. We cannot instruct someone in how to feel, for feeling is a natural response. We can no more teach sadness, tenderness, sexuality, anger, or empathy than we can teach the complex intricacies of cardiac rhythm regulation, or body fluid electrolyte balances. We *can* provide a facilitating experience within which people may more directly become aware of their being, but we cannot teach them their being; just as we can use biofeedback to facilitate the return to natural function in muscle tone, heart rate, or breathing, but we cannot teach *those functions.*

"Selfing," the experience of promoting connected, relational experience, the formative experience of intimacy, *is not teachable but it is learnable.* Whereas one teaches what is not known, one learns by making conscious what is already naturally known. When Sartre said that "consciousness is consciousness of," he meant that there is a relationship between the internal (*me*) and the external (*I*). Our consciousness is *of* that relationship between the two; and in that dyad we find *self.* You cannot be taught the connection; you can only relearn it. What you can *do* is increase your consciousness of the particular relationship between your *I* and your *me.*

Development of this kind of "raised" consciousness is more prevalent in Eastern than in Western society. We have difficulty understanding that being and doing are not interchangeable. We tend to see, for example, the koans of the Zen master as semantic gymnastics, mysticism, or just obfuscation, instead of spiritual exercises about being. We do not want to hear that *we are responsible for our being,* that we must be what we want to be, if we are to be fully human. In his book *Illusions,* the writer Richard Bach suggests that even telling people to accept responsibility for themselves angers them, and that if you force the issue, they will turn against you. In our terms, you seriously jeopardize their security by telling them that intimacy is as important as closeness. As Bach says:

The
original sin is to
limit the Is.
Don't

Being is a profound and complete commitment in life. It is not an exercise or hobby. We cannot "be" in our spare time; nor as a "fad" like yoga classes, or an "in thing" like snorting cocaine. These methods are all aspects of system. Even much of what *looks* healthy on the surface—people's "jogging," "working out," "eating right"—are too often really aspects of capture by the system. They are things people are *doing* to be "part of," to be "in," to be "with it." Such people seldom get around to really *being* healthy. Otherwise, why is it so difficult *not* to overeat, *not* to undereat, *not* to overdrink, *not* to use drugs, *not* to be overdoing, *not* to be unalive? Because we do not get around to *being* those ways. We only fight negatively. The real answer is in *being* healthy, alive, *self*-responsible. The answer is not in fighting with yourself about *doing* the healthy thing. As a healthy person, you do not splinter your shins with forced jogging or jeopardize your metabolism with crash diets. Commitment is total or is not there. That commitment is what *being* is about. And that is what we are afraid of, the power and responsibility of our own *self*-being. Part of our fear is that we cannot control, organize, or categorize *being*. When we are intimate, we do not "understand." *Being* is not understandable; it is only experiential. It is life, not a program for life. We are fearful of being that free. We are fearful of that true *spiritus*.

The Art of Intimacy offers no manual of definitive instructions in how to "behave" or what to "do" to facilitate intimacy. Clearly, were we to do so, and were you to follow our instructions, by our definition your behavior would *not* be intimate. Being your*self* with another precludes your being the agent of any *other*, including the authors of *The Art of Intimacy*. Living as agents of *others* is precisely what prevents intimacy in ordinary life. We are captured by the outside, be they our parents (real or internalized), our lovers, our society, the codes of our culture, or, equally, the need to rebel against any of these. We relate to *others* as captured agents of the outside. If *The Art of Intimacy* were a manual externally instructing you in how to behave, you would still not be being your*self* with the *other*. At best, you might be a better informed and psyychologically more sophisticated agent. Such knowledge might be useful in some things (you could be taught to be more healthily close), but you would learn nothing of intimacy.

Yet *The Art of Intimacy* can perhaps help you toward intimacy in a different way. A way that may be as effective in facilitating intimacy, as "doing" instructions can be at promoting healthy closeness. Counselors in closeness emphasize your awareness of the *other* in relationship to your *self*. In this book, we have been emphasizing your greater awareness of your *self* in relationship to the *other*, whether person or place or thing. "Awareness of yourself" means exactly that. It implies that the only way you can increase your capacity for intimacy is to increase your awareness (your consciousness) of what is occurring in you when you are related to another, in Sartre's phrase "consciousness of." Intimacy is not consciousness of the *other* (what is outside you), but consciousness of *self* (consciousness of *I-me/other*). There are primary areas of consciousness and awareness within the *self* that need to be attended to by anyone concerned with intimacy. We can describe those areas of "consciousness of *self*" that, if increased, make intimacy more likely. Those descriptions will be *The Art of Intimacy*'s self-help guide. "*Self*-help" in the most profoundly literal sense.

Free Choice

You have to choose. If you do not choose, there is no way to *be* with another. If how you are with another is dictated by that *other,* or dictated by your concern with the anticipated response of that *other,* then you have not freely chosen. Your *being* with the *other* has been compromised. Intimacy is impossible. To choose is the beginning of intimacy.

Moralness

Intimacy is a moral experience. It is not moral in the sense of societal rules or religious dogma, but in the spiritual sense of personal integrity. In intimacy, the issue is not whether *others* will disapprove of or punish you for what you have or have not *done,* but whether you disapprove of and dislike your*self* for what you have or have not *been.* This awareness demands a heightened consciousness of one's congruence, the inner experience that one's behavior, feelings, and thoughts are connected. Such congruence is essential in initiating the experience of intimacy. In closeness you negotiate and modulate your behavior and feelings. In intimacy you must *be* your*self. Self* is not negotiable. If you modify your feelings and behaviors and afterward do not respect or like your*self,* then you have not been intimate or moral. You have done the relationship a disservice. For intimacy to happen you cannot *be* less; you cannot be other than your moral *self.* As R. D. Laing says in *Self and Others,* "To be 'authentic' is to be oneself, to be what one is, to be 'genuine.' . . . This is the only actual fulfillment of which I can properly speak. It is an act that is me: in this action I am myself."

Acceptance

Acceptance of the other underlies all intimate experience. No personal openness is possible without acceptance. Becoming conscious of your own judgmentalism is a crucial internal prerequisite to intimacy. You can become aware of your righteousness. When you learn to recognize it, to feel it, you become more capable of acceptance. Acceptance allows intimacy.

Self-responsibility

You feel totally and fully responsible for yourself when you are intimate with another. You know that you make your own happiness and unhappiness. The absence of dependent feelings (like needing to be needed) relieves the relationship of all "taking care of" and the resentment that caretaking brings. Caring allows intimacy.

Attentiveness

You cannot be intimate if you do not listen. Willingness openly and honestly to talk is not enough, you have to listen. In our experience, few people listen. They begin answering in their heads even before the *other* stops speaking. If we think of the act of "listening" metaphorically, we close out in the same way our response to art and the whole of nature. With paintings and deep forests, we respond before we experience. We snap pictures and move on. Learning to allow the time for listening allows intimacy.

Risk-taking

To risk the insecurity of not knowing what the other really is makes intimacy more likely. We all have imprisoning preconceptions of what the *other* is, who our lover is, what our child is "like." Your willingness to give up such prejudgmentalism allows intimacy. Your consciousness of your own preconstructions facilitates your learning to let go of them. Accepting "isness" allows experience. Internal openness to experience in relationship is essential to intimacy.

Presence

Intimacy involves an experiential commitment that is not diluted by time. You learn to know that you are doing what you need to be doing; you are doing it with whom you need to be doing it; you are doing it where and when you need to be doing it. You can learn about intimacy if you can accept that you are never inappropriate to your *self.* In the now is where you exist. Consciousness of the now is essential to the intimate experience; intimacy is timeless. It is always present, never before or after.

Naturalness

Intimacy is natural. Closeness allows socialization and civilization. Healthy closeness does this naturally only if balanced with intimacy. Intimacy allows you to be your natural *self.* Without closeness, stability is impossible; without intimacy, growth is impossible. Being a natural *self* means that you, at least for the moment, are less captive of the system, whether that system is a personal relationship, a family, a past history, or a culture. When you are natural you are more childlike in your willingness to risk. You are more aware of being part of all of nature. You therefore feel more connected to lovers, children, art, the past, the future. You will "learn" from all of them if you are natural. They can thus facilitate your intimacy. You are, in Martin Buber's phrase, "a person." "But a person, I would say, is an individual living really with the world."

Participation

Intimacy is increased by your consciousness of the essential similarity of all humans, your participation in our commonality. We are more alike than different. When lived out, specialness and difference separate us and make intimacy unlikely. The ordinariness of our similarities allows us to share our ordinary differences. Such sharing of difference *is* intimacy. It adds the beautifully strange to the quiet certainty of accepted similarity. You can become aware of how this "consciousness of" similarity is lost by focusing on different languages for experience. You can learn, for example, that feelers and behavers may use different words, may *do* different things, but are essentially alike in *being.* The essential similarities are not expressive but motivational.

Personal Surrender

Intimacy includes your willingness to allow the other the relational opportunity to be himself or herself with you. To do so is to go beyond acceptance; it involves your willingness personally to surrender (which literally means "to give over"). To "give over" to the *other*'s insistent and immediate need to share him or her *self* with you. Personal surrender is not passivity, it is not placation, but an active and positive personal response. It invites sharing; it sets aside your own personal agenda. It is *being with,* the reciprocal of *being*. When you can "give over" in this deep sense, you have enhanced your capacity to be intimate.

Reciprocity

Reciprocity characterizes all intimacy. Relational being is simultaneous. How I am with you and how you are with me derives, in the moment, from our individual and shared being; it is not a matter of cause and effect. Your consciousness of the *self*-existence allows intimacy, because you are not trying to control or cause me to be a particular way, nor am I trying to control you. We share equally in *being* with each other. As we know from dreaming, the unconscious is timeless. The world of intimacy is likewise nonsequential and therefore simultaneous. We are both responsible for *our* participation in relationship, in life. Consciousness of mutuality, reciprocity, and recursion as natural in *relationships* will allow more intimacy. Relationship, in this sense, is existence, for it means your interaction with any *other,* whether person or thing.

Engagement

Intimacy is a playful way of being. Consciousness of your own playfulness allows you access to the child that is in each of us. Play is the only pathway to being able to "be part of" while remaining a *self*. Play includes art, sexuality, humor, and all other forms of nonintentional being. It is the only "doing" way to avoid capture by the system. In play, you can give up the absurd notion of "transcending your nature" or "transcending your *self*." Transcendence, like never-ending intimacy, is a "God" concept. Humans can transcend *I* and *me;* they do so in intimacy. But humans cannot transcend human nature; they cannot raise themselves above relationship because they exist only in relationship (to the rest of what is). Nor can they slip the coils of closeness, familiarity, society, culture, and live in unending intimacy, connected to everything in perfect freedom. Humans need the reassurance of stabilizing closeness. But in play, humans can *momentarily* participate in a God-like engagement in life. In play you are what you are; as "God" is always whatever "God" is. In this sense "God" is always playful. In playing, spirituality is communal. No one *can* play the game in exactly the same way, but we can all become more aware of the spirit of the game (its rules, its nature), and thereby be better players (better able to be healthily close, better able to be intimate).

Systemic Detachment

Intimacy is not systemic. You can become more conscious of your systems—from the level of government, to your community, to your own methods of turning relationships or even yourself into systems. You can learn that you are not the systems in which you participate. Through such detachment, you can also learn to make better use of systems. Through such awareness, you can begin to understand, for example, what the mathematician Kurt Gödel pointed out in his theorem: that each system contains elements of information about the *other* that the *other* lacks. Knowing this about either government systems, religious systems, or personal systems, we see the danger of living wholly inside *any* system. None of them can represent all truth. Only *self,* connected to the rest of what is, can do that.

Creativity

Intimacy is an art. It is not a craft. Crafts produce many wondrous and beautiful objects. Psychological craft is the basis of all healthy closeness, closeness that does not constrict or imprison, closeness that makes intimacy more likely. Art, on the other hand, has more to do with experience than object. Art creates experience in both the artist and in the person seeing the painting, or hearing the music, or reading the words. The art object recedes and the art experience ascends, much as closeness recedes and experience ascends when we are intimate. In your craft, you know what to do and you do it well. Your teachers are important and you listen to them. In your art, you know what to be, and you be it well. Your teachers are important, but you must take what they are inside you and listen to *yourself.* Effectuating creativity is craft;

art *is* creativity. Craft is doing; art is being. To bring forth anything, a painting, a love relationship, a family, a nation, a world, requires both craft and art. The balance of the two we call love, truth, and beauty. In the *intimate self,* "to be" and "to do" are really not so different. After all, the word *behave,* which describes doing, literally means "to have being." To have being is what we are advocating in *The Art of Intimacy.* We ask you to be an artist *in* your life as well as a craftsman *of* your life. We ask you to experience your own capacity for choice, for integrity, for acceptance, for attentiveness, for risk-taking, for presence, for naturalness, for participation, for surrender, for reciprocity, for playful engagement, and for creativity. We ask you to have being.